Mauro Biglino

GODS OF THE BIBLE

A new interpretation of the Bible reveals
the oldest secret in history

Tuthi

ISBN 978-88-946117-5-5

Translation and editing: Davide Bolognesi
Layout: Simone Brucato
Cover design: Simone Brucato, Giovanni Zattera

INDEX

I believe that what I am about to recount might appear to be a fable,
if it did not have the support of eyewitnesses on the one hand,
and the confirmation of the misfortunes that followed on the other.
Before the sun went down, war chariots and armies of soldiers
could be seen in the sky over the entire region,
emerging from the clouds and surrounding the cities.
[...] They first heard shaking and banging, and then
a group of voices saying, "From this place we are leaving."

(F. Josephus, *The Jewish War*, VI 5, 297-299)

Armies clashed in the sky, swords blazed, and the temple shone with sudden flashes.
The doors of the sanctuary were suddenly torn open,
and a superhuman voice cried out that the gods were fleeing;
and at the same time there was a great uproar, as if men were fleeing.

(C. Tacitus, *Histories*, V 13)

We must therefore admit the possibility that,
if we are not the highest intelligences in the universe,
some higher intelligence may have directed the process
by which the human race was developed.

(A. R. Wallace, *Contribution to the Theory of Natural Selection*, 1871)

INTRODUCTION

1. John from America

In the 1920s, naturalist James Hurley landed a seaplane in New Guinea. He discovered that the natives offered daily sacrifices to him and his plane, believing both to be of divine origin. This non-isolated phenomenon took the name of cargo cults.[1]

The most significant proliferation of cargo cults occurred during and after World War II when vast quantities of supplies for the US Army, who were engaged in the war campaign in the Pacific, were parachuted into some of the islands of this area, along with clothing, food, tents, weapons, and other goods. These supplies were destined for the soldiers and the islanders who acted as guides for them.

With the war's end, the air bases were abandoned, and "cargoes" were no longer dropped; the transport of goods — including large quantities of food — from which the locals had greatly benefited suddenly ceased. The inhabitants of these islands thus developed religious practices and magical rituals to encourage the return of the "gods" who had proved so prodigal and generous. These ritual practices included the creation of runways, planes, radios, and wooden control towers in replica, in an attempt to imitate the behavior of the American military operating there. They also began to ritually mimic the signals typical of airports, such as lighting fires to illuminate the runways, and so on.

Cargo cults slowly faded until they finally disappeared with the realization that the generous gods were not returning. Still, at least one case is recorded that helps us understand how specific elements worked, including linguistic aspects that have some point of contact, as we shall

---

[1] On the subject of cargo cults, the reader might want to see: *Cargo, Cult, and Culture Critique* by H. Jebens; L. Lindstrom's *Cargo Cult: Strange Stories of Desire from Melanesia and Beyond*; and M. Kaplan, Neither *Cargo nor Cult Ritual Politics and the Colonial Imagination in Fiji*.

see later, with the transmission of the name of Yahweh.

One of the American soldiers that arrived on the Vanuatu Islands on one of the aforementioned military missions was of African-American origin. The inhabitants of the archipelago, noticing his darker skin color, which more closely resembled theirs, believed him to be a divine being. After his departure, they dedicated a temple to him and kept some of his objects as relics, impatiently waiting for his return. The tribal leader at that time said that after his departure, he dreamed of the American god, and from then on, he was considered a "prophet of the god."

This "deity" was known to these people as "Jonfram." The origin is unclear, as it could not be clarified whether it came from an American name such as "John Frum" or something similar; or whether this name comes from the fact that he introduced himself as "John from America." In any case, the locals remembered the sound /jonfrom/ or /jonfram/ and identified it as the name of this particular "god" who came from above. This detail will be handy when we discuss the name of Yahweh in Chapter 8 of this book.

At the level of general observations, cargo cults have developed under specific conditions in a particular geographical area. However, they teach us much about human behavior concerning the "sacred." One has to consider that the "cargo cults" phenomenon has unfolded in the past century before the very eyes of anthropologists, ethnographers, and linguists; thus, it has been abundantly studied in scholarship environments in all its various aspects. The technological gap between local dwellers and "alien" visitors has provided the space for the thriving of a cult, or if we prefer, a "religious" experience complete with rituals, prayers, and eschatological beliefs. That which — technology, in this case — could not be understood or explained or traced back to a familiar category became "divinized" and made "sacred."

Again, peculiar as it is, the cargo cult phenomenon happened during modern times, so it was possible to study it in detail. Could this, or a similar phenomenon, have occurred already in the history of humanity at a time when no anthropologists, ethnographers, linguists, and other scholars were around to study it?

There are reasons not to discard this hypothesis too soon. And, since this hypothesis is plausible, it is always too late to consider it seriously, but not too late that it cannot be done still. Much evidence, while partially lost, is abundantly available before our eyes.

We have reasons to think that proof of a similar experience to the cargo cults can be found in many ancient texts and sources, including, and especially, the Bible. Evidence is quite plain if only one looks at it by first removing the thick theological lenses that have been sitting on our noses for more than two thousand years, to the point that we sometimes forget we are wearing them.

The canny reader already sees the direction we are taking. Let us, for a moment, put ourselves in the shoes of the islanders that experienced the arrival of the American soldiers, during the Second World War, with their flying machines, powerful weapons, and stunning food supplies.

They saw them flying in the skies, recognized the unbridgeable distance that separated them in knowledge and abilities, experienced or witnessed the destructive power of their arms, but also enjoyed the extraordinary benefits (knowledge, supplies, and practical skills) that came from this incidental contact. With just a short leap of imagination, this could have been the same experience as our ancestors.

Could the ancient man have encountered someone more powerful and technologically advanced than them? If so, what happened when the "alien" visitors left, and the contact was lost? Could the ancient man have transformed the memory of this encounter into magical, higher, spiritually ordered, divine belief systems? Could the extraordinary experience of the encounter with an extraterrestrial civilization, whose immediate memory was lost in the mists of time, somehow take the substitute form of a "theological" or "sacred" experience?

Over the course of more than two millennia, generation after generation of believers, perpetuating gestures more and more devoid of their original significance, created the figure of a "God," who probably had initially nothing to do with the individuals our ancestors might have encountered.

Those ancient "gods" and the one "God" that today billions of people still pray to and worship have nothing in common. They are "aliens" to one another.

2. The alien "God"

We have been taught that "God" possesses specific spiritual characteristics, including omnipotence, omniscience, eternity, compassion, love, and so forth. Through the pages of this book, however, "God" will probably show himself in a light entirely unsuspected to most readers. The final portrait that will emerge will likely reveal the image of a character very different from what many of our readers are accustomed to.

Regardless of the meaning we attribute to the term "alien" — which etymologically means "foreign," "other," "different," "unknown," and only later came also to mean "extraterrestrial" — the reader will find that through a literal reading of the Bible, we can derive a concept of "God" that is quite "alien" next to the idea of "God" as a spiritual being.

That "God" we have been trained to know through two thousand-plus years of theological work might come out now as wholly "other." Furthermore, we are ready to suggest that the term "alien" might mean more than just "different" and "foreign" when applied to the Bible, and entail a whole new semantic twist.

As we proceed by questions, we ask ourselves: were monotheistic religions the byproduct of ancient encounters with technologically advanced visitors from off planet Earth?

Many authors in the past have dealt with possible contact with extraterrestrial civilizations. They have written books that have shaped the hypothesis that such civilizations are at the origin of our species' biological and cultural evolution.

In particular, in the second half of the 20th century, various authors dealt with this subject by quoting and analyzing passages from the Old Testament. Still, they did so by relying on mainstream translations of the Bible available to the public.

As we will show in this book, these translations are often inaccurate, incorrect, or downright false. Incredible as it sounds, there are still mistakes and misinterpretations after two thousand years of tireless work on them.

Thus, can we, through the vantage point of a literal reading of the Bible, learn more about the origin and nature of Yahweh and the birth of monotheism? And if so, are the times suitable for such a revolutionary operation?

We live in a time that encourages us to look more confidently in the direction of the search for extraterrestrial life. In collaboration with Harvard University, astrophysicists of the caliber of Avi Loeb have recently launched the Galileo Project to track, with state-of-the-art technology, and photograph what once were called UFOs (Unidentified Flying Objects) and today are called UAPs (Unidentified Aerial Phenomena).[2]

---

[2]   On the official page of the Galileo Project at Harvard University, the curious reader will find detailed information about Prof. Loeb's goals, activities and publications. For specific references see, "Works cited and consulted," at the end of this book.

NASA has also launched a new independent program to study this phenomenon.[3] On top of that, the Pentagon has released reports and videos of UAPs recorded by military equipment and radars. In recent and official reports, the Pentagon has established that the UAP phenomenon is not the product of the fervid imagination of some crazy ufologist and that, verbatim, "sociocultural stigmas" around it should be promptly removed. UAPs are real and need to be studied carefully.[4]

A group of scientists and scholars of the highest caliber, including Avi Loeb himself, both astrophysicists and representatives of various disciplines, has recently published a volume for Cambridge Scholars Publishing that directly and openly addresses the problem of UAPs and Extraterrestrial Intelligence (ETI), something that would have been unthinkable in academia just a few years ago.

To cite just one example, in one of the many thought-provoking articles included in this book, Dr Jensine Andresen (Ph.D. Harvard University), provides a very detailed account of the history of UAPs and the interest of both scientists and government agencies in this subject over the past seventy-five years, underlining the very close relationship between UAPs, nuclear weapons, and nuclear energy, and in particular, emphasizing that recent observations even suggest that UAPs do not manifest or move within the typical dichotomous Western paradigm Matter versus Consciousness, but from a perspective where Consciousness and Matter coincide. Even the current knowledge paradigms and the whole academic discipline map might be obsolete at this point. The scientist states, among other things:

> Tens of millions of people have witnessed UAP, which have also been documented in photographs, on video, and with radar. My view that many UAP are in fact extraterrestrial in origin is supported further by plausible interpretations of various petroglyphs, geoglyphs, and artifacts, and by accounts described in the literature of many cultures extending back thousands of years.

> (Andresen 281)

A new approach is needed in academia and the cultural sphere in general. And we are sure that a new way of thinking will soon prevail at

---

[3]   Bock, Michael. "NASA to Set up Independent Study on Unidentified Aerial Phenomena." *NASA*, 9 June 2022, www.nasa.gov/feature/nasa-to-set-up-independent-study-on-unidentified-aerial-phenomena/

[4]   Office of the Director of National Intelligence. *Preliminary Assessment: Unidentified Aerial Phenomena*. 2021. Full source in "Works Cited and Consulted."

the academic and social levels. So we are in good company in our effort to search for extraterrestrial life.

We do not look for extraterrestrial intelligent life in the sky with telescopes and other scientific instruments; but we hope to find signs of extraterrestrial visitors where people would less expect to find them: in the Bible.

As we have learned from the cargo cults, human nature is often inclined and quickly ready to resort to the "divine" and the "sacred" whenever it encounters something difficult to grasp through habitual categories and conceptual paradigms.

In these pages, we will address what has not been addressed elsewhere or, worse, has been deliberately forgotten and interpreted in ways designed to obscure the potentially disturbing implications of specific passages of the Bible through new eyes and new methods.

Yet, our first goal is not to find evidence of "extraterrestrial life" but to accompany the patient reader toward becoming more aware of the theological and ideological lenses that have affected the reading of the Bible as a "sacred text" for so long.

Suppose our readers have the patience to walk this not always effortless but enriching journey with us; they might find some of the proof we put forward in this book as mind-bending, stimulating, and revolutionary as we do. There is proof in the Bible of long-established inaccurate, if not altogether falsified, translations that have bent the intention of the original authors/redactors of the biblical accounts.

The best we can do is to leave the doubt open for the open-minded truth-seeker, as we are aware that this result, in a field wholly altered by dogmatic views, when not downright violent attitudes, would be in itself a fantastic achievement. For those who are not afraid to walk with us on the steep but fruitful path of independent thinking and research, and dare to connect the dots of our decade-long study, we believe that a picture will slowly take shape before the eyes that will leave the reader stunned.

3. A personal note

Before we continue on this path, a brief personal note becomes necessary. This is much needed, though it is unpleasant for the writer. However, the reader must know where this journey started many years ago. Before beginning to write books as a divulger, I worked as a translator for the Vatican-approved interlinear Bible edition, published by San Paolo Edizioni, possibly the most prominent official religious publisher in Italy. Their publications are currently used in academia, universities, and graduate and post-graduate Biblical Hebrew and Bible studies courses.

Needless to say, once I started voicing my doubts concerning the meaning of specific passages of the Bible, San Paolo Edizioni (legitimately) decided not to avail themselves of my expertise in this field anymore; the last two books I translated for them went unpublished because our collaboration was halted. In total, I have translated nineteen books of the Old Testament, of which seventeen were published with San Paolo Edizioni.[5]

However, what is important to say here is that, in the following years, I didn't do much more than bring to light and make available to the general public the difficulties and contradictions of some well-known biblical passages that are treated differently in the scholarly editions of the Bible and the versions available to non-specialists. I will make just one exemplification here.

The term "Elohim" is translated as "God" in commonly available Bibles or in the Bible generally known to non-specialists. However, this term was left untranslated in the interlinear Bible edition published by San Paolo Edizioni prepared for specialists and scholars; this at least was true at the time when I was working for them.

In other words: where people read "God" and were led to believe that the biblical authors had written the word "God," scholars read the untranslated term "Elohim" and were made aware that this term is problematic for unbiased translators.

Whatever "Elohim" means, why provide different translations for different readerships? Who is afraid of people realizing that there is so much uncertainty around the very term on which monotheism is founded? We leave this question open for now, as we will discuss the word "Elohim" in more detail in the second chapter of this book.

This contradiction, however, is one of the reasons that led me to begin independent research, after working for many years as a Bible translator for a major Catholic publisher whose books are recognized in Vatican academic circles.

---

[5]   Biglino, Mauro. *Cinque Meghillôt. Rut, Cantico Dei Cantici, Qohelet, Lamentazioni, Ester.* Edited by Pier Carlo Beretta, San Paolo Edizioni, 2008. See also *Il Libro Dei Dodici*, San Paolo Edizioni, 2009.

My reading will result in most passages being unorthodox to a religious perspective. Some would say even heretical. For this reason, for all passages that indicate an unconventional, unexpected, and non-heterodox reading, we will reproduce the original Hebrew text with the literal translation verbatim, word for word.

4. Importantr reading indications

We outline in this book what we keep discovering when examining the biblical text as it is, that is, through a literal reading based on the oldest Hebrew manuscripts: the Stuttgartensia Bible based on the Masoretic text of the Leningrad Codex.

In quoting the Hebrew text, only the consonants have been noted to remain faithful to the source as before the vocalization by the Masoretes, which did not occur until between the 6th and 9th centuries CE.

In the few cases where we wanted to reproduce the pronunciation of the Hebrew language in the text, we refrained from using the official phonetic symbols since these would remain incomprehensible to the layman anyway.

The sounds have therefore been rendered as faithfully as possible, using only the known vowels and consonants of the modern language that are necessary to render the sound. We are sure that the experts in phonetics and transliteration will understand the reasons for this.

The passage below exemplifies what has been provided to the reader:

- The first line contains the non-vocalized Hebrew text that must be read *from right to left*.

- The second line contains the literal translation, also proceeding *from right to left*.

לקלל   עוד את האדמה
earth-the   again   curse-to ← (*read from right to left*)

For the transcription of Sumerian-Akkadian terms, a simplified spelling was chosen without resorting to symbols or breaking the words into their components, to facilitate reading.

1 / DISCOURSE ON METHOD

1. To think out of the box

In his best-selling book, *Gods, Graves, and Scholars: A Story of Archaeology*, Kurt W. Marek, alias C. W. Ceram, lists all the pivotal discoveries in archaeology that came not from professional archaeologists but from outsiders to the discipline.

This situation, however, as C. W. Ceram shows, is wider than archaeology. The most important discoveries in any discipline often come from outsiders. Ceram provides a long list of notable inventions and outstanding achievements for humankind, in all scientific fields, that came from the determination of people who did not belong to the official academic circles or the intellectual élite.

Outsiders have one excellent quality, apart from their obstinacy: they *think out of the box*. The list of examples in all fields is endless.

Among the most rightly famous names in this list is Heinrich Schliemann (1822-1890), who discovered the city of Troy.

Professional archaeologists had convinced themselves that Troy was just the product of Homer's creative mind; therefore, it was not worth their precious time to look for it. Schliemann had a different idea and decided to look for it — and found it.

How did Schliemann achieve this result?

Most importantly, what prevented scholars from doing so? Why, with all their supposed knowledge and experience, didn't scholars do anything? This second question is the most urgent, and we should address it first.

Academic standards and peer-reviewed papers tend to encourage, advance, and promote — according to the definition of famous American psychologist J. P. Guilford — the "convergent thinking" end of the intelligence spectrum rather than "divergent thinking."

"Convergent thinking" works very well in closed systems and tends to find solutions to problems from within the field or the domain in which the situation has developed.

Thus, "convergent thinking" always confirms the righteousness of the system as a whole; it allows some degree of change but does not undermine the foundation of a discipline or an institution.

On the other hand, institutions, including academic institutions, tend to preserve themselves by favoring "convergent thinking."

According to K. Jenkins, "dominant ideologies articulate history academically," that is, in a way that is not just ideological but conservative of the power structure.

In fewer words, scholars tend to conduct their research in a way that does not undermine the (power) structure (on which they thrive).

> It seems rather obvious that seen in a wider cultural and "historical" perspective, **multi-million pound institutional investments such as our national universities are integral to the reproduction of the ongoing social formation** and are thus at the forefront of **cultural guardianship** (academic standards) and ideological control.
>
> (Jenkins, 25)

This "cultural guardianship" aims primarily at perpetuating the institution and directly and indirectly preserving the power structure on which it rests, and so many careers thrive.

The archaeologists of the time of Schliemann were more concerned about "defending" their reputation and, therefore, their career, rather than finding the city of Troy; thus, they did not find it.

They did not *need* to find the city of Troy to consolidate their position in science or advance their discipline. In the worst-case scenario, they could be exposed to ridicule, just as Schliemann was exposed to ridicule before the discovery of Troy.

We could list endless examples of intellectual and academic myopia.

The dynamics are always the same. Let us mention only one example almost archetypical in how it changed the world's history and our concept of science: Galileo Galilei.

Galileo Galilei is a fine example of divergent thinking. The Italian scientist produced evidence that the Earth is not the center of the universe. However, the inquisitors of his time, his intellectual peers, refused to consider his theory and even to look through the telescope that would have proven him right.

What were they afraid of? What prevented them from doing so, if not their deep-down inexpressible awareness, that, had Galileo proved correct, the whole power structure they had built around the geocentric model would have fallen apart?

They preferred not to look. The official discourse could not admit such revolutionary novelty. Again, ideology, not science, stopped them. Often the most ferocious inquisitors are scientists from whom one would expect an open-minded attitude.

The "guardians of the discourse" actively exert their control power. Not only do they not want to look through any telescope that could potentially jeopardize a well-established system that rewards their convergent thinking, but they also do not want anybody else, within or outside their controlled space, to question their (limited) knowledge.

Recently there was the quite amusing news that the Society for American Archaeology (SAA) pompously wrote an open letter to the giant production company Netflix to complain about Graham Hancock's last show, *Ancient Apocalypse*.[6]

In their view, Hancock's "docuseries" should be relabeled as "fiction," partly because they feel offended by Hancock's "aggressive rhetoric," partly because, hear this, Hancock's presentation of the material "does injustice to Indigenous people," and "rob[s] Indigenous peoples of credit for their cultural heritage."

They also accuse Hancock of reinforcing "white supremacy" theories and spreading "narratives that are overtly misogynistic, chauvinistic, racist, and anti-Semitic." All in one very concise letter!

It is a relief to notice that such a conservative discipline with such a long colonial and racist history of plundering and pillaging, like Western archaeology, is now faster than the Indigenous people themselves in defending the rights of Indigenous people.

However, at the time of writing, Indigenous people have not shown any concern about Netflix's show *Ancient Apocalypse*.

One wonders what prompted the SAA to this unusually timely and

---

[6]   Benzine, Vittoria. "Archaeologists Ask Netflix to Reclassify Graham Hancock's 'Unfounded' Netflix Docuseries 'Ancient Apocalypse' as Fiction." *Artnet News*, 2 Dec. 2022, news.artnet.com/art-world/archaeologists-graham-hancocks-ancient-apocalypse-fiction-2222060?utm_campaign=artnet-news. The full letter of the SAA can be found here: https://documents.saa.org/container/docs/default-source/doc-governmentaffairs/saa-letter-ancient-apocalypse.pdf?sfvrsn=38d28254_3

altruistic — but let us call it by its name: condescending — raising of shields in defense of the "poor" Indigenous people.

The SAA's letter also suggests other considerations, as they associate Hancock with a 19th-century white supremacist. If this is the standard, we wonder, what would prevent anyone now from associating the SAA with the 19th-century white archaeologists that filled American museums with Indigenous treasures stolen from around the world?

One need only look at the art collections of many Western museums that display pre-Columbian or Middle Eastern collections of inestimable value but dubious provenance. Why doesn't the SAA write letters to demand the return of these treasures to their rightful owners?

The truth is that the SAA's letter denotes an obsolete, condescending, patronizing, euro-centric approach while accusing Hancock of white suprematism. More than convergent thinking, this sounds like parochial, intolerant, small-minded thinking.

However, we want to avoid adhering to these shallow standards. The story of archaeology has taught us that much good can come from the questions of outsiders that look at things with a divergent thinking approach.

Therefore, how was Schliemann able to find the lost city of Troy while professional archaeologists failed at the task?

The answer is easy enough; free from preconceived ideas, Schliemann believed that Homer's account of Troy's war was *true*. He simply decided to give credit to the ancient sources and thus used Homer's account as a starting point for his search.

He was proved right.

The revolutionary premise of his work was to "pretend" that the *Iliad* and the *Odyssey* contained memories of historical events that indeed took place.

Accompanied by the sarcastic derision of the academic world, Schliemann carried on his search with outstanding tenacity. Eventually, he found Troy on the hill of Hissarlik in western Turkey.

This methodology prompted Schliemann to make some of the most significant discoveries in the history of archaeology. It sounds pretty logical and straightforward, but archaeologists of his time, incredibly enough, could not see it. Not because their sight was weak but because they wore blinders and did not even know it.

With Schliemann's example in mind, let us go back to the Bible, where the most patronizing and condescending guardians of the discourse thrive and have built more than just some lucky academic careers.

2. The short long story of the Bible

Theologians and believers regard the Bible as the Revealed Truth, a Sacred Text. They worship it and pray on it. They read it as if its words were coming directly from God's mouth.

This attitude is found outside of the religious sector as well. Powerful politicians take the oath of office on the Bible before serving the country, and court eye-witnesses swear on it before giving a testimony that could save someone, or get someone sentenced to death.

The Bible is considered the epitome of unquestionable truth and reliability.

This view, however, is in open contradiction with the very nature of the book, made of a fragile text resulting from endless passages, incessant manual copying and transcriptions, censorship, and amendments that lasted more than 2,500 years.

Its longevity adds to its authority and prestige, but if its age sounds like a long time, let us put things in perspective and compare the lifespan of this book with that of our planet, and with that of human civilization as we know it. Since many believe the Bible is the "word of God," we need to measure its relevance against the universe's lifespan.

To put things in perspective, suppose then planet Earth existed for a whole solar year; then the history of our civilization would only last 26 hundredths of a second. Compared to the universe's lifespan, the weight of human presence is practically non-existent.

This example explains the difference between what we believe of ourselves as a species and what we are in the universe's grand scheme.

Now that we know that humankind is almost nothing compared to the history of planet Earth and nothing at all compared to the universe, let us go back to the Bible, the book that supposedly contains the Revealed Truth about humankind and allegedly provides the foundation of some theological assumptions that should be, in the light of our discourse, wholly reconsidered.

If humankind was "created" to "serve and love" God, then we wonder:

- What are these very few instants of a human presence compared to the life of the universe?

- Why this much waste of time and space?

- Why not create human life from the beginning?

- Why billions of years of cosmic void, silence, and absence of any form of dialogue, prayer, offerings, and sacrifices?

- What will become of this "love" when humankind ceases to exist like many other living species have done before it? Will God remain again alone in the silent void of the cold sidereal space?

- Did God feel lonely in the first billion years of the life of the universe?

- Did God only suddenly realize, after 13.8 billion years of solitude, that he could create some form of company for himself?

These are all rhetorical questions because the study of the Old Testament reveals a different reality about the so-called "God." However, let us thus first establish that, as mentioned above, the text of the Bible is fragile and uncertain.

The Old Testament is a series of books that are among the most frequently written, rewritten, manipulated, altered, interpolated, modified, erased, corrected, eliminated, and then officially rediscovered in human history.

When we speak of the Bible, we are thus not referring to a single, coherent text written with a specific purpose at a precise moment in the distant past.

As said, the Bibles in our possession are essentially written based on the Stuttgart Bible, that is, the printed version of the Leningrad Masoretic Codex, prepared between the sixth and ninth centuries CE by the so-called Masoretes — guardians of the Masorah, that is, the tradition — of the school of Tiberias, who belonged to the family of Moshe ben Aaron ben Asher.

The Bibles we have at home are derived from this version of the Old Testament, but with significant differences between the various denominations that follow this set of books.

Catholics must believe that the Old Testament contains 46 divinely inspired books; for the Jewish canon, however, only 39 books are recognized as divinely inspired.

Some books Christians accept as divinely inspired are not recognized in the Jewish canon. These are the books of Tobias, Judith, Wisdom, Baruch, Sirach, the First and Second Books of Maccabees, and some passages of Esther and Daniel.

The Reformed Church, i.e., Protestantism, essentially adheres to the Jewish canon.

In contrast, Coptic Christians consider canonical, and therefore containing inspired truths, other books not included by Catholics and Jews, such as the Book of Enoch and the Book of Jubilees.

The Greek Orthodox Church does not use the Codex of Leningrad as a basis, but the text of the Septuagint, i.e., the Bible written in Greek in Egypt in the 3rd century BCE.

Compared to the Masoretic version, the Bible in Greek has about a thousand variations, some of which are of considerable importance because they reveal significant differences in the meaning of the text; the variations are also sometimes able to show the correction and amendments (i.e., textual forgeries) made by the Masoretes.

The Greek version formed the biblical basis for the Church Fathers in the first centuries after Christ until the Roman Church decided to use the Hebrew canon as its foundation.

On the other hand, the rabbis rejected the Septuagint, arguing that only the books they believed to be consistent with the Law, written in Palestine, in Hebrew, before Ezra (5th century BCE), were acceptable.

But that is not all. In northern Palestine, in the territory of the Samaritans, the truth is not in the code written by the Masoretes but in the Samaritan Torah (Pentateuch). The Samaritan Torah has up to two thousand variants compared to the Masoretic code.

Moreover, in the Samaritan canon, only the first six books are recognized as true and divinely inspired: the Pentateuch and the Book of Joshua.

The Masoretes define themselves as keepers of the Masorah, the tradition, while the Samaritans define themselves as keepers of the Torah, that is, the Law.

The Peshitta, the Syriac Bible, accepted by Maronites, Nestorians, Jacobites, and Melkites, also differs from the Masoretic Bible.

Part of Jewish culture believes that the Talmud contains more truths than the Bible itself.

So before we even come close to translation problems, we realize that we have not one Bible but many Bibles.

We have multiple possible Bibles, and, most importantly, we find that all of these Bibles, with their myriad variations, are declared indisputably true by those who live in the tradition that contains them. Great is the chaos under heaven!

It is neither our task nor our intention to choose between these versions, knowing that in each case, they are all books written by men who pursued concrete goals, often not consistent with the urgency to spread divine truth but rather with the will to exercise power and domination over others.

Contrary to the widespread belief that there is certainty about the authors of the Bible, we must know that there is not a single passage in the Old Testament in which we can say with absolute certainty who wrote it.

The tradition assumes attributions that believers uncritically accept as certain. However, we know that the Bible was rewritten, and probably largely rewritten from scratch, during and after the Babylonian exile (6th-5th century BCE).

A concrete example will help us understand the actual situation. Even those who do not know the biblical text are familiar with the prophet Isaiah, the greatest of the Old Testament prophets, who allegedly foretold the coming of the one who would later be the Christian Messiah: Jesus.

The Book of Isaiah consists of 66 chapters divided into several sections.

Chapters 1 to 39 are attributed to Isaiah because, according to scholars, there are no serious reasons to deny its authorship. (We all understand very well that this statement means something quite different from saying that we know for sure that the author is the prophet.)

This unanimous attribution, however, falters as soon as we consider individual sections. The most significant difficulties concern the so-called "Apocalypse of Isaiah" (chapters 24-27), which many scholars place during the time of the exile (6th-5th centuries BCE) or the period after it, more than two centuries after the time in which the prophet lived.

Further difficulties arise with chapters 13 through 23. Chapters 34 and 35 also offer significant challenges. Chapters 40 through 55 are attributed to the Deutero-Isaiah, an unknown author traditionally referred to as "Second Isaiah," who may have written them during the time of the exile, two centuries later.

The last chapters (from 56 to 66) are attributed to a likewise unknown author named Trito-Isaiah, also known as "Third Isaiah," who probably lived a few decades after Second Isaiah.

As can be seen, the Book of Isaiah is the work of, to be optimistic, at least three authors, two of whom are entirely unknown and who must have been writing over about three centuries.

But this is not the end of it.

The Dead Sea Scrolls, the so-called Qumran texts, have provided us with a different version of the Book of Isaiah, and this discovery only increases the uncertainty. Between the text found in these scrolls and the version of the Masoretes, there are more than two-hundred-fifty variants, including whole words appearing in one version but not in the other.

Let us detach ourselves for a moment from the biblical context and imagine that someone illustrates the composition of the *Divine Comedy*.

An imaginary Dante scholar tells us that the first Cantica (*Inferno*) is attributed to Dante Alighieri because there are no reasons to dispute this attribution. However, at least twenty cantos in this section were written about two centuries after Dante. Moreover, the same interpreter tells us that *Purgatory* was written by a Deutero-Alighieri, who is said to have composed this Cantica two hundred years later. At the same time, *Paradise* is the work of an equally unknown Trito-Alighieri, who is said to have written the text even later.

Would we accept being told that the *Divine Comedy* was written without a shadow of a doubt by Dante Alighieri and that its undisputed credibility rests on this attribution?

Another example will contribute to a better understanding.

The compilation of the first five books of the Old Testament, also known as the Torah, or Pentateuch, is traditionally attributed to Moses. However, scholars know that these texts were written (or at least largely rewritten) during and after the Babylonian exile. In any case, the manuscripts in our possession do not predate the 2nd century BCE.

So, there is not a single book of the Old Testament of which we can say with certainty who wrote it and when. Each time they were rewritten or copied under dictation, these texts changed for various reasons.

Also, we do not know how these books were read.

We would like to emphasize the last statement: we do not know how these books were read.

This apparent absurdity arises from biblical texts being written only with consonants. The Masoretes inserted the vowels only around the 6th-9th century CE, as we have mentioned above.

Scholars have yet to determine whether the vocalization of the Masoretes corresponds to the original pronunciation.

We know very well that because of the unique structure of the Hebrew language, a different vocalization — even a different inflection in the pronunciation of the vowels — leads to significant variations in the meaning of individual terms.

Even today, part of Jewish exegesis still replaces the vowel sounds established by the Masoretes with other vowels, thus obtaining different meanings of the words.

So, this is the situation with the books of the Old Testament: we still need to find out who wrote them, when, and how they were read. However, we can be sure of one thing: the original text does not correspond to what we have today.

Furthermore, all scholars also agree that the original stories, mainly contained in the Book of Genesis, are revised copies of older texts, in this case, Sumerian-Akkadian and Phoenician texts.

Rabbis are well aware of this origin. Rabbi Robert Wexler, who has led the American Jewish University for 25 years and is one of Judaism's most distinguished figures and scholars, has written that the stories of Genesis did not originate in Palestine but in Mesopotamia.

It goes beyond the limits of common sense that the Sumerian-Akkadian narratives are defined as myths, legends, and fables, while the Bible, which is in part derived from them, represents the Truth inspired by "God."

The originals are fairy tales, while the copy is the divine Truth: a logical conclusion!

Yet theologians claim to know and assert with indisputable certainty that "God" inspired these texts and that the Bible contains the divine words.

One almost wishes they were right; if only this would keep them from changing the text at will. However, the empowering possibilities that arose from being able to manipulate the divine words were only a spur to their zealous work.

The fact that they consider the Bible a "sacred text," incredibly, did not stop them from altering and interpreting it at their discretion, falsifying translations or using rhetorical devices such as allegories and metaphors so that the text would reflect their conception of "God," formed over millennia of theological elaboration.

This conception of "God," however, did not exist when the Bible was "written."

3. Pretending the Bible is true

As seen, when it comes to the Bible, we are only left with copies of copies of copies of missing original archetypes that possibly reported ancient oral stories lost in the fog of time.

Thus, the Bible is one of the most uncertain and fragile books that ever existed in the world.

However, theologians have built on it very elaborate religious and dogmatic worldviews. During the millennia, their painstaking work has given rise to the three religions "of the book."

Islam, Christianity, and Judaism comprise more than four billion people; in fact, 4.3 billion people.

More than half of humanity bases their existence and their life values directly or indirectly on the Bible. This book has thus become the fulcrum and the heart of a complex power structure.

Anyone can see how pivotal it is that these religious systems, however different, varied, and contradictory, be founded on solid ground, capable of supporting the monstrous and hypertrophic power system that grew on them.

Nevertheless, these guardians of the orthodoxy are often afraid that the foundation of this power structure is not as solid as they hope. For this reason, the Catholic church forbade Bible reading, unless under the guidance of a preacher, for centuries.

Looking at the big picture, we realize that an immense power structure was built on top of an unstable foundation. Monotheism is today a giant with feet of clay. The text on which it relies is the frailest thing in the world.

One would expect theologians, believers, and Bible translators to avoid even touching the text, let alone changing it. Instead, they feel incredibly comfortable altering it at will, as will become apparent from many examples in the following chapters.

Those who study translation as a discipline know that every translation is, to some extent, an interpretation, which is especially true of ancient texts. However, this is no license for arbitrary translations. Some translations are acceptable or questionable, while others are downright wrong.

One of the best translation practices is to leave controversial or uncertain words untranslated to avoid all sorts of problems and misunderstandings.

Some translations currently seen and read in the publicly available Bibles are wrong or distorted. There are many such examples, and we will learn about some of them in this book.

When translating, like classical musicians that train to get as close as possible to perfection, we have to make an effort to detach ourselves from our ideological background, which would require a certain degree of self-awareness, as the inscription of Apollo in Delphi suggests: "know thyself."

When approaching the Bible, theologians and believers are anything but detached from their conception of "God." Instead of striving for objectivity, they deliberately overlay the ancient text with their own views.

The biblical text is far from the cultural and intellectual milieu in which the Western conception of "God" took shape. Instead of correcting themselves when necessary, they fix the Bible.

Theologians and religious translators should refrain from changing the text and falsifying it when it goes against their beliefs, as they do, to provide an example, with the word [olam], regularly translated with "eternity" in the Bible. Ancient Hebrew dictionaries clearly explain that [olam] does not mean "eternity." "Eternity" in itself is a concept alien to the Bible.

This is a fine example that well explains how theologians use modern concepts, or at least theological concepts dear to them, to overwrite the biblical text. Not in one instance does the word [olam] means "eternity" in the Bible, and yet it is translated with "eternity" all the time.

A similar case is the word [kavod], which is translated with the word "glory" but does not mean "glory." Other terms, such as [ruach] or [elohim], to which we dedicate the following chapters, have also been attributed wrong meanings that reflect a monotheistic will to superimpose a specific religious view.

In sum, every time a biblical passage does not seem to confirm the theologians' concept of "God," they feel comfortable forcing a translation onto the text or resorting to allegorical meaning aimed at fixing the contradiction from a monotheistic perspective.

This approach is entirely anachronistic and antiscientific, yet it does not raise eyebrows within the academic environment.

When approaching an ancient text, we are like archaeologists on the field. We must be aware that before we get to any finding, we must remove strata of dirt with the brush and the trowel. Many layers of earth and dirt have been deposited for centuries on the site we are excavating, and we need to remove them before we get to the object of our study.

In the same way, when we approach the Bible, we must know that there are more than two thousand years of dirt deposited on this delicate object, on this highly fragile text.

The thick theological incrustation deposited on the Bible for more than two thousand years prevents us today from reading it for what it is: an amazing piece of ancient literature that could contain extraordinary truths about our past.

It is about time that humanity retrieves this wonderful book.

The task is not easy because, as we said before, the Bible has become the foundation of an inveterate power structure that affects the religious but also the ethical, political, and economic sectors.

To do so, however, we challenge the theologians on their ground, taking seriously their claim that the biblical text contains the *truth*.

In fact, we consider the Bible *true* in its literal meaning.

We do not assume the redactors/authors of the biblical text misrepresented their own ideas or the facts and events they intended to convey and describe.

We believe that biblical authors always told the truth as they saw it, even when they represent Yahweh as a violent individual who orders the extermination of women and children; or when, to give another example, they tell the story of Yahweh claiming for himself 675 sheep, 72 cattle, 61 donkeys, and, hear this, 32 virgins (Numbers 31:32-40), after a battle against the Midianites.

This part of the booty was not intended for the service of the tabernacle, as explained clearly in Numbers 35, but for Yahweh himself, that is, *for him personally*. One only wonders what a spiritual and transcendental "God" needed 32 virgins for.

Such descriptions and disturbing passages were not intended as metaphors or allegories but accurately represented what the writer had heard or seen.

Similar examples are found everywhere in the Bible.

Believers and theologians have trouble with examples that show Yahweh in a bad light, like a violent, jealous, narcissistic, vengeful, bad-tempered, irascible, and manipulative individual.

Similar descriptions of Yahweh are endless in the Bible, and theologians cannot make sense of them unless they resort to all kinds of hermeneutical categories to "interpret" these passages in a "convenient" way that does not contradict the idea of "God" as a spiritual, transcendental, omnipotent, omniscient entity.

This is where exegesis was born. This is where theology thrives. This is also where the Bible stops making sense.

To avoid these problems, we have decided to approach the Bible with a method that does not allow the translator/interpreter to arbitrarily decide when to read the text literally and when to read it allegorically or metaphorically.

We are determined to read the Bible literally and, most importantly, to follow what seems to us the only serious and honest approach left when reading the Bible: pretending.

Because of the insurmountable contradictions presented above, we are convinced that the only intellectually honest and coherent way to deal with the Old Testament is to "pretend" that what we read is true in the literal sense.

We do not claim that it is true in the theological sense or the sense of absolute truth. We only pretend that it is true as we read it. We believe that when the biblical authors wrote certain things, they meant to say them, not something else.

Schliemann comes to our help. He adopted this method against the advice of the whole academic community, but being faithful to it, he was able to find the buried city of Troy.

Schliemann's methodological approach has led to acquiring knowledge and a historical-archaeological heritage that would have remained buried forever if he had not dared to choose this new and challenging path.

We have used and openly declared this same methodology since our studies in this field began.

Therefore, as already mentioned, we avoid using hermeneutic categories and interpretations such as allegory or metaphor.

As contestable as this methodological stance is, it has the advantage of being clearer than those who resort to vague hermeneutic categories at their discretion.

This approach is also more consistent, with some essential characteristics of Jewish thought, always open to discussion, and never tied to definitive interpretations.

Within the Jewish community, the need to incessantly analyze and compare the beliefs of individuals has led to the formation of a tradition that thrives on commentary and competing interpretations, that which makes knowledge always precarious, critical, never stable, and aptly expressed by a well-known proverb: "One Jew two opinions, two Jews five opinions."

With a respectful and humble mentality, we try to enter into this freedom of analysis by maintaining clear procedures: original Hebrew text, literal translations, careful selection of quoted passages, but above all, the desire to preserve as much as possible logical coherence in our conclusions.

Traditional study systems have led primarily to the development of numerous theologies, often in open and irreconcilable conflict. So, without specific and universally valid facts, the interpretation key presented here can be regarded as one of many possible.

Let us thus proceed with serenity.

— Let us "pretend" the Bible we read is the one originally written.

— Let us "pretend" the biblical authors, when they wrote something, wanted to tell us exactly that.

— Let us "pretend" the ancient authors left in their writings the memory of actual events.

— Let us "pretend" that these books can be considered, in essence, as history books.

אלהים
2 / ELOHIM

1. What "God" means

Let us start with a few short pages devoted to the terms for "God." In particular, we ask ourselves: does "Elohim" mean "God" or not?

We know what "Elohim" means to us today — or better, we know what it means to most translators of the Bible today — but the reality is that no one knows precisely what the word "Elohim" meant for the authors of the ancient biblical texts, *at the time when they were written.*

Let us put it in more general terms.

In the study of ancient languages, it is not uncommon to be uncertain about the primitive meaning of certain words. All the ancient texts that we know once stood in a cultural context that has disappeared forever, the contours of which are often vague, and can be inferred only partially from the text itself. The point of philological and historical research is to bring to light concepts and aspects that have been taken for granted for so long that no one questions them anymore.

Perhaps, this logic would make more sense if we were to turn the question around and focus for a second on the concept of "God" rather than "Elohim."

Even if we accept that "Elohim" means "God," we should ask ourselves: is our idea of "God" today the same as the concept of "God" that ancient Semitic peoples had thousands of years ago? Obviously, no.

That said, the term "Elohim" in the Hebrew Bible entails multilayered semantics that we will try to summarize in the following sections.

It would be helpful to note first that "Elohim" is not the only term in the Bible translated as "God." Conversely, "Elohim" is not always solved with "God" either.

Let us thus take a closer look at the meanings that Bible translators ascribe to the word "Elohim" and examine some of the hypotheses that scholars formulate in their books on the subject. The definition of such a term, as we shall see, is so uncertain that caution is the really indispensable attitude when moving on this ground.

1. Some of the meanings biblical Hebrew dictionaries ascribe to the term "Elohim" are: "rulers," "judges," "gods," "superhuman beings," "angels," "children of God," "mighty ones," "God," "deity," "godlike beings," "those from above."

2. "God" also often renders the biblical terms Eloha. According to some scholars, this variant is a feminine singular form, from which the term "Elohim" is derived. Others hold that the word Eloha is derived from "Elohim" and not vice versa. This term is also used to refer to a "foreign god."

3. Another "divine" name that is found in the Bible is "El," which is usually considered the singular form of "Elohim." However, to some scholars, these are two distinct terms. "El" would be used to mean "strong," "powerful," "an object of fear," or "something to be accomplished." It could also mean "chief" or "lord."

4. The term "Elohim," while always rendered with "God" by traditional translation, contains in fact the Hebrew ending of the plural. Monotheists claim that "Elohim" is singular despite the plural ending. However, it must be noted that "Elohim" is used in the Bible with both singular and plural verbs. So, does it mean "God" or "gods?" Furthermore, it is often combined with an article. (In Hebrew, the article in the singular and in the plural is the same: there is no distinction between the two.) So we could either translate it as "the god" or "the gods."

5. As noted, the article often precedes the term "Elohim." It is not the same to say "god" or "the god." This grammatical element alone proves that "Elohim" is not a proper name but the designation of an individual within a larger group.

2. "I speak clearly and not in riddles"

Having established that the semantic area around the term "Elohim" is all but unequivocal, we are faced with an inevitable decision to accept doubt as our guiding light.

The only possibility of understanding the complex question surrounding the term "Elohim" arises not from dogmatic truths but from analyzing the occurrence of the term in various contexts. A synoptic examination of the diverse instances in which the term is found can go very far in the attempt to get closer to the meaning in which the term "Elohim" was written and used in ancient times.

Furthermore, we shall also consider the behavior attributed to the Elohim in the Bible, and at the same time, the behavior that people adopted toward the Elohim.

We can't help noticing on the side that if the term "Elohim" referred to the unique and universal principle, the one "God" imagined by monotheistic theologians, then several dozen biblical passages would remain incomprehensible (see next section).

Let us thus immediately clarify, as will result clear in the ensuing chapters and pages of this book, that in the Old Testament, the Elohim *are* clearly and recurrently presented as a plurality of individuals.

This will result clear not only from a grammatical perspective but also from the biblical narrative itself, from the unfolding of the stories, and from the interaction between characters, even when read in traditional translations.

It is no accident that religious and spiritualist interpretations of the Bible are forced to consequently define many parts as metaphorical, allegorical, poetic, pedagogical, mythical, esoteric, and so on.

For traditional theologians and conservative religious readers, accepting specific biblical passages is only possible through the aprioristic introduction of hermeneutical categories, often used to define the incomprehensible, such as the "mystery of faith" and "esoteric-initiatory concealment."

With all due respect for differing positions, our method is different. We weigh carefully the concreteness of the Hebrew language and do not dismiss easily the very words of Yahweh, who affirms with unmistakable clarity: "I speak clearly and not in riddles" (Numbers 12:8).

When read literally, with a skeptical and open mind, the Bible is clear.

The Bible speaks extensively about the Elohim. We read about their characteristics, personalities, deeds, intentions, and words. The combination of these data makes the hypothesis that "Elohim" denotes a plurality of individuals entirely plausible.

3. Is "Elohim" plural or singular?

I present in the interrogative form a problem that the Judeo-Christian monotheistic exegetes and theologians always solve dogmatically. For them, there is no doubt that the term "Elohim" denotes the spiritual, transcendent, omnipotent, omniscient, and only "God." Despite the plural ending, monotheistic theologians maintain that the term's meaning is singular.

In the face of this thesis, two different attitudes are possible.

The first attitude is to question the traditional interpretations on philological grounds. Experience, however, teaches that this choice leads to endless and unproductive disputes. It is often impossible, from a philological and linguistic perspective, to prove the absolute correctness of this or that position, therefore the contenders remain rooted in their beliefs.

The second attitude — which I consider cleverer — consists of the deliberate acceptance of the traditional monotheistic theses. By making this choice, one chooses to believe the opposing party's claims to be valid.

So let us continue with this reverse process: instead of challenging the traditional monotheistic positions, let us "pretend" these positions are valid and see what ensues.

The rules, guidelines, interpretations, and grammatical norms elaborated by the monotheistic exegetes have the purpose of helping the faithful to understand the Bible. Therefore, the most helpful behavior is precisely the application of these guidelines to the biblical text.

Let us then examine some passages in light of the claim formulated by the exegetes on the specific subject of the term "Elohim."

For theologians and traditional exegetes "Elohim" is a term that has a singular value and designates exclusively a precisely identified person: Yahweh-God. They exclude multiplicity and the existence of other Elohim distinct from Yahweh.

Let us start with an indisputable fact: Yahweh is often defined with the term "Elohim," and he is more precisely identified as the "Elohim of Abraham, Isaac, and Jacob."

The dozens of times this statement occurs in the Bible always have a clear and unambiguous purpose: to make it clear that Yahweh is the "Elohim" who deals exclusively with Israel and not with other peoples. Consequently, Israel must also address him exclusively.

In view of this incontrovertible "theological" fact, let us see how we can apply it to numerous biblical passages and check its intelligibility and congruence in the text.

For immediate understanding and in full respect of the text, unless otherwise noted we report in the translations the exact terms used by the ancient biblical authors — for example, "Elohim" — without suggesting any specific translations of them, which would require explanations and interpretations.

In our view, this is the most correct and appropriate methodology to deal with texts that are not always solid from the point of view of philological reconstruction.

A doubtful attitude avoids the risk of falling into the temptation, typical of dogmatism, of replacing presumed truths with other and different presumed truths.

This methodology also allows us to proceed with examples the reader can carefully verify in the Bible at their disposal.

~ Genesis 6

Without further ado, let us start from a passage from Genesis, in which the biblical authors say that the "sons of the Elohim" liked women and they would take as many of them as they pleased.

> When human beings began to increase in number on the earth and daughters were born to them, the sons of the Elohim saw that the daughters of the-Adam were beautiful, and they married any of them they chose.
>
> (Genesis 6:1-2)

— If the term "Elohim" refers to one and the same person (Yahweh-God), how could he have children?

— If "Elohim" always refers individually to one and the same person

(Yahweh-God), why is the term "Elohim" preceded by the definite article "the" in Hebrew?

— If "Elohim" here refers to "angels," as some traditional commentators claim, why did the biblical editors/authors not use the common terminology for "angels" that is found in all other books of the Bible, namely [malakhim]?

— Why is there an explicit reference to "children/sons of the Elohim" here? If these sons were men, why mention they married women? Who else would they marry? It is redundant and unnecessary information unless they were not "men."

All these questions are very difficult to answer if we read the biblical text from a monotheistic point of view, as theologians would like to do.

But suppose "Elohim" denotes a plurality of individuals, both in the sense of their acting as a group (which is sometimes rendered in Hebrew by the verb in the singular), and in the sense of identifying one of them as belonging to that group (the "Elohim" Yahweh); then all the insoluble problems we have indicated above would disappear. The situation would become immediately understandable without needing explanation or interpretation.

~ Genesis 31

The end of Genesis 31 (which we urge the reader to read in its entirety) describes a tumultuous encounter between Jacob and his father-in-law, Laban.

After a harsh confrontation, the father-in-law and son-in-law erect a stone on which they swear neither will cross that line with hostile intent against the other.

To ensure compliance with this territorial pact, they invoke the Elohim in the following manner:

> May the **Elohim of Abraham** and the **Elohim of Nahor**, the **Elohim of their father**, judge between us.

(Genesis 31:53)

Nahor was Abraham's brother and Laban's grandfather. We thus have proof that Abraham's family was divided, and followed and worshiped different Elohim.

We thus learn that there were the Elohim of Nahor who ruled in Mesopotamia, where Nahor dwelt with his family, and the Elohim whom Abraham had followed into the land of Canaan.

Incidentally, the reader must know that in Genesis 20:13 Abraham says: "When Elohim had me wander from my father's household...." The verb "had" is found in Hebrew in the plural form. Therefore, it is the patriarch himself who employs the verb in the plural. Was he following more than one Elohim?

We also note that in the Italian edition of the Jerusalem Bible (EDB, 2013), the passage in question (Genesis 31:53) is correctly explained in a note: "the gods on both sides are called as witnesses, as customary in ancient treatises."

The Bible does not report an extraordinary event but a general custom. Nothing unique about this act of law was sanctioned by the presence of the powerful who ruled on both sides. Jacob and Laban acted in absolute conformity with the norms of the time.

The passage is fascinating, however, in relation to the question of the "Elohim" since it reveals two self-evident aspects: the plurality of the individuals called to ensure observance of the oath and their absolute parity.

There is no distinction between the supposedly true "God" and other unidentified Elohim.

It is precisely the clarity of the situation described that raises questions for monotheistic theological exegesis.

— If the term "Elohim" always individually refers to one and the same person (Yahweh-God), how can other Elohim, endowed with the same dignity and power, be asked to take an oath?

— If "Elohim" individually always refers to the same person (Yahweh-God), how can Nahor feel guaranteed by a non-existent Elohim who would be completely helpless compared to the protection granted to Abraham by none other than the almighty "God?"

— Did Nahor (Abraham's brother) and his family not know the difference between the one "God" and their Elohim (who do not exist according to theological teaching)?

—   Did Nahor and his people not know that their closest relatives had a relationship with the almighty Elohim ("God")? Did they never realize the difference between the two Elohim? Have the two brothers ever had the opportunity to compare, on the one hand, the true "God" of Abraham and, on the other hand, idols made of inert stone?

—   Did Abraham never encourage his brothers and nephews to abandon the childish, primitive, ineffective, and unproductive worship of rocks to approach the only true "God" he was fortunate enough to know? Is this even possible?

However, if the term "Elohim" indicated a plurality of individuals and their actions as a single group, all the questions above become irrelevant. The situation becomes immediately understandable and clear without needing explanation or interpretation.

Moreover, their acting as a group would also explain the use of the verb in the singular in several occurrences, given the concreteness of the ancient Hebrew language, which had no fixed grammatical rules but tended primarily to describe situations in concrete terms.

~ *Genesis 32*

The story described in Genesis 31 takes an exciting development in Genesis 32. After erecting the stone, and once the oaths and promises have been made, Jacob continues his journey. As he walks on the street, he encounters two messengers of the Elohim:

> When Jacob saw them, he said: "**This is the camp of Elohim!**" So he named that place **Machanaim**.
>
> (Genesis, 32:2)

Now, [machanaim] is a term written in the so-called "dual form." It thus means "two camps."

The situation is clear. Jacob arrives at a place where he finds two military camps with the troops who defended their respective borders and who therefore acted as guarantors.

—   If the term "Elohim" always refers individually to the same person (Yahweh-God), how could Elohim have two camps?

— Why would Yahweh-God even have two camps?

— If "Elohim" always refers individually to one and the same person (Yahweh-God), doesn't everything seem entirely absurd?

However, if the term "Elohim" indicated a plurality of individuals and their actions as a single group, all the questions above become irrelevant. The situation would again become immediately understandable without the need for explanations or interpretations.

~ Exodus 3:12-15

In this passage, the Elohim speaks to Moses. He wants to provide him with more information about his mission and goals. Moses listens to what he is told, however is unsure with whom he is dealing; he needs to know precisely. Thus, Moses asks the Elohim:

> Behold, I go to the Israelites and say to them, "**The Elohim of your fathers** has sent me to you," and they will ask me, "**What is his name?**" What will I answer then?
>
> (Exodus 3:13)

— If the "Elohim" of the fathers was one, how could Moses have doubts?

— If the term "Elohim" is always Yahweh-God in the singular, how could Moses, the greatest of the prophets, have doubts about his identity?

— If the Elohim of the fathers was the one and only "God," how could the Israelites have doubts about his identity?

What we had previously read in Genesis 31 and 32 makes us understand that Moses had reasons to ask this question. He wanted to know which of the Elohim he was dealing with because he did not know, and obviously, it was possible, if not easy, to make a mistake.

If, on the other hand, as is clear from the biblical text, the term "Elohim" denotes a plurality of individuals, our questions become irrelevant. Moses' strange request to know the identity of the Elohim becomes perfectly sensible; the situation becomes clear without needing explanation or interpretation.

~ Exodus 15:11

After their deliverance from Egypt, the Israelites sing a song of joy to Yahweh, praising him with the exclamation, "Who is like you among the Elohim?" (Exodus 15:11).

— If "Elohim" is always Yahweh-God in the singular, the people's song of triumph — "who is like you among the Elohim?" — sounds absurd.

— If "Elohim" always refers to Yahweh-God in the singular, how could they make such an inexplicable and ridiculous statement?

But suppose that "Elohim" refers to a plurality of individuals, these questions become irrelevant, and the song of joy of Exodus 15:11 becomes understandable without needing explanation or interpretation.

~ Exodus 18

Moses' father-in-law, whose name is Jethro or Reuel, comments on Moses' success in leading the Israelites out of Egypt. He expresses his joy and admiration by exclaiming:

> Now I realize that Yahweh is greater than **all the Elohim**.
>
> (Exodus 18:11)

— If the term "Elohim" indicates Yahweh-God in the singular, how can "God" be greater than all the Elohim?

— Why is "Elohim" accompanied in Hebrew by an adjective meaning "all, everyone, each?" What is the point of using this adjective if "only one" exists?

— Why does an article precede the term "Elohim?"

— What did Jethro mean? Did he mean that Yahweh is greater than all the "judges" (one of the terms used by commentators to justify the plural ending of the term "Elohim")? Can one imagine a more blatant banality than this?

Suppose, instead, the term "Elohim" denotes both a plurality of individuals and their actions as a group, the above questions become irrelevant, and the passage becomes understandable without needing explanation or interpretation.

~ Exodus 20

In enumerating the Ten Commandments, the alleged "God" begins with an assertion that leaves no room for interpretation:

> I am **Yahweh your Elohim**, who brought you out of the land of Egypt, out of the land of slavery. You shall have **no other Elohim** before me.
>
> (Exodus 20:2-3)

— If the term "Elohim" is always Yahweh-God in the singular, why does the one and only "God" need to specify that he was the one who brought them out of Egypt?

— Could there have been any misunderstanding or doubt about his identity?

— If "Elohim" is Yahweh-God in the singular, why does Yahweh say that there shouldn't be "other Elohim" using the plural adjective אחרים [acherim], which means "other, different, foreign?"

— If "Elohim" is always Yahweh-God in the singular, how could one think that the people, as soon as they came out of the state of subjection in Egypt, could turn to "other Elohim," whose existence they were not aware of and could thus not even imagine?

However, if the term "Elohim" indicated a plurality of individuals and their actions as a single group, all the questions above become irrelevant, and Yahweh's order becomes immediately understandable without the need for explanation or interpretation.

~ Deuteronomy 6

Moses speaks to his people and admonishes them:

> You shall not follow **other Elohim among the Elohim** of the nations around you.
>
> (Deuteronomy 6:14)

— If the term "Elohim" is always Yahweh-God in the singular, why does the Hebrew text have the plural adjective אחרים [acherim], which means "other, different, foreign?"

— If the term "Elohim" means Yahweh-God in the singular, how can Moses demand not to follow "other Elohim among the Elohim" of the surrounding nations? It goes without saying that when one chooses "among," it means that the choice is made within a plurality of individuals, at least two; otherwise, common sense tells us there is no possibility of choice.

— If we want to say that the term "Elohim" means "judges," as theologians and monotheistic exegetes claim, we have to admit that Moses thought his people were naive enough to hesitate between "God" and very ordinary and human "judges."

However, if the term "Elohim" indicated a plurality of individuals and their actions as a single group, all the questions above become irrelevant, and the quoted passage becomes understandable without needing explanation or interpretation.

~ Deuteronomy 13

We read here a sequence of commands given to the Israelites. They are told how to behave in various situations concerning Yahweh.

> If your very own brother, or your son or daughter, or the wife you love, or your closest friend secretly entices you, saying, "let us go and worship **other Elohim,**" **(Elohim that neither you nor your ancestors have known, from Elohim of the peoples around you,** whether near or far, from one end of the land to the other), do not yield to them or listen to them. Show them no pity. Do not spare them or shield them. You must certainly put them to death. Your hand must be the first in putting them to death, and then the hands of all the people. Stone them to death, because they tried to turn you away from Yahweh your Elohim, who brought you out of Egypt, out of the land of slavery.

(Deuteronomy 13:7-11)

— If the term "Elohim" is always Yahweh-God in the singular, why does the Hebrew text have the plural adjective אחרים [acherim], which means "other, different, foreign?"

— If "Elohim" is always Yahweh-God in the singular, how could "other

Elohim" be addressed?

- If "Elohim" is always Yahweh-God in the singular, how could there be the possibility of following "other Elohim chosen from and among the Elohim" of the surrounding peoples?

- Why this real, concrete, tangible fear on the part of Yahweh, who goes so far as to order the murder of even the closest family member who incites treason?

If someone claims, however, that the term "Elohim," in this case, means "judges" or inert pagan idols, then we note that Yahweh considered his followers so naive as to hesitate between him (the supposedly omnipotent "God") and very human "judges" or, even worse, ridiculous piles of stones or wooden stakes.

However, suppose the term "Elohim" denotes a plurality of individuals and their actions as a group; all the above questions become irrelevant, and the passage becomes understandable without needing explanation or interpretation.

~ Deuteronomy 32

This chapter is traditionally called the "Song of Moses" and contains numerous passages that, in their extraordinary clarity, contribute to understanding the concreteness of the biblical story.

We invite the reader to read Deuteronomy 32 from the first verse. Here I examine two passages of this chapter that are particularly effective for understanding the plurality of the Elohim.

In verse 8 and 9, Elyon ("the one above," the commander of the Elohim) assigns the peoples the territories they are to settle. Yahweh receives the inheritance of the family of Jacob, which, as the Bible says, was wandering lost in the wilderness, having not even received the allotment of a specific territory.

> When Elyon gave the nations their inheritance, when he divided all mankind, he set up boundaries for the peoples according to the number of the sons of Israel. For Yahweh's portion is his people, Jacob his allotted inheritance. In a desert land he found him, in a barren and howling waste.

> (Deuteronomy 32:8-10)

Verse 12 is particularly interesting for our investigation: "Yahweh alone led him; no foreign El was with him."

Moses then expresses all his anger at the people of Israel, who often betrayed the commitment made with Yahweh and turned to "other Elohim." Moses even points out that:

> They sacrificed to [**shedim**] who are not **Eloha, Elohim whom they did not know, new**, recently come [**from nearby**], whom your fathers had not feared.
>
> (Deuteronomy 32:17)

Moses expresses his deep resentment that the people put themselves in the service of [shedim], who were not even Elohim!

These [shedim] were individuals belonging to a lower hierarchical rank, probably equivalent to that of the Assyro-Babylonian [shadu]. They probably acted as intermediaries between the people and the Elohim.

– If the term "Elohim" is always Yahweh-God in the singular, why does verse 12 say that Yahweh led Jacob alone, without the help of a "foreign El?" How could this possibility even exist?

– If "Elohim" is always Yahweh-God in the singular, how could Moses claim (verse 17) that there were Elohim "new, recently come [from nearby]?"

– Who were these Elohim "recently come [from nearby]," and from where did they come?

If "Elohim," in this case, as some claim, just means "judges, legislators," then we must take note of the fact that, at that time, some unknown judges roamed the land and that the people of Israel were unable to comprehend the difference between "God" almighty and some ordinary "judges, legislators" — and chose the latter.

How can you mistake the one and almighty "God" for some human judge?

But we learn from Sumerian-Akkadian texts that some of the Elohim did not receive any territory or people in the course of the assignments made by the commander of the Elohim (the biblical Elyon of Deuteronomy 32); therefore, they complained and some went about subjugating the peoples they could find.

However, if the term "Elohim" indicated a plurality of individuals and their actions as a single group, all the questions above become irrelevant, and the situation becomes understandable without any need for explanations or interpretations.

~ Joshua 24

Joshua succeeded Moses as leader of the people of Israel.

When the conquest of the land of Canaan was imminent, he gathered the tribes of Israel at Shechem and summoned the elders.

Joshua's goal is to reconfirm the covenant between the people of Israel and their Elohim; above all, he wants to verify the intentions of the Israelites.

Joshua delivers a speech containing many interesting elements for our analysis. In verses 1 to 13, Joshua reminds the people of all the interventions and wonders Yahweh has done for them since their exit from Egypt. Then he tells them:

> "Now fear Yahweh and serve him with all faithfulness. **Throw away the Elohim your ancestors worshiped** beyond the Euphrates River and in Egypt, and serve Yahweh. But if serving Yahweh seems undesirable to you, then **choose for yourselves this day whom you will serve, whether Elohim your ancestors served beyond the Euphrates, or Elohim of the Amorites**, in whose land you are living. But as for me and my household, we will serve Yahweh."

> Then the people answered, "Far be it from us to forsake Yahweh to serve **other Elohim!** It was **Yahweh our Elohim** himself who brought us and our parents up out of Egypt, from that land of slavery, and performed those great signs before our eyes. He protected us on our entire journey and among all the nations through which we traveled. And Yahweh drove out before us all the nations, including the Amorites, who lived in the land. **We too will serve Yahweh, because he is our Elohim.**"

> Joshua said to the people, "You are not able to serve Yahweh. **He is a holy Elohim; he is a jealous El.** He will not forgive your rebellion and your sins. If you forsake Yahweh and serve **foreign Elohim**, he will turn and bring disaster on you and make an end of you, after he has been good to you."

> (Joshua 24:14-20)

First of all, we again find the use of the plural adjective אחרים [acherim], which means "other, different, foreign," that we have previously met.

Here again, we find a reference to the plurality of the Elohim of the fathers, which fully justifies Moses' request to Yahweh to make himself known in Exodus 3:12-15. Given the plurality of the Elohim and the uncertainty about their identity, there was the possibility that they could be confused with one another.

In particular, we learn that the patriarchs served "other Elohim" when they were in Egypt. It is clear that Abraham and his followers, who had come to that land to escape starvation, could do nothing but serve the Elohim who ruled them.

We also learn that in the land of Canaan, where the Amorites lived, there ruled Elohim different from Yahweh and different from those who ruled in Mesopotamia, where the family of Terah and Nahor (Abraham's father and brother, respectively) resided.

Nahor is the same Nahor we find in Genesis 31, whose Elohim vouch for the pact between Jacob and Laban about territorial boundaries, as we have seen above.

Joshua's injunction not to turn to other Elohim, and the reference to the responsibility that will fall on the transgressors, who must repay every treachery with their blood, are repeated at length. Yahweh declares himself without a shadow of a doubt to be a "jealous El."

Finally, in verse 19, the Bible uses the terms "Elohim" and "El" interchangeably.

This wording shows again how the biblical authors used the two terms as synonyms. Speaking of Yahweh, Joshua says, "He a holy Elohim; he is a jealous El."

Biblical authors wrote that Yahweh was an Elohim, meaning that he belonged to the group of the Elohim.

— If the term "Elohim" is unequivocally Yahweh-God in the singular, who were all the other Elohim mentioned as possible and dangerous rivals?

— If "Elohim" is always Yahweh-God in the singular, why does the Hebrew text again have the plural adjective אחרים [acherim], which means "other, different, foreign," associated to the term Elohim?

— If "Elohim" is always Yahweh-God in the singular, then why did the patriarchs not worship him as Lord even when they were in Mesopotamia and Egypt?

- Why, when in Egypt and Mesopotamia, did they instead follow "other Elohim" who did not exist according to monotheistic theology? Had Abraham and his followers so quickly forgotten the only true "God?"

- If "Elohim" is always Yahweh-God in the singular, why were there other Elohim in Canaan (the so-called Promised Land)?

- If "Elohim" is always Yahweh-God in the singular, how could he be "jealous" of other Elohim who did not exist according to monotheistic doctrines?

- If "Elohim" is always Yahweh-God in the singular, why did the biblical authors, when naming Yahweh, feel the need to specify that he is the "Elohim of Israel" or the "Elohim of Abraham, Isaac, and Jacob?" From whom did they want to distinguish him, since he was the only one?

However, if the term "Elohim" indicated a plurality of individuals and their actions as a single group, all the questions above become irrelevant, and the situation becomes intelligible without needing further explanation or interpretation.

~ 1 Kings 11

In this passage, prophet Ahijah informs Jeroboam that Yahweh has decided to take the kingdom out of Solomon's hands and give it to him.

> They have forsaken me and worshiped Ashtoreth, **Elohim of the Sidonians**, Chamosh, **Elohim of the Moabites**, and Milkom, **Elohim of the Ammonites**.
>
> (1 Kings 11:33)

The statement is clear. There are "other Elohim" for whom Solomon, the wisest of all men, built places of worship.

That these "other Elohim" existed is also documented in Judges 11:24. Here, the commander of Israel's forces addresses the king of the opposing army and tells him:

> Will you not take what **your Elohim, Chamosh**, gives you? Likewise, whatever **Yahweh our Elohim** has given us, we will possess.
>
> (Judges 11:24)

–   If "Elohim" is always Yahweh-God in the singular, how can there be
    these other Elohim who are explicitly named in various places in the
    Bible?

–   If "Elohim" is Yahweh-God in the singular, how could the wise Solo-
    mon have other, non-existent Elohim build places of worship? Could
    the wisest of all men not see the difference between the almighty
    "God" and the non-existent stone idols?

–   If "Elohim" is always Yahweh in the singular and represents the only
    "God," how could the commander of Israel's forces grant the non-ex-
    istent Chamosh the right to give land to other people and grant them
    the right to keep the land received?

However, if the term "Elohim" indicated a plurality of individuals
and their actions as a single group, all the questions above become irrelevant, and the situation becomes immediately intelligible without needing further explanation or interpretation.

~ 2 Kings 5

Naaman, commander of the army of the king of Aram, suffers from a
skin disease that the prophet Elisha manages to cure by recommending
him a series of baths in the waters of the Jordan. This result is considered
a miracle due to the intervention of Yahweh, who worked through his
prophet.

Naaman thus promises not to offer a sacrifice to any Elohim other
than that of Israel. The Hebrew expression he uses again contains the
adjective that we have already seen occurring several times in connection
with the term "Elohim," that is אחרים [acherim], which means "other,
different, foreign."

Naaman says that he will no longer offer sacrifices and offerings to
"any other Elohim but Yahweh" (verse 17).

Here again, it is confirmed that Yahweh belongs to the group of Elohim. Naaman, too, shows that he knows that the Elohim are many. Still,
of all possible Elohim, the general chose to address himself exclusively to
the Elohim of Israel from that moment.

Even if we want to admit that "Elohim" is a concept of singular value,
we must still note that besides Yahweh and the "other Elohim" mentioned in the previous sections, there was another Elohim named Rim-

mon, whom the Bible quotes in the following verses.

Rimmon was one of the names by which Hadad, the Elohim who ruled over Damascus, was identified.

Naaman makes a rather strange request to the prophet Elisha, who makes an even stranger concession to the newly converted general.

> "May Yahweh forgive your servant for this one thing: when my master enters the temple of Rimmon to bow down and he is leaning on my arm and I have to bow there also — **when I bow down in the temple of Rimmon, may Yahweh forgive your servant for this.**" "Go in peace," Elisha said.
>
> (2 Kings 5:18-19)

General Naaman has just "converted" to Yahweh, the only "God," and yet asks the prophet for permission to bow down to Rimmon, another Elohim.

The confirmations that the Elohim are a group, a multitude of individuals, are indeed numerous.

~ Jeremiah 7

Yahweh warns Jeremiah not to try to intercede for people guilty of an offense that cannot be forgiven:

> "The children gather wood, the fathers light the fire, and the women knead the dough and make cakes to offer to the Queen of Heaven. They pour out drink **offerings to other Elohim to arouse my anger.**"
>
> (Jeremiah 7:18)

— If "Elohim" is singular, why is it accompanied in Hebrew by the plural adjective אחרים [acherim], "other, different, foreign," which includes the female Elohim Astarte? (Perhaps the definition of "Queen of Heaven" refers to her.)

— If "Elohim" is always Yahweh-God in the singular, how could people prepare offerings and libations for "other Elohim" and thus insult him?

— Who were these Elohim, since they did not exist according to monotheistic doctrine?

— Had Yahweh forgotten that the worship of "other Elohim" had been
    advocated precisely by the wisest of men, Solomon himself?

If, instead, the term "Elohim" alternatively identifies both the plurality of these individuals and their actions as a group, all the questions
above become irrelevant and the situation understandable without the
need for explanation or interpretation.

4. Counting the Elohim

Let us examine and test the Judeo-Christian exegetes' rule in interpreting the term "Elohim."
   They claim that the term "Elohim" is just an "indefinite superlative, a
plural of abstraction, a plural of majesty, a plural of sovereignty, a plural
of excellence, a plural of intensity," and therefore it must be translated
in the singular.
   All these definitions were elaborated to explain the biblical use of the
plural form (Elohim) to convey a singular meaning that identifies an
individual entity, "God," who is supposed to be unique according to the
monotheistic view.
   With this concession, we will try to summarize the most important
passages of the Old Testament in which at least one unique Elohim is
mentioned to determine the total number of Elohim in the Bible. We
find there is at least:

— one Elohim (accepting him as a single individual) who makes the
    Adam and his female;

— one Elohim (accepting him as a single individual) whose sons mate
    with the Adamite females;

— one Elohim (accepting him as a single individual) who presents him-
    self to Abraham with the name of El-Shaddai;

— one Elohim (accepting him as a single individual) who presents him-
    self to Jacob;

— one Elohim (accepting him as a single individual) named Yahweh,
    who has a relationship with Moses and his people;

— one Elohim (accepting him as a single individual) to whom Jethro

(Moses' father-in-law) compares Yahweh;

– one Elohim (accepting him as a single individual) represented by the Golden Calf built in the desert during the exodus and called Elohim;

– one Elohim (accepting him as a single individual) who rules over the family of Nahor, Abraham's brother who stayed in Mesopotamia;

– one Elohim (accepting him as a single individual) who rules in Egypt and to whom the family of Abraham turns, as we have read;

– one Elohim (accepting him as a single individual) who rules over the Amorites;

– one Elohim (accepting him as a single individual) who has two camps seen by Jacob;

– one Elohim (accepting him as a single individual) whom Yahweh expressly forbids to serve.

– one Elohim (accepting him as a single individual) who rules over the nations around Israel;

– one Elohim (accepting him as a single individual) from whom Yahweh decides not to receive help in leading Jacob's family, assigned to him by Elyon;

– one Elohim (accepting him as a single individual) named Chamosh, who rules over the Moabites;

– one Elohim (accepting him as a single individual) named Milkom, who rules over the Ammonites;

– a female Elohim (accepting her as a single individual) named Astarte, who rules over the Sidonians;

– one Elohim (accepting him as a single individual) named Rimmon, who rules over Damascus;

– a new Elohim (accepting him as a single individual) who has recently arrived and to whom the Israelites dedicate cultic acts that anger Moses;

– one Elohim (accepting him as a single individual) presiding over an assembly that must be imagined to have had at least two other Elohim present to be defined as such (Psalm 82);

– one Elohim (accepting him as a single individual) to whom the Israelites offer sacrifices at the time of Jeremiah.

The reader who reads the Bible with a calm and open mind will
understand that in many of the passages quoted, the text undoubtedly
refers to many Elohim.

Let us only think of the assembly of Psalm 82, where several dozen
must have participated; whereas, in our brief exposition, we have enumerated only three.

However, since we want to give credit to the Judeo-Christian monotheistic exegetes and consider only one Elohim for each of these listed
situations, we counted a total of twenty-three Elohim.

If we also allow the interpreters to combine Elyon, El-Shaddai, and
Yahweh in one person, plus the El who met Jacob (Genesis 35), we arrive
at twenty Elohim.

We then ask ourselves:

– Given a large number of Elohim mentioned in the Bible, present and
active in a relatively small area, is it surprising that the term has a plural ending to refer to the group or the actions of the group as a whole?

– Do we need to find, elaborate and invent all sorts of explanations to
justify the plural form of the term "Elohim?" With all we have said
we would be stunned if "Elohim" was not in a plural form!

The application of the hypothesis established by the exegetes, stating
that the term "Elohim" is undoubtedly singular, leads to the following
consideration: should the term "Elohim" have a singular value, the Bible
would be an absurd, incoherent, confused, and almost incomprehensible
text.

On the other hand, if we are to affirm the non-theological hypothesis
that the term "Elohim" refers not to an individual but to a plurality of
individuals, to a group of individuals, then the text would be clearly understood by everyone without the need for mediation and interpretation.

It is also clear that, in this second case, the supposed spirituality of
the Old Testament would lose any raison d'être; it would lack any foundation. Therefore, theologians and monotheistic exegetes cannot accept
it.

5. Are the Elohim immortal?

Immortality is not a concept in the Bible. Indeed it does not even apply to the Elohim, who undoubtedly enjoyed a very long life in earthly years; they even passed it on to the antediluvian patriarchs, but they were mortal beings.

The "sacred text" explicitly says so.

Psalm 82 describes an assembly of the Elohim. For the advocates of the traditional doctrine (Elohim = God), Psalm 82 poses a real problem because the term Elohim cannot be traced back to the singular here. This Psalm actually speaks of an assembly of the Elohim, who are, therefore, necessarily many and are accompanied by pronouns, adjectives, and, above all, by ten verbs in the plural form.

The one who presides over the assembly [Elyon] is very angry with the Elohim because they do not rule as they should. He ends his rebuke with a statement that leaves no room for doubt:

> I said, "You are **Elohim**; you are all sons of **Elyon**. But you will die like **Adam**; you will fall like every other ruler."
>
> (Psalm 82:6-7)

Elyon established a clear distinction between "Elohim" and "Adam." This can only mean that the "Elohim" do not belong to the lineage or group of the Adamites, and thus they must be reminded that they "die like Adam." The specification is only necessary because Elohim and Adamites are distinct groups; otherwise, it would make no sense.

Professor Michael S. Heiser is an American Old Testament scholar who earned a Ph.D. in Hebrew Bible and Semitic languages from the University of Wisconsin-Madison in 2004 and an MA in Ancient History from the University of Pennsylvania. He is also the editor of the Logos Bible Software platform. Professor Heiser writes a few things that I will summarize here for simplicity's sake:

— The Elohim are not human beings.

— They are very different beings from the Adamites.

— They live much longer than the Adamites but they are nonetheless mortal.

– The assembly spoken of in Psalm 82 did not even occur on Earth.

Further comment is unnecessary.

6. Conclusions

In summary, the Bible reveals to us the following characteristics of the Elohim:

– The biblical term "Elohim" did not refer to one spiritual, transcendent, omniscient, and omnipotent "God" but to many flesh-and-blood individuals. (We call them "individuals" because, as we have just seen, they are not Adamites either, so they are not men.)

– The Elohim lived long enough to be considered immortal, even though they were not.

– They were individuals who traveled on flying machines called [ruach], [kavod], [merkavah], and [cherubim], as we shall see in the next chapters.

– The Elohim were never considered "gods" in the conventional sense. They were objects of respect and inspired terror simply because of their great power, guaranteed by the technology they possessed.

– The Elohim did not concern themselves with issues such as religion in the modern sense of the word, spirituality, or life after death. Their goal was to define the power structures in the various territories where different civilizations were developing.

– The Elohim knew the laws of nature and the cosmos and passed them on to their most devout followers, creating castes of kings/governors/priests: the so-called "initiates."

– The Elohim had the same privileges and attributes as Yahweh in terms of functions and powers exercised because they belonged to the same group. Yahweh was only one of them.

The Elohim were originally also, and at the same time, as anticipated in the previous section:

- Legislators: they dictated rules and regulations with full decision-making autonomy.

- Governors: they took care of the many aspects of power; they enforced the laws directly or through their agents and delegates, such as Jethro, Moses, and so on.

- Judges: they controlled the observance of the laws, imposed and enforced punishments or had them enforced.

Finally, some people object that the term "Elohim" could indicate a group of influential men, i.e., a group of "normal" men or possibly evolved Adamites.

No special translation of the Bible would be required to realize that this perspective is incorrect. The Bibles we have at home provide sufficient elements to define the distinction between men and Elohim. These were distinct types of individuals.

Let us look at some of these elements:

- The Bible notices that the Elohim had recurrent sexual intercourses with the Adamite women (Genesis 6). If they had been "ordinary" men — possibly powerful ones, such as legislators, rulers, or kings — it would be a platitude even to mention the fact. On the other hand, biblical and extra-biblical literature extensively reports this "interest" of the Elohim in the Adamite women. We discuss this in more detail in Chapter 4.

- The Bible also tells us with great emphasis that the Elohim "made" the Adam. Again, how would this make any sense if we consider the Elohim just as "ordinary" men? It makes sense only because the Elohim were not "normal men." Therefore it was necessary to devote not a small number of pages explaining that a "particular" group of individuals had created the Adam.

- Likewise, we read in Psalm 82 that the Elohim "die like all Adams." If the Elohim had been just "normal" men, would it have been necessary to recall such a self-evident fact? All men die. As mentioned above, the Elohim lived very long lives that would make them look immortal from a human perspective. However, immortal they were not. They "die like Adam." Elyon, the most important of them all, reminds the Elohim group of this fact during an "assembly," a "council." This alone proves that the Elohim were more than one; in fact, they were a multitude. Otherwise, there would be no council.

– Finally, the Elohim seem to have special neurophysiological needs, such as inhaling the smoke produced by burning fat prepared with the modalities minutely prescribed in Leviticus 3:3-5 and other biblical passages. This smoke "calmed" them. We discuss this in chapter 8.

Before moving forward, let us make a clarification. In cases where an article or singular verb is attached to the term "Elohim," we attribute the actions described in that specific section to that particular Elohim that is the protagonist of the events described in the Bible, Yahweh.

We thus intend to avoid the alternating use of "El" (singular) and "Elohim" (plural), which could lead to confusion.

Finally, we have deliberately chosen to mark the term with an initial capital letter, "Elohim," even though grammatical correctness would dictate a lowercase letter. Tradition has accepted this method, and we have adopted it.

From now on, we also free the term Elohim from "inverted commas."

רוח
3 / RUACH

1. Those who traveled in a [ruach]: Ezekiel and Elijah

The term רוח [ruach] is always translated as "spirit" in the Bible. Theology must necessarily provide a spiritual reading for all the stories of the Old Testament; however, we will see that this reading has no textual justification and is often misleading.

As we said, the term רוח [ruach] is commonly translated as "spirit."

The term "spirit" has been used since the Septuagint, the Greek translation of the Bible from the 3rd century BCE. The Alexandrian authors rendered the meaning of [ruach] as "*pneuma*," the ancient Greek word for "breath," "wind," "breath of life," and thus also for "soul and spirit."

The term [ruach] frequently occurs in the Bible, and its rendering in modern languages depends on the religious conception that shapes the particular interpretation of the biblical text.

However, the ancient Hebrew term [ruach] had a very concrete meaning, as it stood for "wind," "breath," "moving air," "storm wind," and thus, in a broader sense, for "that which moves swiftly through the air space."

In the extreme concreteness of the ancient Hebrew language anything that flew swiftly through the air could only be referred to as a kind of "wind." In later theological-spiritualistic elaboration, the term took on the meaning of "spirit" familiar to us today, which it probably did not initially have.

Let's look at some examples of this usage to understand that such an interpretation is often misleading, and doesn't respect the concreteness that characterizes the writing style of the Old Testament.

Let us start in *medias res* and address briefly the so-called "visions" of Ezekiel.

The word "vision" usually translates the Hebrew word מארה [maré], but in the religious realm, has taken on a misleading connotation for the Bible reader.

When we speak of "visions," we immediately think of a phenomenon that causes us to perceive realities that are considered supernatural.

However, the Hebrew term מארה [maré] refers to the concrete act of seeing something real. More specifically, this term refers to what is being observed, *the object of the observation*.

It could be an object, a person, a situation, a scene, an event, or a phenomenon. It refers to something that is seen with one's own eyes.

So let's proceed with examples that will prove important for understanding the Old Testament.

Ezekiel reports in his book that he had "visions of Elohim," [mareót Elohim], being [mareót] the plural of [maré].

> In my thirtieth year, in the fourth month on the fifth day, while I was among the exiles by the Kevar river, the heavens were opened and **I saw visions of Elohim**.
>
> (Ezekiel 1:1)

Ezekiel states that he witnessed events where the Elohim were present with their flying objects.

The prophet was so impressed that he remembers the exact day and place of this event. It was the fifth day of the fourth month of the fifth year of the exile of Jehoiachin (probably 593-592 BCE). Ezekiel then goes on and says:

> And I looked, and, behold, a whirlwind (רוח) [ruach] came out of the north (צפון)[tzaphon], a great cloud, a fire infolding itself, and a brightness was about it, and out of the midst thereof as the color of amber (חשמל) [chashmal], out of the midst of the fire.
>
> (Ezekiel 1:4)

In this crucial passage, the [ruach], i.e., the presumed divine spirit of theology, manifests itself with obvious physical manifestations, both visual and auditory.

This [ruach] also comes from a specific geographical direction (the north), while Ezekiel is found on the banks of a river, the Kevar, a stream derived from the Euphrates in lower Mesopotamia.

We are not dealing here with a mystical experience or a dreamlike vision but with a concrete event, an experience that the prophet lived through and that he describes in detail.

We have a description of a very close encounter with an unidentified object that was undoubtedly in the air. It looked like a thundercloud coming from the north; in its center, the prophet saw a fire (a propulsion system?) rotating around itself, like luminous radiation.

At its core, something glows like amber (חשמל) [chashmal].

The Greeks translated the term [chashmal] as "elektron." This last image likely served to describe the color and glow of the central part, or it represented electromagnetic phenomena since the electrical properties of the "elektron" were already known in antiquity.

In Ezekiel 11, we also read the description of an unexpected action.

A [ruach] carries a person and then performs another action that we would never expect from the "Spirit of God."

> "The spirit (רוח) [ruach] **lifted me up and brought me to the gate of the house of Yahweh** that faces east. There at the entrance of the gate were twenty-five men, and I saw among them Jaazaniah son of Azzur and Pelatiah son of Benaiah, leaders of the people."
>
> (Ezekiel 11:1)

Again, we have a precise spatial description of the events.

The "spirit" [ruach] moves in specific directions from one place to another, a specific location where people known to the prophet are found. This aspect also enables us to understand the biblical narrative's absolute concreteness and extraordinary realism. There is nothing vague and spiritual.

The passage reveals to us again the nature of the structure of the [ruach], its presence in space, and its very practical function.

Even more interesting is the epilogue to this story, told at the end of the same chapter:

> "Afterwards **the spirit [ruach] took me up, and brought me in a vision by the Spirit of God** [ruach of Elohim] **into Chaldea,** to them of the captivity. So the vision that I had seen **went up from me.**"
>
> (Ezekiel 11:24)

The [ruach] takes the prophet to the exiles. Ezekiel stays with them to explain what Yahweh has shown him. Meanwhile, the "vision," "the thing seen," takes off and *moves away from him upwards.*

To summarize this passage, we have the spirit [ruach] lifting Ezekiel and carrying him to the exiles in Chaldea (meaning that he was actually and physically transported there), and while the prophet is standing there talking to the exiles/prisoners, the so-called "vision," i.e., the "object of the vision," leaves and goes away moving upwards.

Then the [ruach] of the Elohim comes from above, takes the prophet, carries him, deposits him, and then heads upwards: מעלי [mealai], says the Bible, i.e., "from above me."

The text cannot be more explicit than this. The report is so specific in describing the movements of the [ruach] that it is difficult to imagine that all this could be attributed to a spiritual entity.

To call [ruach] such an object was how the Hebrew language of that time represented something extraordinary, which produced storm-like effects but could also carry people; and for which there were no precise terms to define it.

This is only a tiny part of the book of Ezekiel referring to flying objects. The interested reader can read more about this subject in chapter 14 of this book.

The [ruach] transports people in the Bible with some frequency. In the following few paragraphs, we will examine the exciting story of the prophet Elijah, who also traveled in a [ruach].

The episode is found in 2 Kings 2 and is known as "the abduction of Elijah," even though the term "abduction" is not appropriate, as what happened to the prophet was known to him in advance. He knowingly sets off towards the take-off site, accompanied by his disciples, who also know what will happen.

The chapter begins with the departure of Elijah and his disciple Elisha from the city of Galgal.

The prophet invites his young follower to stay, telling him that Yahweh ordered him only to go to Bet-El (which means "House of El," i.e., the place where one of the Elohim either lived or could be met). Elisha, however, continues to follow his master.

On the way, they meet other disciples of the prophet. They tell Elisha that they know that Yahweh is about to "take up" Elijah with his "whirlwind" (here, the concept of a stormy wind returns, as in Ezekiel).

There is no doubt that everyone knows what will happen. Yahweh will "bring up" the prophet Elijah.

Elijah and Elisha go to Jericho, and here again, we find some disciples aware of Elijah's impending departure (2 Kings 2:5). The two set out again for the Jordan, followed by fifty disciples. At some point a burning chariot arrives on the other side of the river, taking Elijah with it.

The episode is very straightforward. Elijah ascends to the skies in a chariot, and his departure is foreseen and known by all the prophet's disciples.

The following verses confirm that we are dealing here with an actual and physical "elevation."

These verse are very important because they describe precisely what Elisha did, and above all, what Elisha's followers intended to do. As Elijah takes off they immediately declare their intention to go in search of him.

> "Look," they said, "we your servants have fifty able men. Let them go and look for your master. Perhaps [**ruach**] **of Yahweh (רוח יהוה) has picked him up and set him down on some mountain or in some valley.**" "No," Elisha replied, "do not send them." But they persisted until he was too embarrassed to refuse. So he said, "Send them." And they sent fifty men, who searched for three days but did not find him.
>
> (2 Kings 2:16-17)

By their behavior, the disciples clearly show that what they had experienced was real. Yahweh's [ruach] had physically taken Elijah and, according to them, deposited him somewhere nearby, "on some mountain or in some valley."

It is decided, against Elisha's advice, to send fifty men to look for him. The search continued for the next three days, but with a negative result. Elijah had disappeared, carried up by the chariot of Yahweh into the skies.

The richness of detail of this story documents the concreteness of the biblical accounts. The Bible cannot be more precise than this: one does not spend three days laboriously searching mountains and valleys to find a missing person who has only been "abducted" in a vision or a dream.

Elijah indeed left with the Elohim on a [ruach].

Let us, therefore, look more closely at the connection between the [ruach] and flying. What are these unidentified flying objects observed and described by Ezekiel as well as Elijah and his disciples?

2. Res inexplicata volans

In 1 Kings 18:11-12, Obadiah, the palace overseer of King Ahab, speaks to Elijah and tells him:

יהוה	ורוח
Yahweh	of-[ruach]-and ←

לֹא–אדע	אשר	על	ישאך
know-not-shall-I	that	up	you-transport-will ←

Let us notice the concreteness of the Hebrew expression associated with the term [ruach]. Again, the [ruach] is involved with the physical transportation of someone from one place to another.

In 2 Samuel 22:11, we have Yahweh riding a cherub.

Yahweh is seen in perspective, on the wings of the [ruach]:

ויעף	על–כרוב	וירכב
flew-and	cherub-on	rode-and ←

על–כנפי–רוח		וירא
ruach-of-(wings)parts-side-on		seen-was-and ←

The scene is eloquent and will be analyzed in detail in the chapter dedicated to the cherubim.

Suffice it to say that Yahweh sits on a cherub and uses it to fly.

This ensemble is seen against the background of another element, the [ruach] equipped with "wings," or "lateral parts."

We will examine other similar examples later and see how the term [ruach] refers to an object that can carry a person even long distances (as shown above).

So what was this unknown and unidentified flying object?

In *The Ancient Hebrew Language and Alphabet* we can find early pictorial representations of the individual letters of the Hebrew alphabet (Benner).

The word רוח [ruach] would be represented by the following three signs:

LETTER	PICTOGRAM	MEANING
ר resh (r)		Head of a man: high-ranking, first, beginning, law, command.
ו vav (u)		Peg of the tent: to add, to join, to make certain and stable.
ח het (ch)		Braided rope (DNA?); man facing upwards; side of a tent: it indicates inside and out, to look and/or to reveal, the breath of life, separation, half, arrow, sling.

The term רוח [ruach] would thus consist of three letters, whose ancient Hebrew pictographic representation refers to concepts that we can summarize with the following concepts and images: higher command, rules, laws, certainty, stability, dwelling, observation, revelation, breath of life, division, throwing weapons.

These images belonged to the ancient Semitic and Canaanite cultures even before the Hebrews. Therefore it is inconceivable to gain a definitive understanding of the meanings attributed initially to them.

The impression, however, is that of a representation of the רוח [ruach] consistent with the concreteness of the language in the Old Testament descriptions we examine in our reading.

Benner is even more precise in his *Ancient Hebrew Dictionary* when he claims that [ruach] derives from the roots *"arach," "racha,"* and *"yarach,"* — that have, among others, the meaning of "traveler, someone who follows a prescribed path from one place to another."[7]

Let us add to these considerations one more element. The word [ruach] takes us back also to Sumerian cosmogony.

In particular, we refer to the stories that describe the formation of the solar system: the planets, their orbits, the "destinies" that intersected during the various phases of the gravitational battles that shook our nascent system.

The solar system came into being through a series of positioning, collisions, definitions of orbits, and dramatic changes in those orbits. It was a long and violent sequence of cosmic events that finally brought the individual planets and their satellites into the current positions.

In describing such cosmic battles with vivid language and dramatic depictions, the Sumerians often used the term "winds" to refer to satellites and minor celestial bodies accompanying the planets.

The Sumerian "winds" were thus material, concrete, specific, identifiable objects moving through space.

However, cosmology alone does not exhaust the parallels with the Hebrew texts. There is an element that allows us to investigate the whole question further and clarify the possible concreteness of the meaning of [ruach].

This word has much older origins than the Hebrew rendering we have cited. Its roots are found again in the Sumerian language, where the sound /ru-a/ is rendered with a very explanatory pictogram.[8]

---

[7] When quoting dictionaries we usually do not indicate the page as we mention and refer to a specific entry organized in alphabetical order. In this case for example, the reader can see Benner's *Ancient Hebrew Dictionary*, under the voice: "Ruach." For a full description of the sources see the "Works cited and consulted" section at the end of this book.

[8] Cf. C. A. E. O'Brien, and Barbara Joy O'Brien. *The Genius of the Few*. Borgo Press, 1985.

The drawing contains two elements: an upper object (RU) located above a mass of water (A).

Since we do not know precisely what the image represents, we will borrow the acronym RIV directly from the *Lexicon recentis latinitatis*, i.e., "*Res Inexplicata Volans*," which literally means "Unexplained Flying Object."[9]

By looking at the image, we can be sure of one thing: this "unexplained thing" is hovering over a body of water, as we see the wings mentioned earlier in 2 Sam 22:11.

The surprise comes when we look at what the Bible says right at the beginning of Genesis about this [ruach] at its first appearance. In Genesis 1:2, we read the following:

המים	על-פני	מרחפת	אלהים	רוח
waters-the	of-faces-on	hovering	Elohim	of-[ruach] ←

"The [ruach] of Elohim was hovering over the waters."

The verb [rachaf] — of which the term מרח'ו [merachefet] is the participle — means "to shake" (Jeremiah 23:9), "to vibrate," and indicates the peculiar way in which birds of prey soar through the air, being carried by the currents without beating their wings (Deuteronomy 32:11).

So we see this supposed "Spirit of God" hovering over the waters.

The biblical authors are specific in identifying the position of the [ruach] "over the waters."

Therefore the flying object is not found anywhere but at that exact location, over the waters. It is not found on the land nor in the forest but over the waters, which indicates that it is limited in space and movement.

These characteristics obviously cannot be attributed to the alleged "Spirit of God," which should be present everywhere.

We can picture the [ruach] of the Elohim hovering above the surface of the water precisely as it is depicted on the oldest Sumerian pictograph of the sound /ru-a/, as shown above. The two descriptions — the Sumerian and the biblical one — are in agreement.

How could one not immediately recall Rashi de Troyes, one of the greatest Hebrew exegetes (10th-11th century CE)? In his commentary

---

[9] *Lexicon Recentis Latinitatis: Volumen 1. Et 2.* Urbe Vaticana, Libraria Editoria Vaticana, 2003.

on Genesis 1:2, he drew a very realistic picture of Yahweh's "throne of glory" when he said that at the beginning of creation, he hovered in the air over the surface of the water, just as a dove hovers over its nest. He goes further saying that this RIV responded to his command.[10]

Even for this Jewish commentator, the supposed spiritual presence of "God" flying like a dove was actually "something" outside of "God," an instrument he used to move by "commanding" and "operating" it.

We can at least assume that the term [ruach] had a very different meaning than the one religious tradition later adopted.

One of the leading experts on the Hebrew language, Rabbi Matityahu Clark (former president of the Council for Jewish Education), in his *Etymological Dictionary of Biblical Hebrew*[11] attributes to the root רוח [ruach] the following meanings: "power, open, space, spread."

In the "Explanation/Commentary" section, the same dictionary also says: "forcing space, leaving spaces, winnowing, wind, direction, power."

The meaning of "forcing space" is traced explicitly to Genesis 1:2, where it says that the [ruach] of the Elohim was the מרחפ'ן [merachefet], i.e., it "floated, vibrated" above the surface of the water.

We should not forget that the root [rachaf], from which the participle just examined is derived, refers elsewhere in the Bible to the act of "hovering over" typical of birds, as in Deuteronomy 32:11. In this passage, the biblical author describes the activity of Yahweh protecting his people, comparing his actions to the flight of the eagle hovering over its young and spurring them on.

In the section "Gradational Variant" of the aforementioned *Etymological Dictionary* relative to the term [ruach], we also read: "to force space, separate, impact."

So we have a set of semantic values that clearly and concretely refer to the concept of space in which something moves, to the action of forcing this space and moving in a particular direction, to the idea of the wind and impact.

Sumerian and biblical texts thus agree in giving a sufficiently clear picture of this RIV. We are dealing with a flying machine that the Elohim uses to move around and that can physically transport people

---

[10]   Rashi di Troyes. *Commento alla Genesi*. Genova (Italy), Casa Editrice Marietti, 1999.

[11]   Clark, Matityahu. *Etymological Dictionary of Biblical Hebrew: Based on the Commentaries of Rabbi Samson Raphael Hirsch*. Feldheim Pub, 2000.

from one place to another.

As seen from these biblical passages and other passages that we will later point out to the attention of the reader, the [ruach] seems to have very little to do with the commonly understood idea of "spirit" and "Spirit of God."

The meaning of the [ruach] in the biblical authors' intentions was very concrete, material, and tangible.

Our definition of [ruach] also has the advantage of being extraordinarily coherent with the portrayal of Yahweh and, more generally, with the description of the events told in the Bible, which always resorts to concrete, material language.

3. Conclusions

Like all other languages, the Hebrew language is polysemous; each word can have several meanings. This does not usually pose a problem.

Problems arise when only one of these meanings, for religious and dogmatic reasons, is ever used. This is the case with the term [ruach], which theological commentators always translate as "spirit" or "Spirit of God."

Let us take an example from our daily life to understand better how fallacious this logic is. Consider the following definitions and expressions that contain the term "spirit."

– "Spirit of the times" indicates a predominant cultural trend in society.

– "To raise a spirit" means to summon a ghost.

– "Team spirit" indicates feelings of camaraderie among the members of a group.

– The expression "he is a noble spirit" is a statement that underlines someone's intelligence or greatness, a person with extraordinary intellectual abilities.

– "A man of spirit" indicates a man full of energy or courage.

– "The spirit of the law" is the aim or purpose of a law when it is written.

– "Spirit trade" is an expression that refers to the trade in alcoholic substances. For example, Italy is known, among other things, for "the Grappa spirit," but when Italians distill the spirit from the pomace, they certainly do not distill the "Spirit of God."

As anyone can see, in each of these examples, the term "spirit" has a meaning that is clearly distinct from all others but, at the same time, perfectly understandable in its context without the need for explanations, interpretations, or introduction of allegories or metaphors.

The same is true for the Hebrew word [ruach]. So how can we understand what meaning we should ascribe to the term [ruach] each time we find it? As always, it is the context that lets us know the meaning. Therefore, it is wrong to always translate [ruach] as "spirit" in the sense of "Spirit of God."

As we have seen in the previous sections, the word [ruach] often refers to a concrete object of which the ancient authors describe the functions and (audible and visible) manifestations in detail.

So when we find the word [ruach] or "spirit" in the Bible, we must carefully and intelligently analyze the context to understand what the ancient authors wanted to say.

With the same attention to the context, let us address now one of the most intriguing and fascinating stories of the Bible: the so-called "creation of man."

4 / THE ADAM

1. Evolution and creationism

In recent decades, opinions have split between the creationist and evolutionist factions. The fault lines of this dichotomy were not scientific but related to faith. On one side was the faith of the creationists, a religious belief that claimed to have its basis in the Bible. On the other side, there was a faith based on a religious-like attitude toward science.

Such an attitude prevents even scientists from being open to new hypotheses and findings. Science has constantly evolved in cycles of destruction and reconstruction of what exists. No scientific achievement is permanent; new knowledge can replace and correct old knowledge at any time.

From the perspective of a scientific method, all results must be considered temporary achievements that pave the way to new and more advanced achievements in the future. When scientific results are indisputable, we abandon science and enter the realm of faith; religious faith or scientific faith are not different.

The so-called "creation" of man — in reality, a fabrication — points to a hypothesis that differs from the creation hypothesis and evolution. The point is to be open-minded about the ancient accounts that report an external intervention of extraterrestrial intelligence in developing the human species.

According to one of the fathers of evolutionary theory, intelligent life must have intervened at some point to give precise direction to hominid evolution, a kind of guided evolution with a planned goal, namely to have a species capable of understanding and carrying out orders.

Ancient traditions and scientific observations coincide extraordinarily from this point of view.

This outside intervention was a genetic engineering operation that affected hominids, animals, and plant species suitably modified to produce sufficient food for the new class of "workers."

In support of this hypothesis, we would like to quote the thoughts of the naturalist Alfred Russel Wallace, one of Charles Darwin's closest collaborators.

Wallace noted several inconsistencies in the theory of evolution on which he and Darwin had worked for years. In his opinion, the theory he had helped to develop, while appropriate for many species, was incapable of explaining the emergence of Homo Sapiens, so the causes had to be sought elsewhere.

In his work *Contribution to the Theory of Natural Selection*, Wallace wrote in 1871:

> The inference I would draw from this class of phenomena is that **a superior intelligence has guided the development of man in a definite direction, and for a special purpose, just as man guides the development of many animal and vegetable forms**. The laws of evolution alone would, perhaps, never have produced a grain so well adapted to man's use as wheat and maize; such fruits as the seedless banana and bread-fruit; or such animals as the Guernsey milk cow, or the London dray-horse. Yet these so closely resemble the unaided productions of nature, that we may well imagine a being who had mastered the laws of development of organic forms through past ages, refusing to believe that any new power had been concerned in their production, and scornfully rejecting the theory (as my theory will be rejected by many who agree with me on other points), that in these few cases a controlling intelligence had directed the action of the laws of variation, multiplication, and survival, for his own purposes. We know, however, that this has been done; and we must therefore admit the possibility that, **if we are not the highest intelligences in the universe, some higher intelligence may have directed the process by which the human race was developed**, by means of more subtle agencies than we are acquainted with.[12]

For many, evolutionism has become a new religion that does not allow doubts. Whereas, Wallace's quoted words testify to a healthy (and genuinely scientific) inclination toward "doubt" and the will to keep the mind open to discoveries and progress.

Wallace emphasizes with extreme clarity the necessity of assuming that "higher intelligences in the universe" have intervened in the evolution of the various species, including the human species.

---

[12]   There are many different editions of Wallace's work. You can use: Wallace, Alfred Russel. *Contributions to the Theory of Natural Selection*. White Press, 2016; but you can also find this passage online: "The Limits of Natural Selection as Applied to Man," by Alfred Russel Wallace: people.wku.edu/charles.smith/wallace/S165.html

> A controlling intelligence has directed the action of the laws of variation, reproduction, and survival to its ends [...] **a higher intelligence may have directed the process by which the human race has been evolved**.

Wallace's position is entirely consistent with the ancient accounts, including biblical ones.

With this in mind, let us now look at the "creation" accounts, which are far from resembling the concept of "creation out of nothing" that theology speaks of. As we will see, we are dealing here with Adam's actual fabrication and, thus, the making of a new species, the Adamites.

2. "Let us make Adam"

The Bible tells us of the creation/fabrication of the Adam at two different moments and presents us with the two ways in which "God" intervened.

These two narratives are apparently so different and incompatible that biblical exegesis attributes them to different traditions, allowing an irreconcilable opposition between different editors of the Old Testament.

The two different sources can be traced to how the authors refer to what we today translate as "God." In Genesis 1:26, the biblical authors use the term "Elohim." In Genesis 2:7, the actions being described are attributed to "Yahweh."

In the first case, it is reported that the Elohim decided to create the Adam "in their image and likeness." In the second case, it is said that Yahweh used clay and breathed life into him.

For this reason, scholars speak of different sources and assume that the authors who belonged to one or the other tradition worked with complete autonomy, reporting ancient stories characterized by different origins and, therefore, incompatible.

On this basis, theologians and traditional commentators have tried to find correspondences at different levels in the two accounts of creation in an effort to smooth out the differences and make the narrative coherent from the point of view of the monotheistic perspective; to this end, they introduced concepts beyond the concreteness of the stories, even going so far as to arbitrarily overlook, ignore, and dismiss essential details and facts in the name of a spiritualistic vision that we believe did not come from the biblical authors.

We reject edifying narratives that supposedly reveal higher realities that cannot be easily expressed otherwise. Once again, we "pretend" the Bible faithfully reports what it intended to portray.

A close analysis of the two sections shows us that the attitude with which many commentators accept and explain the inconsistencies in the narrative is by no means justified. The two passages tell the same story, the same action of the Elohim as a group of individuals, including the one known by the name of Yahweh.

Before we get into a detailed analysis of the so-called "creation of man," let us first stress a critical point.

When, as reported in Genesis 1:26, "God" utters the famous "let us make man," the Bible uses a verbal form called *cohortative*. This grammatical form has the value of an exhortation, a call to action, a kind of "come on, let us get on with it, let us move forward."

In commenting on this verse, the Syriacs spoke of a "council" that "God" held with the "mighty assemblies." Others claimed that "God speaks with the angels." Basil of Caesarea said, "How can he speak this way unless he cooperates with others?"

In some Sumerian versions of the same story of the "creation of man," we are offered a more straightforward reading of this plural. The Sumerians report a conversation of Enki with those who should help him with the experiment of the "creation of man," whose results were at first highly unsatisfactory in the eyes of the "gods" and had to be repeated more than once.

The Sumerian accounts clearly show that the determination, implementation, assessment, and enjoyment of the following benefits of a successful accomplishment of the "creation of man" were a collective effort of all the Anunnaki, a joint decision, and a common goal.

Therefore it should not surprise us that the later biblical version of the same story uses the plural cohortative expression: "let us make man." The opposite would have been surprising!

The point, again, is that the term Elohim does not represent one individual but a group. But let us now see how the Anunnaki/Elohim *made* — and not *created* — man.

3. The [tzelem] of the Elohim

Genesis 1:26-28 contains the first version of the creation of man and reads as follows:

אדם	נעשׂה	אלהים	ויאמר
man	make-let us	Elohim	said-and ←

כדמותנו	בצלמנו
likeness-our-as	us-of-image-with ←

The author of the Bible seems to feel the need to emphasize a particular aspect of creation. The Elohim made the man using their צלם [tzelem]. This particular aspect is so important that the biblical author deems it necessary to mention it twice again in the following line (Genesis 1:27):

בצלמו	את–האדם	אלהים	ויברא
image-his-with	man-the	Elohim	made-he-and ←

אהו	ברא	אלהים	בצלם
him	made	Elohim	of-image-with ←

אתם	ברא	ונקבה	זכר
them	made	female-and	male ←

The author wants to ensure that the reader understands well that the Elohim made man using their צלם [tzelem].

– But what is the צלם [tzelem]?
– Why was it so important to reiterate this detail?

The term [tzelem] used by the biblical authors does not denote the abstract concept of "image," as it is variously interpreted in religious literature and traditional theology.

The definition of the term צלם [tzelem], as found under the voice [tzelem] in the *Etymological Dictionary*, defines explicitly *"something material that contains the image", a "complete form"* (Clark).

The word [tzelem] not only denotes something concrete and material but also contains, in the original meaning of the Semitic word root, the concept of being "cut off from." In the *Brown-Driver-Briggs Hebrew and English Lexicon*, the entry [tzelem] reads "something cut out of" (Brown).

When reading this passage with an open mind, we ask ourselves: what is it that contains the image of a human being and can be "cut off, cut out, pulled out?"

DNA immediately comes to mind. Furthermore, Sumerian accounts tell the story of how the element to be inserted to make man was taken from the purified blood of Anunnaki males.

Surprises don't end here. In Genesis 1:27, the preposition ב [be] precedes the term "image" [tzelem]. Traditional translators tend to render the word ב [be] with "as, according to...."

If this was the case, however, we would expect the preposition כ [ki] and not ב [be] in Hebrew. These two prepositions have very different meanings.

– ב [be] means "with, by means of...."

– כ [ki] means "as, according to...."

It is the prefix ב [be] that precedes the term [tzelem], not כ [ki].

So, the Adam is not simply created "according to the image" of the Elohim. The correct translation would be: "with the image," or better, "*with* that material something that contains the image" of the Elohim.

This critical element is always "overlooked" by traditional religious interpretations simply because it is incompatible with monotheistic theology. The reader certainly grasps the essential difference between the two translations.

Another critical point must also be stressed. In Genesis, it is said that all creatures were created "according to their kinds."

> And God said, "Let the land produce living creatures **according to their kinds**: livestock, creatures that move along the ground, and wild animals, **each according to its kind**."

> (Genesis 1:24)

Only for the Adam, this is not stated. Man is not made "according to his kind." Man's kind at the end of the "divine" intervention differs from the one from which it originated.

If we connect all the dots, we can see a precise picture of the so-called "creation of man." We can better understand why the author of Genesis felt the need to repeat twice that we were made "with his [tzelem]… with the [tzelem] of the Elohim."

They wanted to be sure that the reader understood the concreteness and the extraordinariness of the event, the exceptionality of an act resulting from a decision of the Elohim to introduce something *truly theirs* into the new creature, which thus received the breath of life, directly from the "gods."

Let us end this section with a question.

– Who was the creature that received the [tzelem] of the Elohim?

The most likely hypothesis points to Homo erectus or Homo habilis, which were then skillfully selected and blatantly domesticated.

Again, we learn from the Sumerian accounts of creation that man was created to work for the Anunnaki. In other words, the Elohim created Homo sapiens so that he could understand and carry out the instructions received from his makers. Evolution of human thought then transformed these "makers" into "gods."

4. The second account of creation

According to the traditional view, the second version of "creation" is an allegorical story in which "God" is depicted as a potter molding man from clay. This second account, at first sight, seems to be inconsistent with the work of the Elohim described in the previous section.

We believe that, if read correctly, the two stories complement each other. In Genesis 2:7, we read as follows:

וייצר	יהוה	אלהים	את–האדם
formed-and ←	Yahweh	Elohim	man-the

עפר	מן–האדמה
(dry-earth, dust) matter ←	earth-the-from

So, the Elohim does not *create* (the verb is unambiguous) but *forms* the Adam with "something" found on the planet Earth. We immediately notice the correspondence between Adam "man" and [adamah] "earth," also reminiscent of the assonance between "earth" and "earthly."

Tradition has identified this "something" with that which the Elohim has formed the man with: "dust or clay." This is the meaning that is usually attributed to the word עפר [aphar]. This word also has the meaning of "dust or clay." However, the original meaning of [aphar] recalls the broader meaning of an "earthy substance," something belonging to the earth (Clark).

But let us proceed by carefully examining the verse. The Elohim Yahweh formed (Genesis 2:7):

עפר	האדם
aphar	Adam-the ←

Notice that there is nothing, in this verse, between the two words "Adam" and "aphar."

And yet, this passage is always translated as "Yahweh Elohim formed Adam *with* dust." But the preposition "with" is not even found in the biblical text!

As seen when discussing the [tzelem] in the previous section, the English preposition "with" is rendered in Hebrew with ב [be]. As the reader can verify, however, there is no [be] preposition between "Adam" and "aphar." In fact, there is no preposition at all.

Therefore the traditional translation, "Yahweh Elohim formed the Adam *with* dust," is incorrect and does not correspond to the Hebrew text.

This is one of those cases in which the theologians and traditional translators simply falsify the translation to make the text coherent with their religious perspective.

In the quoted passage, there is no preposition. Therefore, the text reads with undoubted clarity: "Yahweh Elohim formed the Adam-aphar," where the close association between "Adam" and "aphar" suggests that the latter term functions as a noun modifier.

Since the word "aphar" has the meaning of "dust, earth," it is very likely that it refers here to a particular kind of Adam: the "Earth-Adam" or "earthling." This lexical choice is in complete agreement with how the

Greek version, the so-called "Septuagint," translates: "ανθρωπον χουν," i.e., "the Earth-man."

The word [aphar] thus indicates a *particular type* of Adam, the one suitable for planet Earth, possibly suggesting that other "Adams" lived in other parts of the universe, suitable for different planets that are not Earth.

Inconsistencies in traditional translations of this part of the Bible do not stop here. There is another statement, in Genesis, that is in stark contrast to conventional theological narrative.

> Then the Elohim Yahweh planted a garden in Eden, **in the East**, and there he put Adam, the man whom he had formed.
>
> (Genesis 2:8)

According to this passage, the Elohim placed the Adam in the Garden of Eden *after* he formed him, so he must have developed or fabricated him in another place. This Adam existed before the creation of Eden, in which he was only placed in a second moment after having spent an undetermined period at a different location. Where?

The Bible does not say. Some answers might be found in the Sumerian-Akkadian texts, but this is not the place to address such subject. Let us try instead to find some other elements in the Bible that are useful to our understanding of this second account of "creation."

Let us focus on the phrase "in the East" that we have just read. This expression is a common translation of the Hebrew מקדם [mi-qedem], which includes the preposition [mi] and the word [qedem].

Once again, however, the traditional translation is misleading. If the translation "in the East" were correct, the Hebrew text would necessarily require the preposition ב [be], which also expresses the complement of "state in place," English for "in."

But we find no preposition [be] in Hebrew; instead, we have [mi].

The preposition מין [min] abbreviated in [mi] does not convey the sense of "state in place" but the complement of "provenance" or "motion from a place," which we would translate in English as "from."

Therefore, the literal translation of this verse would be: "the Elohim planted a garden in Eden *from* the East," and not "*in* the East."

But there is more.

If we analyze the meanings of the second term of the syntagm, קדם

[qedem], we observe that it contains both the definitions of "place" and that of "time."

The first meaning — "place" — has the sense of "that which is in front of, opposite." In the geographical context in which the Hebrews oriented themselves to the rising sun, which was in the East, the word acquired the meaning of "that which is in the East." In this case [mi-qedem] would mean "from the East."

In the sense of "time," however, the word [qedem] has the meaning of "that which is before, old, from ancient time." This second set of meanings can be traced to the Assyrian root *kudmu*, from which comes the Hebrew noun meaning "before, preceding, belonging to an earlier time." In this second case [mi-qedem] would mean "from before."

A possible literal translation of Genesis 2:8 would then be: "Elohim Yahweh planted a garden in Eden from [the] ancient one," where "ancient" could possibly refer to an "earlier, primeval Eden," thus indicating the existence of some kind of Eden archetype from which other Edens might be derived.

These other Edens were probably planted in different places, wherever the Elohim went and wanted to settle, using different types of Adam according to their need.

5 / THE FALL OF HUMANKIND

1. The Garden of Eden

The adventure of human life started in Eden. According to this view, in Eden, man took his first steps, enjoyed a short moment of endless happiness, and then made a mistake that bore consequences for which he is still paying. This regrettable decision goes under the name of "original sin."

Due to this sin, "God" expelled the creatures he "created" and condemned them to live a life of pain and suffering outside the garden of Eden.

This eternal damnation still haunts the existence of billions of people today. According to St Paul, death entered the world through the sin of one man, Adam; thus "death came to people."

> Just as sin entered the world through one man [Adam], and **death through sin**, and in this way **death came to all people**, because everyone sinned.
>
> (Romans 5:12)

However, if we read the Bible with the approach we have used so far, we can't help but wonder:

- Did this sin actually take place?
- Does that following damnation still stand?
- Are Adam and Eve responsible for the evil in the world?

The place called Eden appears in Genesis immediately after the second account of the creation of man, which we analyzed in chapter 4. Genesis informs us that Yahweh made a fenced place in Eden and placed the Adam in it (Genesis 2:8 ff).

ויטע	יהוה	אלהים	גן–בעדן
planted-and ←	Yahweh	Elohim	Eden-in-fenced-place

מקדם	וישם	שם	את–האדם
east-from ←	placed-and	there	Adam-the

אשר	יצר
that ←	made-had-he

Then Yahweh chooses and delimits an area, the so-called Eden, which is not a mythical and indefinite "earthly paradise," a kind of special situation, a statute of a spiritual order, but a concrete region, a geographical area, a physical place.

As seen in the previous chapter, the original meaning of the term מקדם [mi-qedem] is, "that which is in front," but also "that which is before." So we could say that Yahweh planted a fenced garden in Eden, "from that which came before," or "from that which existed before." In it, he placed the Adam he had made somewhere else, before.

So if we were to suggest a translation of this passage, for the reasons we have given in chapter 4, we would say: "Yahweh Elohim created the Earth-man and placed him in the garden created in Eden, which was laid out from the one that was before."

2. The two trees

Once enclosed and protected, the Eden is used as an experimental garden to produce fruit of all kinds; among many others are two unique trees (Genesis 2:9).

ועץ	החיים	בתוך	הגן
of-tree-and ←	living-the	of-middle-the-in	fenced-place-the

ועץ	הדעת	טוב	ורע
of-tree-and ←	of-knowledge-the	good	evil-and

The special trees, as explained in the verses above, are:

- Tree of the Living (usually translated as "life");
- Tree of the Knowledge of Good and Evil.

While no further details are given for the latter, only the former, the Tree of the Living, is said to be planted "in the middle" of the fenced place called Eden.

We must now carefully follow the sequence of events.

~ Genesis 2:9

The Tree of Life is planted in the center of the garden. In contrast, the Tree of Knowledge does not seem to have an exact location.

It is also important to note that the first tree is only "of Life" and not "of Life and Death," while the second tree establishes an inseparable link between "Good and Evil." Life and Death are not connected, as one exists in the absence of the other, while the other two elements, Good and Evil, are inseparable.

~ Genesis 2:17

Yahweh expressly and exclusively forbids eating the fruit from the Tree of the Knowledge of Good and Evil.

Since the prohibition does not refer to the Tree of Life — which, as we have seen, was planted in the middle — can we conclude that, for the Elohim, it was more serious and possibly dangerous that his creatures experienced "knowledge" than "long life?"

~ Genesis 3:1-2

The serpent tempts Eve and induces her to eat the forbidden fruit. The woman's answer is very curious, as she says that the prohibition refers to the tree that is בתוך הגן [gan-ha toch-be], "in the middle of the Garden."

However, we know from Genesis 2:9 that the tree in the middle of the garden is the Tree of Life, not the Tree of Knowledge. This passage thus openly contradicts Genesis 2:17.

~ Genesis 3:6

Eve eats the fruit of the "tree in the middle of the garden" and offers it to her companion. Do they eat from the Tree of Life? If so, they do not infringe the Elohim's prohibition as found in Genesis 2:17 — unless the Elohim confused the trees, or the redactor of text did.

In summary, there is confusion in the transmission of the story or inconsistency in the narrative. Where does this mess-up come from? Did the Elohim confuse the trees at the time of the prohibition? Was the serpent confused when he tempted Eve? Was Eve herself confused about the position of the two trees in the garden? Was the confusion caused by the editor of the first draft, or later editors and publishers of the biblical account?

We do not know, but the confusion is evident, and the hypotheses to explain it are numerous and varied. Let us consider some of them.

The confusion could be due to a copyist's error that resulted in a shift within the text, limiting the definition of positioning to one tree instead of attributing it to both. In this case, the fact that the phrase "in the middle of the garden" comes after the Tree of Life would mean little.

Another hypothesis is that there may have been only one tree in the original narrative, with no indication of its location. Only later was a new, second tree inserted.

By the time Genesis was written, the narrative material had been circulating in oral form for some time, and the theme of the Tree of Life, or cosmic tree, was known to other cultures. However, there are no explicit earlier references to the Tree of the Knowledge of Good and Evil, which could be a later addition.

There is a phrase in Deuteronomy 30:15 that supports the hypothesis of the original uniqueness of the tree. Yahweh says to Moses, "I present to you life and good, death and evil." In Deuteronomy, thus, concepts of life-good/death-evil overlap in obvious parallelism. The binomial concepts associated with the two trees seem to merge in Deuteronomy. Were these concepts/trees also initially joined together in Genesis?

However, we cannot help wondering: if there were two trees, and the prohibition did not include the Tree of Life, but only the Tree of Knowledge, why didn't they eat the fruit of the Tree of Life, thus both benefitting from it and becoming immortal? Had they eaten from the Tree of Life first, they would have become immortal, and the Elohim's threat — "You shall die!" — would no longer have had any effect.

As can be seen, this is no slight complexity.

3. They realized they were naked

The development of the story gives us a clue that we consider essential. The two have just eaten the forbidden fruit and find themselves naked (Genesis 3:7).

הם	עירמם	כי	ויעדו
they	naked	that	learned-and ←

Only after they eat the fruit do Adam and Eve realize they are naked. So, they suddenly discover/experience something they were unaware of before: their nakedness. Thus, they make belts to cover it.

In particular, they hide their sexual apparatus. The covering of the rest of the body is not an immediate necessity. It will be fulfilled later by Yahweh when he drives the two out of Eden (Genesis 3:21) and provides them with clothes.

This biblical remark is always taken for granted, and its exact meaning is never understood. The nakedness does not concern the whole body, only the sexual organs.

Adam and Eve do not discover with fear and horror the nakedness of their back, chest, neck, limbs, and breasts, but only that of their genitals. In other words, once they eat the fruit, they become aware of their sexuality. More specifically, they become aware of their reproductive power, as the sheer "view" of their sexual organs was already evident before eating the fruit.

We must assume that what astonishes them is not the realization that males and females are different — which was already apparent, as the text admits: "Adam and his wife were both naked, and they felt no shame" (Genesis 2:25) — but that the morphological difference serves a specific purpose. Genitals offer a new possibility that does not please "God."

Genesis also draws our attention to the fact that the two hide from "God" and not from each other. Adam and Eve hear the footsteps of the Elohim — whose steps can thus be heard before he is seen! — and immediately run into hiding (Genesis 3:8-10).

Yahweh, not seeing them, cries aloud and says, "Where are you?"

Adam says he heard "God's" footsteps — "God" has footsteps! — and, therefore, he hid from him.

אנכי	כי–עירם	ואירא
I	naked-because	afraid-was ←

Adam is "afraid" of "God," his "creator," because he is naked!

Why is Adam afraid of the divine reaction? Amos Luzzatto, an eminent Jewish biblical scholar, points out that nakedness was not a sin per se in the Old Testament. Adam, however, seems to be conscious of his nakedness.

It seems clear that the sin of our ancestors was not in nudity per se but in the sex that followed the realization that they (Adam and Eve) could reproduce, and they could do so without the help and permission of the Elohim.

The essential difference between the new species — the Adamites — and the Elohim is lost by crossing this thin line. The making of the Adam and the reproduction of the Adamites were previously prerogatives of the lords from above, the "gods." Now, Adam and Eve have discovered they are self-sufficient in reproduction.

They can reproduce without the intervention of the Elohim.

The tree (whether one or two) represents the element that transforms the two creatures and gives them the ability to generate life, formerly reserved for the "gods" and now available to humans.

"God" immediately recognizes the consequences of the new situation.

> And Yahweh Elohim said, "**The man has now become like one of us**, knowing good and evil. He must not be allowed to reach out his hand and take also from the tree of life and eat, and live forever."
>
> (Genesis 3:22)

It is a rather striking statement that needs no interpretation in its clarity. By eating the fruit, Adam became like the Elohim ("one of us!"). The Adamites have obtained the procreative power of the Elohim. They are like them.

Yahweh understands that this is an epochal event that dissolves the bond of the new species to its creator and makes it autonomous in future demographic expansion. This leads to a situation whose consequences are not even entirely predictable and whose dramatic developments are brought about by the sequence of all those events we have discussed in the previous chapters: the intermingling between the "sons of Elohim" and the "daughters of the-Adam," the subsequent wrath of "God," the Flood, the eventual restoration of genetic purity with Noah, and so on.

Once the gravity of the situation is recognized, the Elohim endeavors to find a solution. He does not want to kill them. He decides to remove the representatives of the new species from the protected and fenced garden where he had placed them.

"God" is afraid of the Adamites — perhaps because he foresees how difficult it would be to control them in the future — and does not want them anymore in his "garden," his experimental laboratory.

To avoid the risk of their return, he places a guard (cherubim) at the entrance of Eden, which proves, once again, that this was not some paradise, a kind of blissful state from which man would have fallen, but a very precise, physical location, where one could enter and leave.

4. Knowledge of good and evil

The story we have just read in the first part of this chapter forms the basis for the theological concept of original sin. From this concept stems the subsequent idea of eternal damnation that weighs on Adam and his descendants.

Adam is banished from Eden, learns about death, and must work hard to produce food. Together with Adam, humanity also falls from eternal life and happiness into a state of death and pain. This "damnation" burdens all humankind.

However, the banishment of Adam from Eden could hint at a much more immediate and, in some respects, reassuring fact for humankind. Let us proceed in order.

"God" warns Adam and Eve that, should they eat the forbidden fruit, they will "certainly die."

> "You must not eat from the **tree of the knowledge of good and evil**, for when you eat from it **you will certainly die**."
>
> (Genesis 2:17)

Why does "God" not forbid the consumption of the fruit of the Tree of Life instead?

From Genesis 2:17, the prohibition applies only to the Tree of Knowledge, so we might infer that the Elohim feared more that humans could reproduce than live forever or, better, a long life. At any rate, it must be noticed that Adam and Eve eat the fruit, but contrary to Elohim's prediction/threat, they do not die!

It is worth pointing out a curiosity often overlooked by commentators. In this sequence of events, "God" was wrong, and the serpent was right. "God" told Adam and Eve they would die if they ate the fruit, but they did not. The serpent, on the other hand, not only said to them that they would not die but that they would instead become like "God," which is later confirmed by "God" himself: "The Adam has now become like one of us, knowing what is good and what is evil" (Genesis 3:22).

The serpent, the tempting adversary, spoke the truth; while "God" was misleading!

> "**You will not certainly die**," the serpent said to the woman. "For God knows that when you eat from it your eyes will be opened, and **you will be like God, knowing good and evil.**"
>
> (Genesis 3:4-5)

We might, however, think that the Hebrew wording of the Elohim's prohibition would not indicate a threat but a prediction, as if the Elohim barely meant to say something like, "You will surely die in the future." If this were the case, however, we would have to assume that Adam and Eve were created immortal.

But this is impossible because "God" himself throws them out of the Garden of Eden in Genesis 3:22 to prevent them from eating from the Tree of Life, thus becoming immortal. So, they were not created immortal.

The reader should also remember that immortality does not occur in the Bible, for we have seen that the Elohim themselves were mortal. All these considerations show us that the Elohim were afraid that Adam would have access to those techniques which would guarantee him a life as long as theirs, making the new species totally uncontrollable and dangerous.

Apart from these pedantic arguments, we must acknowledge that the fundamental aspect of this passage lies in the description of the threat/prediction mentioned, regardless of when and how it may have materialized.

Let us not forget that the Hebrew exegesis also writes: "Death was in reality not a curse, but a normal consequence of human nature… it is natural that time, age and decay" would bring man to such an end.[13]

To summarize what we have said so far:

— there is confusion in the identification of the two trees and we do not know who caused it;

— the confusion could be explained by the fact that originally there could have been only one tree;

— Adam and Eve become disobedient and discover their sexuality;

— Adam and Eve are not ashamed of each other but fear the reaction of the Elohim, from whose gaze they hide.

We have so far seen considerable differences between what religious tradition has reported about the fundamental concepts of "original sin" and "punishment" — with everything that resulted in the religious, theological, ethical, and legislative spheres — and the biblical text.

Now we must analyze one aspect of great importance, the so-called "Knowledge of Good and Evil."

Traditional interpretation recognizes the true meaning of man's disobedience to "God" in wanting to determine for himself what Good and Evil are. This is the sin that we, as humankind, have carried with us since our beginnings.

Thus, the Tree of Knowledge would allegedly and symbolically represent the ethical choice between Good and Evil and confront man with the possibility of freely choosing Good — the will of "God" — or Evil — that is, actions that do not take into account, or worse, contradict the divine will.

Faced with this choice, the concepts of just and unjust, good and bad, lawful and unlawful found their entrance into man's conscience; and humankind began the journey that led man to develop an ethical code, the beginning of the awareness of some innate morality inscribed once and for all in the heart of humanity.

However, the biblical text tells us something else.

First of all, the concept of knowledge of Good and Evil, as expressed

---

[13] *Genesi-Bereshit*. Mamash Ed., 2006.

in the biblical verses, does not contain a concept of distinction and separation: Good and Evil are inseparable. So no choice is given between the two.

Ancient Hebrew grammar also comes to our help here.

When biblical authors intend to distinguish between two elements, they use a specific wording that introduces the concept with the expression [ben... u-ven...]. Biblical Hebrew always says that a distinction is made [between... and between...], but this wording is not present in the passages about the Tree of Knowledge, where Good and Evil are closely related.

In introducing the image of the Tree of Knowledge, there is no mention of a distinction "between Good and Evil" but of the simultaneous and inevitable experience of both. Thus, there is no consideration of man's acquired ability to distinguish between Good and Evil; this was not the aim of the author of the book of Genesis.

Secondly, as Professor Amos Luzzatto notes, the specific meaning of the Elohim's punishment of Adam and Eve could be described as a "physiological and pathophysiological aspect of human behavior, as inevitable as the pain of childbirth [...], which for millennia has been linked to the suffering of women for obvious physiological reasons."

The "evil" referred to here is thus physiological, concrete, and material, not ethical. It concerns the physical component of human life and namely pain. The same physical meaning is used in Deuteronomy 28:35 and Job 2, where the same Hebrew word used in Genesis, רע [ra], indicates skin disorders and ulcers.

From these considerations, we learn that Good and Evil are not separate as Life and Death are. The biblical Evil is an essentially physical fact; suffering is an element inherent to life in its material ordinariness.

A confirmation of what has just been said is in Genesis 3:16-19, where the Elohim formulates the so-called "damnation," the "punishment" of Adam and Eve.

> To the woman he said, "I will make your pains in childbearing very severe; **with painful labor you will give birth to children.** Your desire will be for your husband, and **he will rule over you.**"

> To Adam he said, "Because you listened to your wife and ate fruit from the tree about which I commanded you, 'You must not eat from it,' cursed is the ground because of you; **through painful toil you will eat food from it all the days of**

your life. It will produce thorns and thistles for you, and you will eat the plants of the field. **By the sweat of your brow you will eat your food until you return to the ground**, since from it you were taken; for dust you are and to dust you will return."

(Genesis 3:16-19)

To summarize, biblical Evil entails the following:

— Eve will suffer from her pregnancies, give birth in pain, and endure the harassment of her overbearing husband.
— Adam will have to suffer and toil to obtain food, and until he can produce it himself, he will have to feed on the herbs of the field. In Eden, with the Elohim, he did not have this problem.

5. The tempting serpent

Let us now talk about another protagonist of the story of "creation."

Now **the serpent was more crafty than any of the wild animals Yahweh Elohim had made.** He said to the woman, "Did God really say, 'You must not eat from any tree in the garden?'"

(Genesis 3:1)

— Who is this serpent?
— What does it represent?
— What is the meaning of the temptation?

Sumerian-Akkadian mythologies tell us of the constant opposition between two Sumerian Anunnaki deities (Enlil and Enki) who had different approaches toward the new species they created, the Adamites.

One of the most critical differences concerned the possibility of making the new being fertile, thus giving it a chance to reproduce independently.

Enlil was rather hostile to man, regarded him only as an enslaved species, and therefore rejected him; Enki, who had expressly wanted and created the new species, was attached to his creature and wanted to promote its development and evolution.

Enki was also responsible for the excavations in the mines, for which man was specially created. He was considered the expert on "that which is in the deep" and was often represented with the image of a snake.

Now, the Hebrew root that identifies the serpent, נחש [nachasc], initially indicates the act of knowing intentions in advance (Clark). This definition confirms once again that knowledge is a fundamental element of the symbolism characterizing Enki.

In most ancient mythologies, the serpent is the bearer of knowledge reserved for the few (we would call it "esoteric" knowledge).

Indeed, knowledge of the deep structure of genetic inheritance belongs to that kind of science that could not be disseminated superficially. The double serpent winding around the Tree of Life would, in this respect, represent the double helix structure of DNA used by the Elohim in creating the Adam working on the [tzelem]. We discussed this in chapter 4.

The image of the serpent and the temptation of man is the translation into the biblical language of the difference between Enlil and Enki. The intervention of the serpent/Enki would thus represent the moment when the new species was born.

For many Jewish commentators, Eve also had sexual intercourse with the "serpent." From this sexual intercourse, Cain was born, but this discussion is beyond the scope of our analysis.

6. Conclusions

The whole matter of sin, punishment, and temptation in Eden reveals its growing complexity; the difficulties of interpretation that have arisen over the centuries testify to this. The theological interpretation reveals a whole series of untreated aspects. So let us summarize what we have found out so far:

— Adam and Eve are in a closed and protected place where the Elohim meets all their material needs;

— Yahweh prohibits any possibility of autonomous reproduction of the new species;

— The prohibition is identified with the prohibition against eating a particular fruit that gives "knowledge."

– The confusion of the text in identifying the trees could be explained by the fact that, initially, there was only one tree, or the two trees were conflated together;

– Adam and Eve were disobedient and discovered intraspecific sexual functionality.

– According to Hebrew exegesis, Eve could also possibly have experienced interspecific sexual functionality with the serpent;

– The Elohim learns of the new situation, recognizes the dangers, and sends them away;

– Adam and Eve suddenly find themselves "forced" to live in complete self-sufficiency, where their lives depend exclusively on their efforts and physiology.

– Eve will suffer from her pregnancies and give birth in pain.

– Adam will have to suffer and toil to obtain food.

Once they gain their independence, Adam and Eve discover and experience life's positive and negative aspects with all its advantages and disadvantages in a new environment. They experience the "good" and the "evil" of life in very concrete ways.

"God" seems to say, "You made your bed; now lie in it!" The proverb, trivial as it may be, is very useful in illustrating the non-existence of the concept of "punishment," or "eternal damnation." The "punishment" of Adam and Eve would thus not be a condemnation at all but only the consequence of their choices.

Yahweh did not punish man with a penalty consisting of labor and physical suffering but merely expressed what is commonly called a "*sententia post eventum*," simply recognizing an inevitable situation created by acquired autonomy. "God" informed Adam and Eve that the new existence would inevitably have positive and negative aspects and that they would experience both.

Again, the Bible refers here to the materiality of daily life. The "evils" in their punishment do not concern the suffering of the psyche or the soul.

In analogy with the Tree of Knowledge of Good and Evil, we should also mention that the Tree of Life does not contain the concept of Death. We are not dealing here with the Tree of Life and Death.

The two concepts — Life and Death — seem to be mutually exclusive, whereas Good and Evil are not only not mutually exclusive, but necessarily coexist. As we have said, Good and Evil were not distinguished, not even at a grammatical level.

When one experiences Good, one inevitably experiences Evil. It is profoundly wrong to consider only the negative aspect separately and interpret it as the result of a punishment from "God" or an "eternal damnation" of the Adamites.

It is wrong to think that man could dispose of the absolute Good and that he brought absolute Evil into the world with his behavior. Some thinkers will wonder at this point: if the concepts of original sin and the punishment resulting from disobedience do not exist, then who introduced Evil into creation?

For centuries, theology has debated the dramatic problem of the presence of Evil in the world, the so-called "*mysterium iniquitatis*," an issue that is always inseparable from "theodicy," that is, from the need to justify "God" by absolving him of any responsibility.

This task, which theologians of all times have set themselves, runs like a thread through the history of ethical-religious thought. To this question, the Bible gives an answer that requires neither special analysis nor complex theological or anthropological considerations. Yahweh himself settles the matter in Isaiah 45:7.

יצר	אור	ובורא	חשך	
forming ←	light	creating-and	darkness	

עשה	שלום	ובורא	רע	
doer ←	(good)completeness	creating-and	evil	

אני	יהוה	עשה		
I ←	Yahweh	doer		

I form the light and create darkness,
I bring good and create evil;
I, Yahweh, do all these things.

(Isaiah 45:7)

Yahweh says, "I create good and evil" through one of the most authoritative voices in the history of Jewish thought, the prophet Isaiah. The verse is entirely at odds with the willingness to hold Adam responsible for the Evil in the world.

So, can we think, or at least hope, that in the not-too-distant future Catholic theology will abolish the concept of "original sin" that burdens every living being born on Earth?

As we have already mentioned, the Apostle Paul introduces the concept of original sin, which later finds an essentially definitive formulation in St Augustine. A careful reading of the biblical text can only lead to the conclusions that original sin is a *theological invention*.

We are confident that the Church will not want to impose on its faithful the burden of an evil they did not commit. All the more so since Adam and Eve may not have been the progenitors of all humanity but only of a group created by the Elohim with the task of taking care of their needs.

The "god" (Enki/Snake) who created them genetically also passed on reproductive independence to them; the other "god" (Enlil, Enki's brother), who was against them, drove them out of Eden.

However, was the Elohim so weak that he feared his creatures?

We know that the Elohim were something other than a spiritual "God," so this fear must not surprise us as it was well-founded. The Elohim wisely decided to separate themselves from their "creatures," which would soon become dangerous and difficult to handle since they had reached a degree of independence that was not planned initially.

In the following pages, however, we shall see that this separation between the Adamites and the Elohim was anything but final. The Adamites and the Elohim had many opportunities to meet throughout history; the Bible is simply one of the ancient accounts that tell the stories of this continuous relationship between the Creators and their creatures from the perspective of a small and tiny part of the Semitic people, the family of the patriarch Israel, and Yahweh, their Elohim.

6 / BACK AND FORTH WITH THE ELOHIM

1. The sign of Cain

After Adam and Eve have left the fenced and protected place from which "God" expelled them, they must provide for themselves. The Adamites' new life outside Eden immediately begins uphill, as the story of Adam and Eve's sons, Cain and Abel, shows.

After killing Abel, Cain is banished from his tribe. After hearing the judgment and punishment "God" has reserved for him, Cain makes an extraordinary remark about the consequences of this punishment: "I will be a fugitive and a wanderer on the Earth, and whoever finds me will kill me" (Genesis 4:14).

At Cain's request, the Lord then puts a mark on his face so no one can kill him. But who on Earth could kill Cain, if Abel was already dead, and the other two people ever born were Adam and Eve, their parents?

Assuming that the Adamites are a specific ethnic group created through genetic engineering and cloning, as discussed in the previous chapters, it is clear that when Cain goes into exile, he finds himself among foreign people who do not have the same characteristics as the Adamites and are, therefore, barbarians. Cain fears being killed by them and expresses his fear.

Those who cannot accept these assumptions say that Cain is afraid of being killed by his own relatives, which would imply that Adam and Eve had other children, and that Cain was scared of being killed by them.

Now, there undoubtedly were other relatives. According to Rashi de Troyes, one of the most important Jewish exegetes, Cain was born with a twin sister, and Abel was born with two. (Twin births were common in the reproduction supported by the Elohim, so this also fits perfectly with our discourse so far.)

What is strange is not that there were other relatives but that the

Lord would put a mark on Cain's face so that his twin sisters or relatives, whoever they were, would recognize him! Much less could Cain have been afraid of being killed by animals because even if "God" had put a mark on Cain's face, the animals certainly would not care.

Again, these are just a few curiosities that we wanted to mention to understand that the story as it is told to us is less logical than it appears when read in a way that is consistent with the text. The oddities of the antediluvian Adamites and patriarchs, however, certainly do not end with Cain.

2. Antediluvian patriarchs

Let us look more closely at the family tree of Adam.

Genesis chapter 5 is exciting because it contains a list of antediluvian patriarchs whose ages and lineages are recorded. In particular, it says that Adam lived 930 years; Seth 912; Enosh 905, and so on. The last patriarch mentioned is Noah. His figure is particularly famous because it is associated with the Great Flood. Lamech, the last patriarch mentioned before Noah, lived 777 years.

Thus we have seen that a very long life span characterized the lives of the antediluvian patriarchs. There would be much to say on this point. Many traditionalist commentators, unable to accept unorthodox truths, try to explain this oddity in various ways. However, the truth is that the Bible does not speak here of lunar years or resort to other kinds of calculation: it speaks of years as we understand the term, solar years. It also seems arbitrary to resort, as some exegetes do, to all sorts of hermeneutical and numerological categories to make sense of the long lives of the antediluvian patriarchs. As mentioned in chapter 1, we have already established that our methodological approach dictates that what the Bible says is true to the letter.

In addition to indicating the long ages of the patriarchs, the Bible tends to give the name of the firstborn of each one of them; but also adds at the end the formulaic expression: "And then he had other sons and other daughters" (Genesis 5:7).

From all this, we infer that the genealogy of the Adamites is not a series of people coming one after the other in a way that their ages add up continuously. Instead, because of their very long lives, we need to conclude that they were all coeval with each other, as were their sons and daughters.

So we must imagine a population of Adamites that consisted of hundreds, if not thousands, of people, as each of them begat sons and daughters, and of course, each of those sons and daughters in turn reproduced and multiplied. So the group of the Adamites became, with time, more and more numerous.

While all the patriarchs are treated similarly, it is worth underlining a passage in Genesis 5:13 because a particular expression is used there for Seth that is not used for the other descendants of Adam. Seth is the third son of Adam and Eve.

When "God" created the Adam, as seen in the previous chapters, it is said in the Bible that the Elohim made him "in his image and likeness" (Genesis 1:26). Similarly, when Adam was 130 years old, "He begat a son in *his image and likeness*" (Genesis 5:3). For Seth, and *only for Seth*, the same expression is used as for the creation of Adam and Eve, *in the image and likeness*.

The same is not said of any of the other patriarchs. This indicates that Seth was probably created by some particular intervention of the Elohim, of the sort we have seen in the previous chapters.

All children are formally born in the image and likeness of their parents, or at least in the image and likeness of one of their parents. However, here, as in the case of Adam, the author deemed it necessary to emphasize that Seth was created "in his image and likeness."

The creation of Adam, as seen in the previous chapters, occurred thanks to the [tzelem] of the Elohim, that is, by genetic engineering. We can assume that the same thing happened with Seth, so perhaps there is a continuity of intervention, which would not surprise us.

Adam then begat more sons and daughters after the age of 130 and lived 930 years. The Bible lists a long list of patriarchs who lived long lives, as anticipated above. So, Adam was coeval with Seth, Enosh, Kenan, Mahalalel, and Jared. This means that Adam died shortly before Noah was created, as one can verify from reading Genesis 5.

Again, the lives of the antediluvian patriarchs do not follow one another, but they overlap; this is a long genealogy of people who knew each other personally since they all probably lived in the same area at the same time. The picture below can help visualize the lives of the patriarchs as described in the Bible.

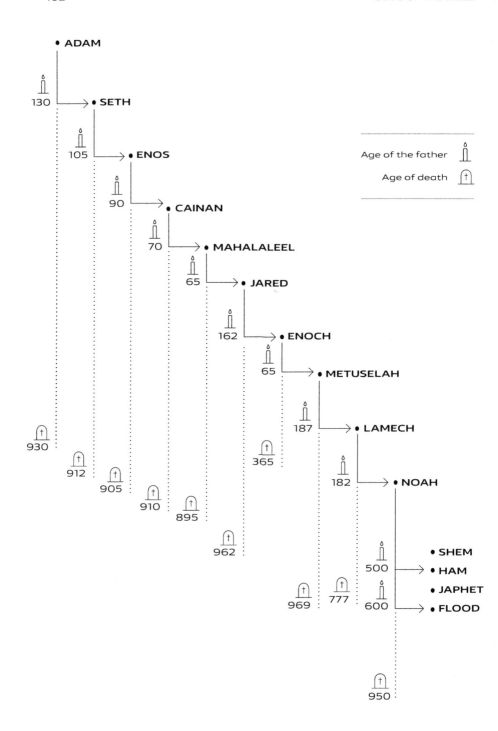

Age of the father

Age of death

When Seth was 105 years old, he begat Enosh. Another very curious and unusual statement is made about this event:

> A son was also born to Seth, whom he named Enosh. **Then the people began to call on the name of Yahweh.**
>
> (Genesis 4:26)

We learn here that the name of Yahweh began to be invoked at the time of Enosh! This leads us to believe that Yahweh was not invoked before Enosh, i.e., at the time of Seth, Cain, Abel, Adam, and Eve. When the Elohim "created" the Adamites, Yahweh's name was not invoked.

If we read the Bible carefully, we can understand why. Yahweh is called in the Bible "*ish milchamah*," which means "man of war." Yahweh was a soldier, a military Elohim.

In the beginning, the Elohim worked, grew crops, raised livestock in Eden, experimented with food, and created a new species, the Adamites, to work for them.

The intervention of an Elohim with the characteristics of Yahweh was unnecessary at this point. So, Yahweh comes around later. If "Yahweh" is mentioned in the Bible before Enosh, this is probably due to later interpolations by copyists and editors of the biblical texts.

Adam begets Seth when he is 130 years old and Seth begets Enosh when he is 105 years old, which means that Yahweh is not invoked for at least 235 years.

But let us continue with the genealogy of Adam, for the surprises are not yet over. Let us focus on one particular name in the long list of antediluvian patriarchs in Genesis 5: the name Jared.

> When **Jared had lived 162 years, he became the father of Enoch.** After he became the father of Enoch, Jared lived 800 years and had other sons and daughters. Altogether, **Jared lived a total of 962 years**, and then he died.
>
> (Genesis 5:18-20)

The name Jared hints at some important events about which biblical and extra-biblical literature talks diffusely; we will discuss this in the next section.

3. The great descent

Significant events in the Bible and other examples of ancient literature are often recorded in names.

The verbal root from which the name "Jared" is derived means "to descend." Since our studies in this field began, we were always convinced that in the name "Jared was "recorded" the memory of an important "descent." All the more so because Jared's son Enoch, is later told to be actually "traveling with the Elohim."

Let us focus for a moment on Jared and the "descent" that must have happened at the time of his birth. The Bible gives us no detailed account of this event. However, Genesis 6 says that the "sons of the Elohim" saw that the "daughters of the-Adam" were *tovot*, "beautiful," that is, "suitable." Thus, they took as many as they wanted as wives.

The Bible does not tell us exactly when or how this happened; it only allows us to understand that it happened before the time of Noah because when it speaks of the Flood, it is clear that the Elohim wanted to bring order to a situation that became confusing because of the interbreeding that had occurred.

At the time of Jared, however, it occurs to us that there was, as the name implies, a "descent."

Can we find references to a significant "descent" in biblical or extra-biblical literature? The answer is yes; we can find references to this descent in the biblical Apocrypha, particularly in the Book of the Watchers.

This book tells the story of two hundred rebellious angels who descend to Earth to join Adamite women, thus confirming what is being accounted for briefly in Genesis 6: the sons of the Elohim took the "daughters of the-Adam," the Adamite women as companions and wives.

The Book of the Watchers is more detailed than the Bible in its account of the story: "And it came to pass that the children of the Adamites, which were born in those days, multiplied, and there were born unto them beautiful girls." When the "sons of heaven" saw them, they fell in love with them and said to each other, "Let us choose wives from among the daughters of the Adamites and beget children."

Semeyaza, the leader of this group of angels, said to them, "I fear that I alone will pay the penalty for this great sin." Semeyaza is afraid that he alone will be punished when the generals hear about their decision to join Adamite women, which must have been forbidden.

At Semeyaza's complaints, however, all the angels answered, "No, we all swear and promise that we will not evade this feat and will put it into practice." Furthermore, "They swore and promised to each other, all two hundred of them."

The exciting part is yet to come. The Book of the Watchers reports that:

> **They went down to Ardis, to the top of Mount Hermon,** and they called it Mount Hermon because they swore on it.

This is a fascinating piece of information.

Syncellus, an 8th-9th century Byzantine scholar, in commenting on "Ardis," said that the reading "they descended to Ardis" is incorrect. Instead, it should read, "They descended in the time of Jared."

Since Syncellus, many other interpreters have said that the reading "in Ardis" is incorrect, as is evident from the Aramaic and Greek. Instead of "they descended to Ardis," we should read, "they descended in the time of Jared."

We can thus positively affirm that our intuition was correct. The name Jared indeed hints at a "great descent," as described in the Book of the Watchers. During this time, two hundred "angels," or, as the Bible calls them, "sons of the Elohim," came down to Earth and took Adamite women as wives.

The biblical Apocrypha help us to understand that in the time of Jared, the sons of Elohim — namely, for those who believe that Yahweh is "God," the sons of "God" — descended to Earth and took as many Adamite women as they wished.

The famous Jewish exegete Rashi de Troyes says in his commentary on Genesis that:

> The term "beautiful" means that the Adamites' daughters were made beautiful by adorning them so that when one of them entered the wedding canopy, **a mighty one would come and possess her first.**

"A mighty one" stands for "one of the Elohim." They would enter the room and possess the woman. Rashi de Troyes continues by adding that the Elohim would even take, that is, have sexual intercourse with "married women, men, and animals."

4. Walking with the Elohim

Jared's son, Enoch, is in no way inferior to his father. His story, too, is a special one worth telling. Possibly it is even more exciting and vivid than what his father Jared had experienced during his lifetime, namely that the sons of the Elohim had come to Earth to seduce the daughters of the Adamites and sleep with them.

The Bible tells us about Enoch that, at the age of 365, he… leaves with the Elohim!

For all the other patriarchs, the age of death is 930, 912, 905, 910, and so on. Noah is 950 years old when he dies. Enoch, on the other hand, leaves at the age of 365. He does not die. He leaves with the Elohim. He is among the undead, like Elijah and Moses.

Elijah departed with the [ruach] of the Elohim; Moses, according to Flavius Josephus, disappeared from the land of Moab in a "cloud" (a term referring to the flying machine of the Elohim). In the same way, Enoch *left* before dying.

According to the Bible:

> Enoch walked faithfully with the Elohim 300 years and had other sons and daughters. Altogether, the days of Enoch were 365 years. **Enoch walked faithfully with the Elohim; then he was no more, because Elohim took him away.**
>
> (Genesis 5, 22-24)

Hebrew exegesis comes to help us, stating that Enoch "did not die of old age in his bed, but disappeared too soon compared to the average life of the time." So Enoch did not die, the Elohim "took him away."

The story of Enoch can also be found in the Book of the Secrets of Enoch from the Apocrypha of the Old Testament.[14] Enoch himself tells us about his departure.

> When I was 365 years old, on the solemn day of the first month, I was alone in my house, grieving and weeping with my eyes. While I was resting in my bed sleeping, two men as great as any I had ever seen on earth appeared to me.

In this first passage, Enoch says he was "sleeping" and then he goes on to say:

---

[14] Sacchi, Paolo, editor. *Apocrifi Dell'Antico Testamento.* UTET, 2013.

> Their faces were like sunshine, their eyes like burning lamps, from their mouths, came forth fire, their clothes a plumage of feathers and their arms like golden wings at my bedside. They called me by my name; **I arose from my sleep.**

So Enoch was asleep before he was called, and he woke up. This is a fundamental concept. The editor says in the footnote: "The pleonastic expression is meant to emphasize that what happens to Enoch on this occasion is not a vision, but something that happened."

We always pretend that what is written is true. If we pretend, we keep saying, we can understand. If we believe that what the ancient writers wrote is just the product of their imagination, we can take all these books and throw them away because they are useless. However, if we throw them away, we also throw away the Bible, and if we throw away the Bible, we throw away everything based on it. If, on the other hand, we intelligently pretend that these facts happened, then we understand many things, and the narrative becomes coherent.

The whole situation is so realistic that Enoch will later appear before the great leader, the Lord of the Empire, and will say that his face became so hot and burnt that an angel had to intervene to cool it.

> Who can stand before the face of the King of kings and endure the tremendous shock or burning heat? The Lord called one of his terrible angels and placed him beside me, and the **angel cooled my face.**

This episode recalls the story of Moses asking Yahweh for the opportunity to see his *kavod.*

Yahweh consented but warned him that he could not see it from the front, but only from behind, for if he saw it from the front, he would die; in order not to die, Moses is advised to hide behind a rock and see the *kavod* from behind once it has passed (Exodus 33:18-21).

Can we even imagine that the glory of "God" can only be seen from behind? At any rate, we know from Exodus that Moses' face was burned after he came down from the mountain where he saw the *kavod* of Yahweh. His skin was burned.

The story of Enoch is highly realistic, as we can see from his remarks, "I had a burnt face" and "they were standing beside me." At this point, he was awake and this was no longer just a dream.

Furthermore, Enoch's description of the two figures "standing" next to him, reminds us of the birth of Noah, where Noah appears with big shining eyes, his face white, his face radiant, just like the figures Enoch describes.

But there are more connections between Enoch and Noah. Genesis 6:9 says of Noah that he "was righteous and perfect in his generation."

By the syntagm "righteous man and perfect," the Bible does not mean so much from a moral point of view. In the concreteness of the Hebrew language, the passage suggests that Noah was righteous and perfect in physical-anatomical and genetic terms.

The Bible also says that, "Noah walked with God," that is, "he walked back and forth with the Elohim," which is precisely what is said of Enoch, as we have seen. The Elohim chose these figures to be taken on long journeys until Enoch is taken forever.

So it is said of Enoch and Noah — respectively in Genesis 5:22-24 and Noah in Genesis 6:9 — that they "walked with the Elohim."

In passing, it should be remembered that twenty-three kinds of flying chariots are described in the Book of Enoch. Enoch traveled a lot; he was initiated into astronomy mysteries, the heavens' secrets, et cetera. In other words, he received scientific knowledge that he had to record in writing for the benefit of humankind.

In this respect, Enoch is comparable to the figure in the Sumerian-Akkadian stories of Emmeduranki or Emmedurana, who is also the seventh of the so-called antediluvian kings, as listed in the famous Sumerian King List. Emmeduranki receives from the Anunnaki — the Sumerian counterpart of the biblical Elohim — a whole series of information that he will pass on to humanity.

But what does it mean that Noah and Enoch "walked" with the Elohim?

First, we must note that the expression for Enoch and Noah is precisely the same. The Bible uses the verb [itchallech] in addition to the term Elohim and the word [et], which means "with." So the traditional translation for this passage is that Noah and Enoch "walked with God."

The original Hebrew text, however, contains a determinative article before the word Elohim [ha-Elohim] that is arbitrarily left out in traditional translations. The literal, philologically correct translation would be, "He walked with *the* God."

Let us not forget that the Hebrew article has no distinction between singular and plural, so another correct translation could be, "He walked with the gods." But suppose "Elohim" is singular here; the article is still wrongly omitted in traditional translations. The line should thus read: "He walked with *the* god."

But what does "with *the* god" mean? If "god" is not a proper name, then with which "god" did Enoch walk?

In a different place in the Bible, the Elohim says to Jacob, "You must build an altar to the god who has shown himself to you" (Genesis 35:1), thus referring to a very specific "god," the one who had shown himself to Jacob, not another one.

With which "god" did Enoch walk? This is not a rhetorical question.

To avoid this kind of problem, we suggest a more appropriate translation for this passage: "He *walked with the Elohim*."

We do not translate "Elohim" because nobody in the world knows exactly what Elohim means. By leaving "Elohim" untranslated, anyone can give this term the meaning they want. But at least we have respected the biblical text, and we have not arbitrarily removed a determinative article that is very important.

We always say, let us leave "Elohim" untranslated.

But there is more. What does "walked with" actually mean? The term "walked" translates the Hebrew verb [halach]. This verb is used for Enoch and Noah in the so-called *hitpael* form, which in Hebrew expresses the idea of doing something intensively, reflexively, and reciprocally.

Thus, the *hitpael* form here indicates precisely that one is not simply "walking" but constantly "going back and forth, reciprocally." Enoch and the Elohim go *back and forth with each other all the time*.

No expression could make this continuous physical relationship more concrete. The term is used twice with Enoch and once with Noah.

A more correct and respectful translation of this critical biblical expression found in Genesis 5:22-24 and Genesis 6:9 — respectively applied to Enoch and Noah — should read: "He walked/went/traveled back and forth with the Elohim."

5. The anointment of Enoch

The relationship between the Adamites and the Elohim at the time of Jared and Enoch was one of continuous, concrete and physical contact. Some people traveled with the Elohim, while "the sons of the Elohim" came down and took for themselves the women they liked. A lot was happening.

This picture emerges from the Bible itself only if we report what is written in Hebrew instead of making up translations to fit a priori theological perspectives and beliefs.

It is also interesting to note that the Italian commentators of the *Talmud* say that Noah "was not a Hebrew," and this is why Noah's covenant with "God" is important (Di Segni).

Both Enoch and Noah traveled back and forth with the Elohim, and in these travels, Enoch was brought before the great leader of the Empire, commonly referred to as "God." What happens, then?

Enoch is anointed by the hand of Michael, the Archangel, the *Archistrategos*, Commander of the army. The ruler of the Empire commands Michael to:

> Take Enoch, strip him of his earthly garments, **anoint him with holy oil**, and clothe him with robes of glory. **The oil appeared like a great light, its anointing oil like the beneficent dew, its fragrance like myrrh, and its rays like the sun.** I looked at myself and was like one of the glorious ones.

This ritual is of no little importance.

From the custom of anointing someone derives the concept of "Messiah," which literally means "the anointed one." This idea is then passed on to the New Testament. The very term Christ, "*Christos*," means "anointed one" and refers to the word root [mashiach], the Messiah.

This term has evolved over the centuries to take on a symbolic meaning. When two drops of oil were poured on someone's head, he was considered anointed as a king, or special messenger, he was a Messiah. But let us look more closely at the meanings behind the word [mashiach].

The *Brown-Driver-Briggs Hebrew and English Lexicon* provides the following meanings for the verb [mashach]: "to wipe, brush, cleanse, smear, anoint," i.e., to wipe, rub to cleanse, smear until it smears. It is much more than spilling a drop (Brown).

The *Strong's Hebrew Dictionary* of the Bible, for the verb [mashach], lists: "to rub with oil," conveying the idea almost of something done with particular violence (Strong).

The *Comprehensive Etymological Dictionary* defines it as "smash," in the sense of "to hit," "to spread, to smear" (Klein).

The *Lexicon Hebraicum Veteris Testamenti*, the Hebrew-Latin dictionary of the Pontifical Biblical Institute in Rome, defines the verb [mashach] with the Latin "*Levo, oblevo*" (Franz).

The meaning that emerges from all these definitions is that this verb is closer to a physical activity in which a person is taken, stripped, rubbed, washed, and anointed with oil to the point that he is almost disfigured.

This action differs from spilling two symbolic drops on someone's head.

In this particular context, this procedure may have protected the Elohim and thus maintained a distance, or at least a sterile situation, between them and the person brought into their presence. It was a hygienic and sanitary act of prevention.

Let us look at what is written, for example, about the anointing of those who were allowed to enter Yahweh's temple.

> Then the Lord said to Moses, "Take the following fine spices: 500 shekels of liquid myrrh, half as much (that is, 250 shekels) of fragrant cinnamon, 250 shekels of fragrant calamus, 500 shekels of cassia — all according to the sanctuary shekel — and a hin of olive oil. Make these into **a sacred anointing oil**, a fragrant blend, **the work of a perfumer. It will be the sacred anointing oil.**"
>
> (Exodus 30:22-25)

The Bible specifies that the final product must be the work of someone — a perfumer — who can actually and physically produce a mixture according to a specific recipe. This perfume must be prepared in a certain way and be used in a particular manner. The use of this mixture is not a symbolic act.

> "**Use it to anoint the Tent of Meeting, the ark of the covenant law, the table and all its articles, the lampstand and its accessories, the altar of incense, the altar of burnt offering and all its utensils, and the basin with its stand.** You shall consecrate them so they will be most holy, and whatever touches them will be holy. **Anoint Aaron and his sons** and consecrate them so they may serve me as priests."
>
> (Exodus 30:26-30)

All the spices used to prepare the mixture are known for their antibacterial, antimicrobial, and antiseptic properties. So when we put these spices together with the full range of meanings we have seen in these dictionaries, we understand that anointing someone was not simply a symbolic act. Nor was it merely a matter of putting the spices in water, which would have been enough if the mixture served to sprinkle two drops on someone's head symbolically.

Instead, the spices had to be soaked in oil because it made it possible to cover and anoint all the objects inside the temple, and the clothes and bodies of the people who entered the sanctuary.

This means that those who entered the temple had to remove their robes, rub them off, and sprinkle them with oil until they were covered and smeared with the prepared mixture.

All of this happened over centuries when the hundreds of Adamites lived together, in close contact with the Elohim, just as the Greek myths describe the famous Golden Age when men and gods lived together.

Some Adamites and the so-called "gods" lived and traveled together; the "gods" came down and united with women; the "gods" selected certain privileged people and treated them in a special way — we have just mentioned Enoch's anointing — took them in their flying machines and assigned them particular tasks.

If we trust these ancient authors and pretend that what they told us is real, we will discover a period in the history of humanity when extraordinary things happened. Ezekiel, Elijah, and Zechariah tell of flying machines. Ezekiel, in particular, tells us of his travels with these flying machines.

We will deal with this topic in the following chapters, especially in chapters 13 and 14. But first, we need to address another aspect of the "great descent," which requires a whole new chapter: giants.

עֲנָקִים נְפִילִים רְפָאִים
7 / THE GIANTS

1. "Their days will be a hundred and twenty years."

Let us now turn to a subject that has always caused considerable confusion among traditional commentators.

After the creation of Adam and Eve, Genesis recounts the events of the expulsion from Eden and presents us with the rich and complex genealogy of the descendants of the first couple, which we have addressed at length in the previous chapter.

Seth was begotten by Adam "in his image and likeness." After having begotten other sons and daughters, Adam died at age 930.

This age should not surprise us. Adam was a direct product of the grafting of genetic material by the Elohim. We can assume that Adam — like all the other antediluvian patriarchs — possessed the quality of longevity that resulted from the genetic heritage of the Elohim.

At one point, the Elohim decided to intervene again and shorten the age of the Adamites, as it is written:

> My spirit will not contend with humans forever, for they are mortal; **their days will be a hundred and twenty years.**

(Genesis 6:3)

What caused the Elohim's intervention?

The Adamites had begun to multiply on the Earth and, of course, had daughters. As we have seen in the previous chapter, the Elohim who had descended on Earth were probably males. It is not difficult to imagine that the natural needs, and perhaps the desire to give new stability to the life they now spent on Earth, must have directed the attention of these individuals to the female half of the new species.

The author of Genesis 6:2 tell us:

האדם	את–בנות	בני–האלהים	ויראו
Adam-the	of-daughters	Elohim-the-of-sons	saw-and ←

ויקחו	הנה	טבת	כי
took-and	they	(good)beautiful	that ←

מכל		נשים	להם
(all)everything-(among)from		(females)women	them-for ←

בחרו	אשר
chose-they	that(those) ←

First, let us point out that טבת [tovot] is usually translated as "beautiful," but it also means "good" in the sense of "capable, suitable." So these women had to be "good," i.e., "suitable" to enter into a relationship, start a family, and engage in sexual relations and procreation.

The continuation of this story, however, portrays the anger and displeasure of "God" for the interbreeding. The Elohim express their displeasure at the wickedness of man, at the extensive failure of humankind, and in the face of this terrible "sin," decide to wipe humanity from the face of the Earth. Therefore, "God" sends the Flood (Genesis 6:5-7).

When we read this passage, we cannot help but ask ourselves the following questions:

— Could this omniscient "God" not foresee what would happen after he created the new species? Did he not know that the behavior of his creatures would depend on the qualities he gave them?

— What sense does it make to endow a creature with the freedom to decide its fate and punish it because its choices do not correspond to the will of its creator?

— Is this not entirely gratuitous cruelty? Can a spiritual "God" hate his creatures so much to want their death?

— What sense does it make to exterminate animals with an unescapable flood because of faults that can only be attributed to humankind?

In short, the thesis of the existence of a spiritual "God," able to create everything out of nothing but unable to foresee the consequences of his choices, and therefore forced to change his mind and take remedial action, has some very puzzling aspects.

According to our hypothesis, however, this can be explained quite simply. The Elohim who "created" humankind belonged to a technologically advanced race but were undoubtedly not endowed with omniscience and omnipotence.

2. "There were giants on the earth in those days"

As seen in the previous chapter this story is also told with some details in The Book of Enoch.

The first part tells of the "fall of the sons of heaven" who saw that the daughters of the Adam were desirable and decided to take them as wives. Two hundred of them agreed to this. However, their leader, Semeyaza, knew that this decision would arouse the wrath of the lords of the empire and he feared that he alone would be held responsible.

Thereupon, his companions agreed to share the responsibility. They gathered on Mount Hermon — a mountain range in the southeast of Anti-Lebanon — and swore not to abandon the project and to carry it out without hesitation.

Then they began to seek out the Earth women and teach them practical knowledge, such as the cultivation and harvesting of plants and their use for therapeutic purposes. In short, they taught them, as the text says, the "secrets of the early days."

They thus began to have sexual relations with them, and "giants" were born. The Bible confirms the giants' presence on Earth in Genesis 6:4:

בימים	בארץ	היו	הנפלים
days-the-in	earth-the-on	were	Nephilim-the ←

אֲשֶׁר	אַחֲרֵי־כֵן	וְגַם	הֵהֵם
that	(this)after	also-and	those ←

הָאֱלֹהִים	בְּנֵי	יָבֹאוּ
Elohim-the	of-sons	(entered-were)entered ←

וְיָלְדוּ	הָאָדָם	אֶל־בְּנוֹת
birthed-had-and	Adam-the	of-daughters-from ←

הַגִּבֹּרִים	הֵמָּה	לָהֶם
strong-the	they	them-to ←

הַשֵּׁם	אַנְשֵׁי	מֵעוֹלָם	אֲשֶׁר
(famous)name-the	of-men	always-for	who ←

The first problem in this section is its ambiguity.

> The Nephilim (giants) were on the earth in those days — **and also afterward** — when the sons of the Elohim went to the daughters of the-Adam.
>
> (Genesis 6:4)

It is impossible to understand with absolute certainty whether the [nephilim] were the product of the interbreeding between Adamite women and the sons of the Elohim or whether they existed independently of them.

If the giants were the product of the interbreeding between the two species, we should have found an expression indicating that giants were present "only afterward." Instead, we read that they were present "in those days" and "also afterward," which leads us to believe that their presence preceded the interbreeding between the two species, or at least occurred simultaneously with it, but not as a direct consequence of it.

This is all the more stimulating when one considers that the problem is not only chronological — were giants already on Earth, or are they the product of the interbreeding? — but also concerns the meaning of the term [nephilim] itself.

We shall return to it at later, at the end of this chapter, but let us first emphasize some other aspects that are important. The Bible takes up the term "giants" in many places and calls them by different names:

– Anakim (ענקים),

– Rephaim (רפאים),

– Emim (אמים),

– Zamzummim (זמזמים)

In Numbers 13 we read the story of Moses sending scouts to the Promised Land; his people were still in the desert of Paran, and the conquest of the land of Canaan had to be carefully planned. They needed to know what the land was like, who lived there, whether the inhabitants were numerous or sparse, what defenses the cities had, where the camps were located, and what kind of vegetation could be found.

In short, although this was a land promised by "God," Moses knew well that it would be necessary to conquer it with military force and using wise and thought-out strategies. The Elohim Yahweh was powerful but not omnipotent.

In this regard, Moses had no doubts and knew the land had to be conquered through his efforts. Therefore, he sent out scouts to gather the necessary information.

After forty days, the scouts returned with news and products of the land. They reported that the land was desirable but strong and savage peoples inhabited it. Some of the scouts even claimed that the conquest of this land was an impossible undertaking (Numbers 13:28):

שָׁם	ראינו	העֲנק	וגם–ילדי
there	saw-we	Anak-the	of-born-also-and ←

The explorers emphasize that they saw the sons of Anak, that is, the Anakim. They justify their statement by saying that they carefully observed the land to be conquered (Numbers 13:32-33):

בתוכה	אשר–ראינו	וכל–העם
them-middle-the-in	saw-we-that	people-the-all-and ←

מדות	אנשי
stature	of-men ←

את הנפלים	ראינו	ושם
Nephilim-the	saw-we	there-and ←

מן–הנפלים	ענק	בני
Nephilim-the-from	Anak	of-sons ←

כחגבים	בעינינו	ונהי
locusts-the-like	eyes-our-in	were-we-and ←

בעיניהם	היינו	וכן
eyes-their-in	we-were	so-and ←

(In passing, let us note the assonance between the Hebrew term "Anakim" and the Sumerian "Anunnaki", which defines the probable Sumerian-Akkadian counterpart to the biblical Elohim.)

The explorers expressed their awe as they saw men of unusual "size and stature." In the eyes of the Anakim, who belong to the descendants of the Nephilim, they must have appeared — it is said — "like locusts."

The comparison with the locusts could not refer to quantity — which in this case would have been advantageous to the Israelites — but to size. Their sheer size was the reason for the fear that seized the messengers.

The scouts concluded their report by saying that these people were stronger than them.

The same incident is repeated in Deuteronomy. When the Israelites are in the Arava, on the other side of the Jordan, Moses gives a speech in which he recalls the events that took place during the desert pilgrimage. He also recalls the times when the Israelites rebelled against the will of the Elohim, who guided them. He says that the people grumbled and would not go forward in the conquest of Canaan because (Deuteronomy 1:28):

ורם	גדול	עם
and-being-tall	mighty	people ←

גדלת	ערים	ממנו
great	cities	us-of(more) ←

בשמים		ובצורת
skies-the-(to-up)in		inaccessible-and ←

שָׁם	ראינו	עֲנָקִים	וְגַם–בְּנֵי
there	saw-we	Anakim	of-sons-also-and ←

Moses then recalls how Yahweh fought for them many times. In this context, we can only express our disappointment that a non-canonical book entitled The Book of the Wars of Yahweh (cited in Numbers 21:14) has been lost because it could have shed light on what this Elohim specifically did in battle.

Of these battles, unfortunately, only a vague memory is preserved in the Bible. In this regard, we now ask some questions that express a fundamental doubt:

– Wars of Yahweh disappeared, or has it been deliberately made to disappear?

– Is it guarded by those who cannot allow accurate accounts of the wars of Yahweh to undermine further the image of a spiritual "God" created by theologians?

– Would the accounts of the wars of Yahweh be consistent with what the Church preaches today about the infinite and universal mercy of this "God?"

In Deuteronomy 2:9, Moses lists the commandments he received from Yahweh. In particular, he was not to fight Moab because the sons of Lot, Abraham's grandson, had already taken possession of the "land of Ar." He says that in the land of Ar (Deuteronomy 2:10):

בָּהּ	יָשְׁבוּ	לְפָנִים	הָאֵמִים
it-in	dwelt-they	before	Emim-the ←

וָרָב	גָּדוֹל	עַם
numerous-and	great	people ←

כָּעֲנָקִים	וָרָם
Anakim-the-like	tall-being-and ←

The story continues, in the next verse, with further clarification:

אַף–הֵם	יַחְשְׁבוּ	רְפָאִים
they-also	considered-were	(giants?)Rephaim ←

כַּעֲנָקִים
Anakim-the-like ←

The term [emim] itself can mean "terrible." The Emim were thus great and considered Rephaim, like the sons of Anak, who were of the lineage of the Nephilim.

In this situation, Moses urges his people not to fear, for the Elohim Yahweh will fight before him and destroy his enemies (Deuteronomy 9:2-3), even though they:

וָרָם	עַם–גָּדֹל
tall-being-and	great-people ←

The Israelites actually wonder:

עֲנָק	בְּנֵי	לִפְנֵי	מִי יִתְיַצֵּב
?Anak	of-sons	of-faces-in	resist-will-who ←

Anakim, Rephaim, and Emim are always compared, identified with each other, and all considered to be of the same lineage of the Nephilim, beings of tall stature who had fallen/descended from above. They are strong and powerful people who struck terror and whose supposed invincibility induced the people of Israel to give up the conquest of their land.

Deuteronomy also reminds us of the name and size of one of these Rephaim (Deuteronomy 3:11):

נִשְׁאַר	רַק–עוֹג	כִּי
survived	king-Og-only	for ←

הִנֵּה	הָרְפָאִים	מִיֶּתֶר
behold	Rephaim-the	of-remnant-from ←

בַּרְזֶל	עֶרֶשׂ	עַרְשׂוֹ
iron	of-bed	its-bed ←

ארכה	אמות	תשע
its-length	cubits	nine ←

רחבה	אמות	וארבע
its-width	cubits	four-and ←

Knowing that a cubit measures the distance from the elbow to the tip of the finger (i.e., about 17 inches), the result is a bed 12.8 feet long and 5.6 feet wide. The narrator then mentions that the bed was still in Rabbah in the Ammonite area at the time of the narrative. It could still be seen.

> **Og king of Bashan was the last of the Rephaim**. His bed was decorated with iron and was more than nine cubits long and four cubits wide. It is still in Rabbah of the Ammonites
>
> (Deuteronomy 3:11)

3. David and Goliath

The First Book of Samuel contains a story that everyone knows, one of the most famous anecdotes in religious literature: the story of David and Goliath.

The text recounts one of the many confrontations that Israelites and Philistines had in the struggle for control over the territory of Canaan.

We read (1 Samuel 17:1-11) that the Philistines and Saul went to battle against the Israelites, and the Philistine Goliath of Gath terrified the Hebrews by repeatedly challenging them to single combat.

After forty days, the young shepherd David accepted the challenge and defeated his adversary. First, he struck him down with a stone from a slingshot and then decapitated him with the Philistine's sword.

This Goliath of Gath was able to spread terror, for (1 Samuel 17:4):

וזרת	אמות	שש	גבהו
palm(one)-and	cubits	six	his-height ←

He was almost nine feet tall. His powerful armor matched his size. He wore a bronze helmet and plate armor that weighed 5,000 shekels of bronze. Shin guards protected his legs, and he was armed with a bronze spear. The blade weighed 600 shekels of iron (1 Samuel 17:4-7).

The shekel's weight varied from 0.3 to 0.4 ounces, so the armor weighed about 110 pounds and the blade of the spear 13 pounds.

Was he a giant? We know that he belonged to one of the peoples who lived in the territories to be conquered, such as the Rephaim, the Emim, and the Anakim, all descendants of the Nephilim.

We have, therefore, various biblical accounts that tell us of people with extraordinary physical features who belonged to a race whose presence aroused fear and terror.

Excavations on the banks of the Jordan and, in general, in the areas where the events described took place, have shown that these areas were dominated, at least since the 4th millennium BCE, by strong peoples who produced a megalithic civilization capable of erecting cyclopean structures. Just think of the incredible site of Baalbek (in the Bekaa Valley in Lebanon), where monoliths weighing hundreds of tons each were moved.

Archaeology documents that new inhabitants gradually replaced these people.

The Anakim (men "with long necks") inhabited the area of Hebron and the region that the tribe of Judah would later conquer. Three leaders are mentioned, Ahiman, Sheshai, and Talmai, whose names are of Aramaic origin. They were defeated by Caleb when the city of Hebron surrendered to him.

Subsequently, Joshua destroyed them and they only survived in the territory of Gaza, Ashdod, and Gath (the city of the giant Goliath), perhaps not by chance.

The Rephaim (to whom Og belonged) occupied Transjordan from Mount Hermon to Ammon; like the Anakim, they were defeated by Joshua amid the wars of conquest, although David still clashed with some of them who lived on the West Bank (2 Samuel 21:15-21). They were also present in Gilead and were exterminated by the Amorites.

The etymology of [rephaim] is uncertain. For some, the term refers to the concept of "healing" contained in the root [rafah], and the hypothesis is quite realistic. That the Anunnaki/Elohim were endowed with special medical knowledge is a fundamental part of the whole framework on which the idea of their genetic engineering ability is based.

The Zamzummim also belonged to the group of the Rephaim. They lived in the region of Amman (Transjordan) and were defeated by the Ammonites, who took possession of their territory. It is also said of them that they were a people of "high stature," like the Anakim (Deuteronomy 2:20-23).

The Emim eventually dwelt in the territory of Moab (east-southeast of the Dead Sea), and the Moabites named them since they were otherwise known as Rephaim.

According to Genesis 14:5, they were defeated by the king of Elam and his allies; their city was destroyed and then rebuilt by the Israelite tribe of Reuben (Numbers 32:37).

Traces of these peoples' names are also found in a geographical reference: the "Valley of Rephaim," identified with the plain of El-Beqa southwest of Jerusalem.

Since we wish to deal only with the Bible, we avoid going into all the evidence furnished by the finds of skeletons, skeletal parts, or footprints of gigantic individuals, more than ten feet in height, in various parts of the world: Mesopotamia, Gargayan (Philippines), Ceylon, China, West Pakistan, Java, Tibet, South Africa, Southeast Australia, North, Central and South America, California, Aleutian Islands, Morocco, Caucasus, Glozel (France), Lucerne (Switzerland), Northern Europe, Sardinia (Italy).

Some archaeological findings match the size of Goliath's weapons. In Morocco, tools were found that could only be used by people with a height of at least 13 feet; in China, 500 two-handed axes weighing 18 pounds each were excavated.

In his *Histories*, even the historian Herodotus tells of the discovery of a giant about 10 feet tall (I 68). From numerous sources and from all over the world, the evidence seems to emerge — for the unbiased freethinker — of the existence of an ancient race of "giants," to which we would like to add a curiosity of great interest.

During the time of King David, the Philistines were fighting numerous battles against Israel. In one of these battles, there were present (besides Goliath, the giant of whom we have spoken) four [rephaim] from the city of Gath and another man of great stature.

He is described as follows (2 Samuel 21:20):

מדון	איש	ויהי
(stature-great)Madon	of-man	was(there)-and ←

רגליו	ואצבעת	ידיו	ואצבעת
his-feet	of-fingers-and	his-hands	of-fingers-and ←

מספר	וארבע	עשרים	ושש	שש
number	four-and	twenty	six-and	six ←

The author is very precise in communicating the particularity that identified this giant: he had six fingers on each limb, twenty-four digits in all. The presence of this hexadactyly individual and his family background are confirmed with the same thoroughness in 1 Chronicles 20:6, where it is stated that there was a:

מדה	איש
(very tall) stature	of-man ←

שש-ושש	ואצבעתיו
six-and-six	his-fingers-and ←

Again, we have a giant with twenty-four fingers.

4. The meaning of the term [nephilim]

The Bible says that the Nephilim were the famous "men of antiquity, famous heroes" (Genesis 6.4).

All the traditions and lore of the world speak of these "famous heroes." The Greeks have the myth of Heracles; the Sumerians tell the stories of Gilgamesh, et cetera. The Bible thus turns out to be one of the many texts written by humanity that tell essentially the same stories.

The Septuagint, the Greek Bible, translated the word [nephilim] with γιγαντες, "giants."

In Hebrew extra-biblical literature, particularly in the so-called Book of Jubilees, these giants were children born from the sexual encounters between the Elohim and the Adamite females.

The Romanized Jewish writer Flavius Josephus reports that the "angels of God" united with women and gave birth to ungodly children who were proud and arrogant and trusted only in their strength (*Jewish Antiquities*, 1:73).

At the beginning of this chapter, we asked ourselves whether these giants were present on Earth before the interbreeding of the "watchers" with the Adamite female, or were they the consequences of those encounters?

> The Nephilim (giants) were on the earth **in those days — and also afterward** — when the sons of the Elohim went to the daughters of the-Adam.

> (Genesis 6:4)

The parenthetical insert of Genesis 6:4 — "and also afterward" — seems to add confusion to the origin of the word [nephilim]. But we can find some hints by looking at the word's etymology.

The word [nephilim] probably derives from the root of the verb [naphal], which means "to fall, to come down."

If this is so, Genesis 6:4 — "the Nephilim were on the Earth in those days, and also afterward," — might be read more appropriately, "at that time on Earth there were those who had fallen/come down."

We know, however, that there is a significant difference between "to fall" and "to come down." The verb "to come down" conveys intention, which is not present in the act of "falling."

Professor Michael Heiser of Wisconsin-Madison University argues that the word [nephilim] does not derive from [naphal] because its vocalization differs from the usual derivations of this root and, consequently, the intention inherent in "descending" cannot be attributed to it.

Instead, he asserts that the correct reading could only indicate a masculine plural noun or a masculine plural active participle. In the latter case, it would still have been vocalized differently and thus read [nophelim].

Heiser also points out that Hebrew always refers to the act of descending with the verb [yarad].

According to Ronald S. Hendel, Professor of Hebrew Bible and Jewish Studies at the University of California, the use of the verb [naphal] with the meaning of "to fall" is present elsewhere in the Bible; thus, [nephilim] represents the qatil form of the verb, which can be seen as the adjectival passive of the root [naphal] with the meaning of "to fall." In short, this would be a kind of conjugated adjective.

The scholar quotes a passage from Ezekiel 32 in which the verb [naphal] indicates a voluntary descent by warriors.

In conclusion, it does not seem a stretch of the imagination to think that [nephilim], similarly to the verb [yarad], has both the meaning of "involuntary falling" and "deliberate descent."

The diatribe, however, remains unresolved. So we end here the philological disquisition and proceed with our discussion by introducing elements from the Aramaic language and the Greek world.

The Greeks did not care about establishing whether the term [nephilim] contained the meaning of a "involuntary fall" or a "voluntary descent." They translated the term [nephilim] as γιγαντες: "giants."

In the Septuagint, Genesis 6:4, we read:

οι δε γιγαντες ησαν επι της γης εν ταις ημεραις εκειναις και μετ᾽ εκεινο

The giants were on Earth in those days and after that

The Greeks called the [nephilim] "giants," with a peremptory choice devoid of interpretative nuances. This choice, however, raises another question:

– Why did [nephilim] mean "giants" to the Greeks?

It must be known that in the Aramaic language, the word נפילא [nephila] is a proper name for the constellation of Orion. In Greek mythology, Orion was a "giant" from Boeotia and the son of Poseidon.

Orion was a great hunter and always went out with his dog Sirius, which corresponds to the giant star of Canis Majoris. This star accompanies Orion's journey in the celestial sphere: it is very bright and visible under Saiph (Kappa Orionis).

In love with the Pleiades, Orion began to chase them, so the goddess Artemis, who had, in turn, fallen in love with him, had him killed by a scorpion. When Zeus discovered what had happened, he became angry, struck the scorpion down, and decided to place Orion in the sky.

Since then, Orion's constellation shines in the night in his continual attempt to reach the Pleiades — a group of stars in the constellation Taurus — who preceded him in the celestial path.

Numerous other studies correlate the constellation of Orion with the birth of human civilization.

In a range of hypotheses formulated by authors such as E. Von Däniken, G. Hancock, R. Bauval, B. Fagan, and A. Collins, the constellation of Orion is identified as a possible place of origin of the extraterrestrials who descended on our planet.

According to these theories, Orion's origin and importance for humanity are recorded in numerous architectural artifacts on sites considered sacred by various ancient populations from different continents.

The most well-known example is the Giza plain, where the spatial arrangement of the three great pyramids is said to reflect the orientation of the three stars of Orion's belt. But we could also mention the Mayan pyramids in Teotihuacan, Mexico, and the constructions on the mesa of the Hopi Indians in Arizona.

We must, of course, remember that there are currently no certainties. We do not enter here into the discussion of the reliability of these hypotheses. Still, we must note the striking coincidence between apparently separate elements, which we limit ourselves to describing as a mere curiosity for the time being.

At any rate, Hebrew, Aramaic, and Greek mythology intersect here, providing a possibility of interpretation of [nephilim] that integrates various meanings.

– Orion was, for the Greeks, a giant of colossal dimensions;

– In Aramaic, there is the term נפילא [nephila] which identifies the figure and constellation of Orion;

– The Aramaic term [nephila], when taking the Hebrew termination of the masculine plural, becomes [nephilim];

– The Greeks translated [nephilim] as "giants."

– If the translation of the singular נפילא [nephila] is Orion, the translation of the plural could be "Orions, Orionians, Orionites?" Was this what the biblical authors were referring to: "Orionians?"

– Did the Greeks understand this? By calling them γιγαντες "giants," was it their intention to identify their connection with the giant Orion and the celestial site from where they may have come?

– Did the Greeks know more, or did they know something different? This question is legitimized by the knowledge that the scholars who produced the Greek version of the Bible, the so-called Septuagint, used an original text that differed from the Masoretic text.

We have no specific answers to these questions.

For the time being, the hypothetical summary reported here has the connotations of mere curiosity and therefore has no claim to truth. Still, the coincidences are stimulating.

In a field where fluidity is the main feature, any conjecture with a minimum of foundation can prove helpful because it stimulates supporters and detractors, equally committed to verifying, disproving, or confirming it. In any case, the unfettered advancement of knowledge always benefits.

8 / THE BIRTH
OF MONOTHEISM

1. In the beginning was polytheism

Moses is considered the founder of Jewish monotheism, from which all later elaborations of monotheism later developed. We shall return to this in a moment, but not without pointing out that polytheism was the natural primal state of religious thought in ancient peoples.

The cultures we call "primitive" had a multiplicity of deities. The concept of a "single deity" was virtually non-existent in ancient civilizations, and their many gods possessed characteristics that made them unique on an individual level.

The so-called "primitive" man had to deal with a pantheon of gods structured in a clear hierarchy and characterized by different levels of knowledge and power. Within this diverse spectrum, the "primitive" man found many individual deities whom he distinguished in times of worship and to whom he turned according to his needs.

These gods were specialists in various fields of knowledge and practical application. According to the stories of different ancient peoples, the gods gave man the theoretical and technical expertise necessary to set the process of civilization in motion.

Mesopotamia, the "land between the two rivers," is the cradle of civilization. Here, we find the oldest documented information about the stories that we still call "myths" today. The progress of research forces us more and more to consider these so-called "myths" as accurate accounts of the ancient past.

Thousands of cuneiform tablets found in what is now Iraq contain accounts about the lives of Sumerian deities from the distant past, known to us as the Anunnaki.

The Anunnaki correspond to the Neteru of the Egyptians, the Ilu of the East Semitic cultures, and the Elohim or Baal of the West Semitic peoples.

We should note that we continue to use the term "deities" only to conform to the conventions used in the standard texts, recognizing that these individuals have nothing to do with the concepts of the "divine" and the "sacred" prevalent in contemporary culture.

The first example of monotheism in the history of the ancient world seems to date back to the 14th century BCE, and it is thought to be the result of the so-called "Amarna revolution" by Pharaoh Amenhotep IV (18th dynasty). He is believed to have introduced the worship of the single god Aten to replace the prevailing polytheism.

The pharaoh is said to have even built a city called Tell el-Amarna dedicated explicitly to the new religious movement. He called himself "Akhenaten" in honor of the solar deity whose cult he attempted to establish.

This is the prevalent thesis, even though some Egyptologists are beginning to question its historical framework. However, since the figure of the monotheistic Pharaoh was accepted, even Moses himself was identified with Akhenaten.

Various hypotheses have also gained acceptance in non-academic historiographies, such as the theory that sees Moses as the priest of the Aten cult. Even Sigmund Freud, in Moses and the Monotheism, notes the similarities between the worship of the Egyptian sun god Aten and Mosaic monotheism.

According to this hypothesis, Moses was an Egyptian close to Pharaoh Akhenaten, with whom he shared a monotheistic religious view. After the death of the pharaoh and the subsequent polytheistic restoration, Moses is said to have decided to leave Egypt, accompanied by his followers — who still adhered to the Aten cult — and the Semitic peoples in the provinces over which he had some influence.

Moreover, the priestly office Moses possibly held was identified with the term "Yahud," from which the name "Yahudim-Yehudim-Judei" was derived to indicate the followers of Moses who fled with him from Egypt.

The analogies between the so-called *Hymn to the Sun* attributed to Akhenaton and the content of Psalm 104 are also cited in this regard, but it is not the task of this book to go into the merits of these theories. We limit ourselves to stating that traditional religions regard Moses as a monotheist and the founder of Jewish monotheism, from which Christian monotheism was later derived.

Is that so?

2. The father-in-law of Moses

Exodus 3 tells of the meeting between Moses and one of the Elohim, who would later become the ruler of the people of Israel under the name Yahweh.

Moses is tending the flock of his father-in-law, Jethro. The latter, as the Bible reports, was a priest in Midian, an area we can locate between the northeast of the Sinai Peninsula and present-day Arabia, east of the Gulf of Aqaba.

The place name also appears in extra-biblical sources such as Ptolemy, Jerome, Eusebius, and Flavius Josephus, whose citations allow us to determine with good approximation the location of the ancient settlement of Midian near the oasis of El-Deb or in Mogarir Shuayb. Here, there is a spring from which Moses supplied his flocks and a cave where, according to tradition, Jethro met his El (possibly, the singular of Elohim).

Jethro is also called [reu-el], "friend of El" (Exodus 2:18).

When Moses succeeds in leading his people out of Egypt, he sets off for the land of Jethro/Reuel, a place he knows well from his years of hiding when he was wanted for a murder committed in Egypt. Here, Moses had the opportunity to meet his future wife, Zipporah, and her father, Jethro/Reuel (Exodus 2:17 ff).

In these familiar surroundings, he is received by his father-in-law (Exodus 18), who, having learned of Yahweh's help in delivering the Israelites from Egypt, says (Exodus 18:11):

כי–גדול	ידעתי	עתה
great(more)-that	know-I	now ←

מכל–האלהים	יהוה
Elohim-the-all-of	Yahweh ←

Reuel says that Yahweh is the greatest of the Elohim as he proved this by his deeds in the exodus of the people from Egypt. The comparison with the other "gods" is clear; a comparison from which Yahweh emerges victorious because of his doing and not because of his uniqueness, which is not even hinted at in the priest's words.

Yahweh has to prove that he is endowed with the necessary power to do what he promises and thus can carry out his intentions, even if he is in open conflict with another rival Elohim to whom the people of Israel can turn at any moment.

We must be aware of centuries-old religious practices that show us the figure of the priest in a light that has almost nothing to do with that to which the cultures of the Middle East referred at the time.

Among the Sumerians, the priest was called *ensi*. His functions were that of a "governor." He was a local representative of the "god" who ruled a particular area. The position of the Sumerian ensi corresponded to that of the figure defined by the Akkadian term ishakku (Isaac in the Bible).

In the West Semitic language, the priest was named כֹהֵן [cohen], a term that identified the task of "one who performs service as a chief," he was thus again a kind of governor acting on behalf of the lord of the land (Clark).

It is no coincidence that after the exodus from Egypt, Moses encounters his father-in-law, who gives him specific instructions on organizing the tribes he is to make into a nation.

Jethro/Reuel is a [cohen], a "priest" acting on behalf of the local Elohim, and therefore he is skilled in governing. He passes on to his son-in-law all the necessary information to make Israel a nation (Exodus 18:13 ff):

– Moses is to act as a mediator between the people and the Elohim;

– he shall represent the people's interests before the Elohim;

– shall transmit to the people the laws and ordinances;

– shall select from among the people righteous men who fear the Elohim and appoint them leaders of groups of various sizes (thousands, hundreds, the fifties, and tens);

– these selected people shall administer daily life and laws, personally attending to matters of lesser importance and asking for his intervention only in cases of greater relevance.

We are dealing here with an actual pyramid organization to make the government of a few thousand people functional.

3. When Moses met Yahweh

Having established that even for Moses' father-in-law, Jethro/Reuel, the variety of "gods" was completely normal, let us see how and when Moses met his Elohim.

In Exodus 3, Moses, the shepherd of Jethro/Reuel, led the herd through the desert to the mountain where Yahweh dwelt.

> Moses was tending the flock of Jethro his father-in-law, the priest of Midian, and he led the flock to the far side of the wilderness and came to Horeb, **the mountain of the Elohim**.
>
> (Exodus 3,1)

We learn here that this Elohim lived on a particular mountain, Horeb. Several studies place Mount Horeb on the Midianite territory's borders, in the Sinai Peninsula's east-northeast.

The Bible says that while Moses was there, a [malakh] of Yahweh came to him. This [malakh] was a spokesman, not the Elohim himself but a messenger of the Elohim.

Theological tradition incorrectly identifies the [malakhim] with "angels." As we shall see soon (chapter 11), these [malakhim] were flesh-and-blood individuals who walked about, ate and slept, got dirty and washed, and could even be physically attacked by humans. They have nothing to do with the uplifting ethereal figures that tradition later constructed.

Going back to Exodus, Moses meets one of these messengers.

> The [malakh] of Yahweh appeared to him in flames of fire from within a bush. Moses saw that though the bush was on fire it did not burn up.
>
> (Exodus 3:2)

Religious tradition describes this event as a supernatural phenomenon. However, Moses knows what he sees is not some spiritual "apparition." He deals with a physical person and a peculiar phenomenon that affects him. This [malakh] is found:

הסנה	מתוך	בלבת–אש
bush-the	of-within-from	fire-of-flame-in ←

באש	בער	הסנה
fire-the-in	burning	bush-the ←

אכל	איננו	והסנה
consumed-being	it-not	bush-the-and ←

Moses sees a bush that burns without being consumed. We wonder: was it really a bush? The Hebrew term that religious traditions usually translate as "bush" is סנה [seneh]. This word, however, has another ordinary meaning other than "bush," as it could also mean "rocky ridge." In another place in Bible, Seneh is the name of a specific rocky structure, a proper name.

> On each side of the pass that Jonathan intended to cross to reach the Philistine outpost was **a cliff; one was called Bozez** and the other **Seneh**.
>
> (1 Samuel 14:4).

The original meaning of the root refers to the semantic area of being "sharp," which can be attributed either to a shrub or a very sharp-edged geological formation.

Now, Mount Horeb, as mentioned before, is identified as the place where Yahweh dwelt. This Elohim, as we know from many other places in the Bible, was often associated with mountains (Sinai, Horeb, Or/Ar, Seir). So, we cannot help wondering what Moses actually refers to when he says in Deuteronomy 33:16 that Yahweh is:

סנה	שכני
[seneh]	(on, in)of-residing ←

According to traditional translations of this passage, Yahweh lives in a bush. We find it easier to think that Yahweh had a permanent, or at least preferential, residence on the mountain's rocky ridge rather than a bush.

Given the possibility offered by the double translation "bush/rocky ridge," the latter seems to be a far more acceptable reading, marked by that common sense that requires no special flights of fancy.

This is not only a subjective interpretation. The confirmation comes from Yahweh, who addresses Moses with a clear command in Exodus 3:12, which reads:

הַהָר הַזֶּה	עַל	אֶת־הָאֱלֹהִים	תַּעַבְדוּן
this mountain-the	on	Elohim-the	serve-will-you ←

The service is not to be done in a "bush," which, according to the version we criticize, would be the dwelling place Moses attributed to him, but on the mountain.

So, going back to Exodus 3:2, we can imagine that what burns is not a bush but a sharp-edged part of a rock, and — as we will see later in chapter 13 about the miracles of prophet Elijah — we have no difficulty imagining a rock that burns without being consumed if it is permeated or covered with flammable oily substances.

If you sprinkle any bituminous product on a stone and bring it near an extreme heat source, you will witness precisely what took place before Moses' eyes on Mount Horeb: a flame that burns while the stone remains seemingly unharmed.

The surface of this [seneh] could catch fire as soon as one of the vehicles on which the [malakhim] or the Elohim traveled landed. And it is precisely a [malakh] that arrives first at the meeting with Moses, as we have just seen. The biblical authors give us further confirmation of this reading:

On the morning of the third day there was thunder and lightning, with a **thick cloud over the mountain**, and a very loud trumpet blast. Everyone in the camp trembled. Then Moses led the people out of the camp to meet with the Elohim, and they stood at the foot of the mountain. **Mount Sinai was covered with smoke, because Yahweh descended on it in fire.** The smoke billowed up from it like smoke from a furnace, and **the whole mountain** trembled violently.

(Exodus 19:16-19)

You came near and **stood at the foot of the mountain**, and **the mountain blazed with fire** to the very skies, with **black clouds and deep darkness.**

(Deuteronomy 4:11)

The sight of the mountain wrapped in fire becomes a familiar experience for Moses because it is repeated every time the Elohim appears there. The mountain is covered with smoke and fire. No bush is ever mentioned again; instead we often find that Yahweh dwells or descends on a mountain.

Let us go back to Exodus 3 when Moses first sees the [seneh] burning. The experience is extraordinary, but Moses' sight is impeded, and he cannot see well from where he stands. So he says to himself, "I'll move (turn around), and I'll see this great sight, for the [seneh] is not consumed."

The wording of the sentence contains the verb in the *cohortative* form — אסרה-נא [na-asura], "that I move" — suggesting that Moses is urging himself to "turn around" to take up a better position since he cannot see well in his present location. We would say colloquially, "Let me move a little so that I can see better."

- Is it possible that one must physically move to see an "apparition" of a spiritual kind?

- Is it possible that one must move when what is to be seen stands in a bush?

This seems hardly credible and rather improbable.

But there is more. At one point, Yahweh enters the scene. So, in addition to the [malakh], the Elohim also arrives. Yahweh observes the movement of Moses, calling out to him from the midst of the [seneh], asking him to stop, and making himself known:

The [**malakh**] of Yahweh appeared to him in flames of fire from within a [seneh]. Moses saw that the [seneh] was on fire but did not burn up. So Moses thought, "I will go over and see this strange sight — why the [seneh] does not burn up." When **Yahweh** saw that he had gone over to look, Elohim called to him from the midst of the [seneh], "Moses! Moses!" And Moses said, "Here I am." "Do not come any closer," he said. "Take off your sandals, for where you stand is holy ground."

(Exodus 3:2-5)

We have intentionally left the word [seneh] untranslated in the above quotation. Anyone can see that if one replaces [seneh] with "bush," the passage makes little or no sense.

If, on the other hand, one replaces [seneh] with "mountain" or "sharp-edged rock," then the selection becomes immediately understandable without needing any hermeneutical effort, interpretation or explanation.

Also, if we translate [seneh] as "bush," then we must admit it is a very crowded bush! There are at least two individuals in the [seneh], the [malakh] and Yahweh.

Moreover, modern translators often confuse or overlap these two figures. But this interpretation is not supported by the text. There are two distinct subjects here: the [malakh], who presents himself to Moses, and Yahweh, who speaks to him later.

As seen, Moses would like to move to a better position to observe the scene, but Yahweh stops him and commands him "not to come any closer," the reason being that the ground on which he stands is קֹדֶשׁ [kodesc], "sacred."

The original meaning of the term "sacred" did not include values such as holiness, spirituality, and transcendence, which the theologians attributed to this term. The word "sacred" simply referred to something that was physically or conceptually "set apart, set aside for, reserved for," and consequently forbidden to those who were not expressly authorized to have access to it.

Imagine a hall prepared for a conference; the speakers' table is "sacred" because it is separated from the audience and reserved for a specific function and purpose. Suppose someone from the audience wants to sit there; they are politely invited to leave and take the designated seats.

The first king of Rome, Romulus, was not so polite to his twin brother. The latter dared cross the furrow defined as "sacred," and he paid with death for his action.

An area becomes "sacred" when it is chosen, defined, and allocated to specific functions. A lamb becomes "sacred" when it is selected from the flock to be designated for a ritual; [kosher] food, for example, is sacred food because it is "fit for consumption." The *Shabbat* is "sacred" because it is "separated" from the other days.

Thus, the term "sacred" does not and cannot have a single, unambiguous meaning. It is defined, specified, conventionally accepted, and subsequently respected under different circumstances and under threat of consequences of varying severity, ranging from the simple request to leave to the penalty of death.

Again, the definition of "sacred" did not initially have the spiritual significance later attributed to it.

Returning to the story, Yahweh tells Moses that that territory (mountain, rocky range) is his and, therefore, must not be violated: the local ruler did not want intruders in his home.

There is also another element that is worth mentioning. What is particularly striking to the attentive reader is the fact that Yahweh must identify himself. We read in Exodus 3:6:

אָבִיךָ	אֱלֹהֵי	אָנֹכִי
your-father	of-Elohim	I ←

יִצְחָק	אֱלֹהֵי	אַבְרָהָם	אֱלֹהֵי
Isaac	of-Elohim	Abraham	of-Elohim ←

יַעֲקֹב	וֵאלֹהֵי
Jacob	of-Elohim-and ←

Is it conceivable that the universal, spiritual, transcendent, and only "God" needs to be recognized? Yahweh does not simply say, "I am God," as one would expect in a "conversation" between the one and only "God" and he who would bring monotheism into the history of humankind.

Instead, Yahweh needs to specify that he is the same Elohim who spoke to Abraham, Isaac, and Jacob — and not another Elohim. He is the Elohim who made a covenant with them; therefore, he is interested in the people of Israel and can be trusted.

Moses needs to be sure of the identity of his interlocutor. In a famous passage, the prophet demands to know the identity of the Elohim to whom he's talking.

> Moses said to God, "Suppose I go to the Israelites and say to them, 'The God of your fathers has sent me to you,' and they ask me, 'What is his name?' Then what shall I tell them?"

(Exodus 3:13)

Yahweh seems somewhat annoyed and does not answer Moses directly. "I am who I am," he blurts out (Exodus 3:14). Yahweh seems to affirm here that his actual name does not matter. Moses and the people need not worry about his name; they need only recognize that he had a relationship with their fathers, Abraham, Isaac, and Jacob.

Thus, Yahweh can be trusted and would always keep his promises. Reading between the lines, we could paraphrase: "The important thing is that everyone does what is expected to be done within the covenant we are establishing."

Eventually, the Elohim reveals that his name is יהוה [yhwh] (15), of which Yahweh is a later vocalization; and says:

לעלם	זה–שמי
always-for	my-name-this ←

לדר דר	זכרי	וזה
generation generation-for	my-remembrance	this-and ←

Thus, his name is Yahweh, and he must be remembered by that name forever.

We will return to this subject later. For the moment, we learn that "God" needs to be recognized and makes proposals that inevitably bring him into conflict with other rival Elohim, with whom he contends for control of peoples and territories in the Middle East.

From the matter-of-factness with which the sequence of individual actions is described, it is easy to deduce that the multiplicity of "gods" was an absolute normality for Moses and his father-in-law Jethro.

4. Moses speaks of Yahweh

Deuteronomy is known in the Hebrew canon by the more appropriate title of [devarim], which means "words." It contains a series of sermons attributed to Moses in which he celebrates the importance of the laws, his passion for choosing the covenant with the Elohim, and his joy at the gift of the Promised Land.

The book highlights the historical premises that justify the pact, lists the obligations that make up its content, and finally states the positive or negative consequences of compliance or non-compliance with its rules.

The entire structure of the book is based on the models of treaties of alliance concluded between lords and their vassals.

In his speeches, Moses repeatedly refers to the Elohim in a way that often contradicts monotheism. Let us look at some of the most relevant passages.

~ Deuteronomy 6:14
Moses addresses the people with a direct command:

תלכון	לא
walk will-you	not ←

אחרים	אלהים	אחרי
other	Elohim	behind ←

סביבותיכם	אשר	העמים	מאלהי
you-around	that	peoples-the	of-Elohim-among ←

This is an explicit statement, not subject to interpretation, declaring the existence of other Elohim who rule over the surrounding peoples; their presence is confirmed by the attitude of Yahweh, of which Moses speaks immediately afterward (verse 15):

אלהיך	יהוה	קנא	אל
your-Elohim	Yahweh	jealous	El ←

We read correctly: Yahweh, Elohim of the people of Israel, is a "jealous El." But how can one be envious when there are no competitors? Can one fear the competition of those who do not exist?

We even know the names of some of his rival Elohim: Chamosh for the Moabites, Milkom for the Ammonites, Hadad for the Arameans, Melqart for the Tyrians, Shadrapa (a medical "god") for the Phoenicians, and many other. Therefore, there are many Elohim, the choice of people is potentially open; consequently, the individual Elohim can feel jealousy towards his rivals.

If the other "gods" are only human inventions, why is it difficult for the only true "God" to prove his uniqueness with incontrovertible evidence? Why is he jealous? You can only be jealous if there are rivals.

At any rate, we can be sure of one thing: this feeling of Yahweh represents a natural, concrete, and deeply felt jealousy, and its consequences are dramatic: betrayal is punished by death.

~ Deuteronomy 7:16

The command to serve Yahweh exclusively is repeated in Deuteronomy 7.

> "You must destroy all the peoples Yahweh your Elohim gives over to you. Do not look on them with pity and **do not serve their gods.**"
>
> (Deuteronomy 7:16)

So we are dealing with a "God" who would have a disturbing conception of his relationship with humanity if he really were the only and universal one. He chooses one people and then forces them to destroy all the other peoples who stand in the way of achieving his goals.

Fortunately, we know Yahweh was not the one and only "God" but just a minor local ruler. His insignificance and weakness caused him to issue cruel orders, as we shall see. The need to maintain his power was more important than any other concern.

~ Deuteronomy 13:7 ff

Moses describes some hypothetical situations, providing guidelines for behavior should these situations actually occur.

> If your very own brother, or your son or daughter, or the wife you love, or your closest friend secretly entices you, saying, "**Let us go and worship other gods**" (**gods that neither you nor your ancestors have known, gods of the peoples around you, whether near or far, from one end of the land to the other**), do not yield to them or listen to them. Show them no pity. Do not spare them or shield them. **You must certainly put them to death.** Your hand must be the first in putting them to death, and then the hands of all the people.
>
> (Deuteronomy 13:7-11)

> If you hear that in a city [...] evil men are out there who have seduced the inhabitants by saying, "**Let us go and serve other gods**" [...] you shall investigate, examine, interrogate carefully [...] and if it is certain [...] you shall pass the city's residents with the edge of the sword [...] even its livestock [...] **you shall burn the whole city.**
>
> (Deuteronomy 13:13-17)

The fear of the Elohim Yahweh of being abandoned by his followers was so great that loyalty had to be maintained at all costs, even with the killing of family members, the extermination of the inhabitants of entire cities, and the terror that ensued.

We cannot help but see that the threat of betrayal was real, and the behavior of Yahweh mirrors the attitudes and decisions of tyrants of all times.

~ *Deuteronomy 32:17*

In this passage, Moses accuses the Israelites of arousing Yahweh's jealousy.

אלה	לא	לשדים	יזבחו
Eloha	not	[shedim]-the-to	sacrifices-make-they ←

ידעום	לא	אלהים	
they-know	not(that)	Elohim ←	

באו	מקרב	חדשים	
came-they	near-from	new ←	

אבתיכם	שערום	לא	
your-fathers	knew-they	not ←	

These lines are particularly rich in information and should be given attention. We are dealing here with another explicit statement about jealousy arising from betrayal.

This time the betrayal is committed in favor of entities even lower in the ranking than the Elohim. These entities are called [shedim] and differ from the Elohim.

The term [shedim], usually translated as "demons," is reminiscent of the Assyrian-Babylonian "*shedu*," who were supposed to act as intermediaries between the people and the higher leaders. They were probably lowly guardians, so the cult devoted to them was particularly reprehensible.

We also learn that some Elohim only recently appeared on the scene, which means that they are new and almost unknown, and even the patriarchs had no knowledge of them.. These Elohim were on the move, roaming the territory in search of people to subjugate and serve.

5. Yahweh speaks of himself

We will deal shortly with the question of Yahweh's name. Here we will merely give some insight into the attitude "God" takes concerning his alleged uniqueness.

In Exodus (chapters 19 through 40), Yahweh speaks to Moses on the mountain and gives him a series of commandments, rules, and regulations that form the actual body of law modeled after the military covenants.

This monumental body of law finds its basis in the statement of Exodus 6:7, where Yahweh says, "I will take you as a people to myself and be an Elohim to you." This choice binds Israel to Yahweh, a member of the Elohim's ranks, by an exclusive bond.

In Exodus 20:2-3, we find again the need for identification and representation already mentioned, but here it is expressed in a way that makes it more straightforward and understandable. We read, "I am Yahweh, your Elohim, who brought you out of Egypt, out of the land of slavery." Then the text continues:

יהיה–לך	לא
you-to-be-will	not ←

על–פני	אחרים	אלהים
my-faces-(against)over	other	Elohim ←

The construction of the verb "to be" with the preposition to (as in "to be to…") in Hebrew means "to have." Having identified himself, Yahweh imposes the peremptory obligation to have no other "gods" above him; the Israelites are not to represent them or to prostrate themselves before them.

We know the reason for this command. Again, Yahweh affirms (Exodus 20:5):

קנא	אל	אלהיך	יהוה	אנכי
jealous	El	your-Elohim	Yahweh	I ←

Once again, it becomes clear that there are indeed rivals who can arouse Yahweh's jealousy. A real risk that he tries to avert with a terrible threat. For the sin of the fathers, he will punish their children until the third and fourth generations.

> You shall not bow down to them or worship them; for **I, Yahweh your Elohim, am a jealous El**, punishing the children for the sin of the parents **to the third and fourth generation of those who [hate] me.**

(Exodus 20:5)

Who are the addressees of such harshness?

This threat is directed towards "those who hate me," but the verb שׂנא [sana], that traditional translations usually render with the word "hate," does not in fact mean exactly "hate."

If we want to paraphrase this passage we could say: "punishing the children for the sin of the parents to the third and fourth generation of those who [don't show an exclusive respect and worship toward] me." One did not have to go so far as to "hate" the Elohim to be punished. It was sufficient to turn away from him and turn to other "gods."

The severity of the punishment testifies that the risk of someone betraying due loyalty to Yahweh was real, possible, and probably not infrequent.

Having established that Moses does not present himself as a monotheist, we should say that, strictly speaking, he was not a monolatrist either.

Monolatry denotes the worship of a single "god" over others. Still, this definition presupposes belief in the existence of commonly understood deities, whereas if we look at the Bible, we are confronted with a different situation.

The Elohim who called himself Yahweh was not one of the many "gods" of a polytheistic religion, but a member of ranks of the deities differently called Anunnaki/Igigi/Neteru/Ilanu/Elohim, flesh-and-blood individuals who came to Earth, formed the Adam in their image using the [tzelem], and eventually passed on to him all that was necessary to create culture and civilization.

Moses, then, was neither a monotheist nor a monolatrist but a skillful strategist who made a pact with one of the many possible local "lords" of his time.

6. Joshua's choice

If Moses was not a monotheist, what can we say about his successor, Joshua? We can find an answer to this question in the Book of Joshua 24.

Joshua calls all the tribes of Israel together, assembles them in the region of Shechem, and summons the elders, the chiefs, the judges, and the officials before the Elohim.

Before the assembled congregation, Joshua summarizes what has happened since the calling of Abraham up to his days: the arrival in Canaan, the emergence of the descendants through Isaac and Jacob, the captivity in Egypt, the deliverance, the first victorious battles against the nations that tried to prevent the passage of the Israelites, the crossing of the Jordan, the conquest of the city of Jericho, and the first territories of the so-called Promised Land.

After Joshua has finished enumerating all the achievements attained with the help of Yahweh, he turns to the people. He says:

> Now fear Yahweh and serve him with all faithfulness. Throw away **the Elohim your ancestors worshiped beyond the Euphrates River and in Egypt**, and serve Yahweh.
>
> (Joshua 24:14)

We learn here that the patriarchs originally served other Elohim in Mesopotamia, "beyond the Euphrates river," their homeland, and during the centuries spent in Egypt.

Joshua then continues with a statement that would surely astonish a convinced monotheist. He says: "If it is difficult for you to serve Yahweh" (15), and then:

בחרו	לכם	היום	את–מי	תעבדון
choose ←	you-for	today	who	serve-you

אם	את–אלהים	אשר–עבדו	אבותיכם	אשר	בעבר
if ←	Elohim-(the)	served-that	your-fathers	that	of-part-in

הנהר	ואם	את–אלהי	האמרי
river-the ←	(otherwise)if-or	of-Elohim-the	Amorites-the

אשר	אתם	ישבים	בארצם
that ←	you	inhabit	their-land-in

So we learn that there were many different options, many "gods" to rely on: the Elohim whom the fathers had served in Mesopotamia and who continued to rule over those peoples, the Elohim of the area where the Hebrews had begun to dwell after the conquest of Canaan, and finally the Elohim named Yahweh.

After Joshua presents the three options and explains to the people the need for a decision, he tells them what decision he has already made:

את-יהוה	נעבד	וביתי	אנכי
Yahweh	serve-will-we	my-house-and	I ←

Joshua and his family chose Yahweh; now, it is the people's turn. That this is not a purely rhetorical device becomes evident in the following verses, when the people affirm that they want to follow Yahweh.

Joshua points out the consequences and responsibility of this choice, saying, "You are witnesses against yourselves that you have chosen to serve Yahweh" (Joshua 24, 22).

The people confirm their choice. They express their commitment to Yahweh and promise to serve him.

> Joshua said, "Then **throw away the foreign Elohim** that are among you and yield your hearts to Yahweh, the Elohim of Israel." And the people said to Joshua, "**We will serve Yahweh our Elohim and obey him.**"
>
> (Joshua 24:23-24)

Verses 25 and 26 enumerate the sequence of actions that generally follow the formalization of an alliance, the conclusion of a covenant between a lord and his subjects. It is an interesting passage to read.

> On that day **Joshua made a covenant for the people**, and there at Shechem he reaffirmed for them decrees and laws. And **Joshua recorded these things in the Book of the Law of God**. Then he took a large stone and set it up there under the oak near the holy place of Yahweh.
>
> (Joshua 24:25-26)

This was not the first time the Israelites had chosen Yahweh. Abraham had responded positively to the proposal to leave his land and move to Canaan; the people had decided to follow Moses, who promised to lead them out of Egypt with the help of this Elohim; during the desert wanderings, the people had again agreed to serve this Elohim after abandoning him and questioning his ability to keep his promises.

The alternation of acceptance and abandonment, loyalty and betrayal, of decisions withdrawn and then reaffirmed, testifies to the fact that Moses, Joshua, and the entire population were aware of the possibility of changing sides at any time.

The Elohim to whom one could turn to offer one's service in exchange for help and protection were numerous.

We must also not forget a theme presented with disarming clarity in the Bible: these choices were motivated by convenience alone. Spiritual needs were not taken into consideration. People chose the Elohim, who seemed to offer more guarantees at a specific moment: monotheism had no home in this world.

This attitude will remain constant in the history of the ancient people of Israel, requiring endless interventions on Yahweh's part. Prophetic literature represents the strong and desperate voice, a constant reminder to respect the pact of alliance made with this particular Elohim, Yahweh.

Before the religious reform of King Josiah (648-609 BCE), Yahweh was not only not unique but also far from being exclusive. Cults dedicated to Anat, Tamuz, and Asherah were widespread. (In the chapter on the miracle of Elijah, we will discuss the worship of Baal, the ruler of the northern territories.)

Under King Hezekiah (715-687 BCE), these so-called "pagan" cults were abolished but quickly reintroduced by his successor Manasseh (687-642 BCE).

> He erected altars to Baal and made an Asherah pole, as Ahab king of Israel had done. He bowed down to the whole army of the skies and worshiped them. He built altars in the temple of Yahweh.
>
> (2 Kings 21:3-4)

The "army of the skies" was also known to the prophet Isaiah, who clearly distinguishes it from earthly kingdoms when he recalls, "On that day Yahweh will punish the army of the high, on high, and the kingdoms of the Earth, on Earth" (Isaiah 24:21).

Each army/kingdom is punished in its own "location," so to speak, those in the high, on high, and those on Earth, on Earth. Similarly, King Manasse worshipped the "whole army of the skies." Monotheism was not even a viable option.

Perhaps the future will allow us to accept this statement with some serenity.

7. The name of Yahweh

Having established that Yahweh was one of many, let us examine the name by which this Elohim told Moses that he wished to be called: Yhwh. Scholars variously describe this name as "the name of excellence," "the great name," "the only name," "the glorious and terrible name," "the hidden and mysterious name," et cetera.

Moses acts as an intermediary between Yahweh and the people. Since he does not consider Yahweh to be "God" in the modern religious sense, he needs to know his identity, as seen above, before acting as his spokesman. Moses needs to know his name so that he, in turn, can communicate it to those who are to follow him. To this request, the Elohim responds (Exodus 3:14):

אהיה	אשר	אהיה
ehyeh	asher	ehyeh ←

Then he adds, "You shall say to the children of Israel: אהיה [ehyeh] has sent me to you" (14).

The Elohim further clarifies this identification by introducing the famous tetragrammaton יהוה [yhwh] (15), of which "Yahweh" is a tentative and later vocalization.

אבתיכם	אלהי	יהוה
your-fathers	of-Elohim	Yhwh ←

We must therefore think his name consists of the four letters "Yhwh," even though they are closely related to the previous definition that reads [ehyeh asher ehyeh] and to which we will return.

It was certainly not the first time Yahweh introduced himself by this name. He had to have done so before since the antediluvian patriarchs knew the tetragrammaton [yhwh]; according to Genesis 4:26 at the time of Enosh (Adam's grandson):

יהוה	בשם	לקרא	הוחל
Yhwh	of-name-(with)in	invoke-to	began-they ←

We then ask ourselves:

– Did Adam, Eve, Cain, and Seth (father of Enosh) not invoke Yahweh?
– Provided that they knew him, did they not address him in any way?
– Did they call upon him differently?
– Did they not know his name?

We have no answers, so all we can do is take note of the strangeness of such a peremptory statement: only from that moment (at the time of Enosh) did they begin to call upon Yahweh.

Also, we cannot but wonder in what language this word [yhwh] was pronounced, for it is evident that the Hebrew language did not yet exist at the time of Adam, his sons, and grandsons. Nor should we believe that the situation changed in the time of Moses. So we ask ourselves:

– What language did Moses and the people who followed him out of Egypt speak?
– The families these people belonged to had been living in Egypt for centuries. What language could they speak, if not some form of Egyptian? At best, they could speak a variant of Amorite, widely spoken at the time, or Aramaic, which was gradually gaining acceptance. But everything points to Egyptian.

At any rate, the tetragrammaton [yhwh] was written in the Bible several centuries after its pronunciation and only indicated the consonants of a language that did not yet exist when this name was first spoken.

Is the name [yhwh] an originally Hebrew invention, or is it a later product of the monotheistic imagination of the Jerusalem priestly class? We can confidently answer both these questions in the negative.

Knowledge of the tetragrammaton, regardless of its explicit formulation before Moses, is attested in extra-biblical sources.

In the ancient area corresponding to modern Lebanon and Syria, a civilization known as Ugaritic had developed before the appearance of the Hebrews in Palestine. Its main urban center, named after the city of Ugarit, was located in what is now Ras Shamra on the Mediterranean Sea.

The *ostrakas* are ceramic bowls containing auspicious signs. In some of these archaeological findings of Ugaritic origin, travelers on their way south are addressed with the words, "May Yahweh of Teman and his Asherah accompany you."

There are two surprising clues in these seemingly trivial inscriptions.

First, we learn that the Ugaritic culture knew Yahweh as "Lord of Teman," a term used in the Semitic language for "south" (Israel and the region of Sinai actually lie south of Lebanon and Syria.) So we are in the area where Moses met his Elohim, and the travelers who went there were under the protection of this "Lord" who ruled there.

It is also said that Yahweh had an Asherah, a "consort." The existence of a female companion is also attested elsewhere, and not only by the numerous statuettes representing a female "deity" found in almost all places of Palestine where archaeological excavations have been carried out.

Significant material in this regard was found in a place between the Negev and the Sinai: Kuntillet Ajrud. It was a sanctuary still active between the 9th and 8th centuries BCE, inhabited by Israelites who performed a prophetic function: invocations to Yahweh and his paredra, known as Asherah, were found there.

The Egyptian Hebrews residing in Elephantine (Egypt) had no difficulty addressing Yahweh and his consort Anat-Yahu even in the 5th century BCE. Several of these situations — both geographically and historically distributed — coincide with the figures and actions of the Anunnaki, governors who had divided their territories over which they ruled with their respective companions.

Archaeology and paleography have also enabled us to verify that the name Yahweh was present in the territory to the south of Palestine (the Negev and Sinai) as far back as the 3rd and 2nd millennia BCE, in the forms *Ja/Ya, Jaw/Yaw, Jahu/Yahu, Jah/Yah*.

Also, belonging to the Ugaritic culture is a fragment of the Baal Cycle in which it is written: "My son's name is Yaw" (Garbini, *Storia e ideologia*).

Inscriptions with the tetragrammaton of Yahweh [yhwh] and the script Yaw-rad meaning "descent" are also attributed to these millennia (long before Moses and the exodus of the Hebrews). The Amorite epigraphy of Mari (Mesopotamia), dating from around the 18th century BCE, presents numerous records of names composed with *yahwi* or *yawi* or even simply *ya*.

The persistence of the devotion to this local ruler is also documented in later centuries when Porphyry (a Phoenician historian from the 3rd century CE) writes that a god named Ιευω (Ieuo) was worshipped in Berito (Beirut).

Therefore, we are dealing with a cult present in that territory since at least the beginning of the 2nd millennium BCE, which was followed by nomadic and sedentary populations.

Its vocalization also poses significant problems. Without going into the technical merits of the philological analysis, we shall report what pertains to the various interpretations that everyone is familiar with:

– Is [yhwh] to be pronounced Yahweh or Jehovah/Gehovah?

Jehovah is formed using the vowels of the word [adonaj], meaning "lord." Given the absolute prohibition of pronouncing the name "God," when the tetragrammaton [yhwh] vocalized with "o" and "a" occurs throughout the biblical text, it should be read [adonaj]; when it is already preceded by [adonaj] it takes the vowels of the word "Elohim" and then becomes Jehwih (Deiana et al.).

It must be said, however, that in the Masoretic Bible itself, the tetragrammaton is vocalized as Yehowah hundreds of times.

The subject is complex. For many decades, indeed for centuries, there has been debate over the possible meaning of the term Yahweh and the phrase with which Yahweh introduces himself to Moses, [ehyeh asher ehyeh].

Scholars of various backgrounds have provided interpretations based on the careful and surgical exegesis of the tetragrammaton. It is not an easy matter because this expression has no comparison throughout the Old Testament.

To make sense of this riddle, we propose to change the perspective.

8. Making sense of foreign names

Let us start by asking some common sense questions:

— Since the term "Yahweh" occurs in various forms in non-Mosaic cultures, could this name possibly be an attempt to reproduce the sound of a proper name in another language?

— Is it not possible that Moses and the biblical authors were just trying to reproduce the sound of a name they heard by writing down the consonants they had?

— What would happen if a Westerner were to say his name to a population with a completely different writing or phonetic system, perhaps one containing only consonants?

— How would a name that sounds far removed from what a particular foreign population is used to be represented graphically?

— What kind of analyzes, conclusions, and hypotheses would a scholar make if he found this attempted representation many centuries later without accurate and documented evidence of when and how it originated?

In interpreting the Hebrew language, we have to deal with a particular situation characterized by an understanding of the scriptures based on theological thought. This constitutes an actual inversion of the logical process.

Instead of founding theological considerations on what is written, a theological approach tends to shape the word meanings based on a priori positions. This happened for the Bible especially during the vocalization process, as Prof. Giovanni Garbini points out.

> **Words underwent drastic transformations, changing their meaning according to the ideological needs of the individual biblical authors**, which in the final phase of composition were far removed from those at the beginning of the first millennium BCE.
>
> (Garbini, *Note di lessicografia*)

Many philological, religious, initiatic, and esoteric elaborations and mystical and kabbalistic practices have developed from the tetragrammaton. But in reality, the name [yhwh] could be nothing else than the result of the way some languages of that time rendered the sounds of another language: possibly the language in which the Elohim pronounced his name.

The situation certainly does not improve even if we carefully observe the other part of the sentence before the tetragrammaton. The Catholic Encyclopedia — published in the New Advent CD-ROM — sets forth the innumerable difficulties in providing a clear, specific, and unambiguous interpretation of the name of "God."

"I am that which I am," "I am what I am," "I will be what I will be," and "I will be what I was…," are just a few of the many solutions proposed over time to convey the meaning of what that Elohim intended to mean by [ehyeh asher ehyeh], which precedes the communication of the tetragrammaton [yhwh] in Exodus 3:14-15.

There are many questions to be answered, starting with the possible origins of the tetragrammaton (Indo-European, Chaldean, Egyptian, Akkadian, Proto-Semitic), followed by the complexity of the problem of pronunciation, continuing with the possible grammatical constructions, from which various and different hypotheses arise.

It is not our intention to go into the merits of this matter, but we would like again to remember the words of Prof. Garbini.

> It is **impossible to know Hebrew as it was spoken in pre-exilic times**, at least from the point of view of vocalism. […] we know Hebrew as it was spoken at the end of the first millennium CE […] The reconstruction carried out by the Masoretes was not about knowing the linguistic structure of these texts but their ideological content.
>
> (Garbini, *Introduzione alle lingue semitiche*)

In the face of so much uncertainty, it is not difficult to imagine that even the reformulation of the meaning of the tetragrammaton was influenced by the desire to ascribe a theological meaning to a term that may have initially had none.

The need or desire to find an exact meaning of [yhwh] arose long after its original pronunciation. Any hypothetical meanings arrived at are based on preconceived religious considerations that still influence many exegetes today.

We always remain skeptical, but perhaps we are not so far from the truth if we assume that the Masoretes and their epigones tried — and still try — to elicit a message from a term that perhaps had no other meaning than the one it exclusively represented: a proper name.

Let us try to forget for a moment that this subject belongs to a text considered "sacred" by much of Western culture, and let us ask, as is our custom, some questions as devoid as possible of theological conditioning:

– Suppose a "primitive" culture were to reproduce the sound of a Western proper name such as "Francesco" in its writing system. Let us imagine that the "writing system" of this "foreign" culture has no vowels, only consonants. What would they write? Assuming they use alphabetical writing, is it plausible that they could write: [frncsc]?

– What if, a few centuries after the writing of the name [frncsc], some "sages," or "priests," starting from the written and mysterious signs at their disposal, wanted to derive some meaning from them?

– What would these exegetes produce if they were swayed by the temptation to find meaning at any cost in the word [frncsc]?

– Would future scholars dealing with this culture understand that the sounds with which the name "Francesco" was transcribed belonged to a foreign, alien language?

– Would these scholars be willing to accept that the search for meaning in the specific language of this population would lead to nothing?

– How many would be willing to accept that a hypothetical Westerner who introduced himself by the name "Francesco" could not intend to communicate anything other than his proper name?

– If one were to research the name [frncsc] several centuries after the name was announced and written down, how many would be able to explain its true origin?

We are not dealing with an abstract hypothesis here, but there are concrete and practical examples of this sequence of events in the so-called "cargo cults," which we have discussed in detail in the "Introduction" to this book. In light of what we said in the "Introduction" about cargo cults, we ask ourselves:

– As we reflect on the origin of the name "Jonfram," as it came to be known within the cargo cult phenomenon, can we assume that the term "Yahweh" has met the same fate?

– Are we so far from reality if we consider [yhwh] as a lexical representation of the sound with which the Elohim pronounced his name in a language very distant and different from that of the biblical people and authors?

– When the tetragrammaton was first uttered, at the time of Enosh (Genesis 4:26), Hebrew did not yet exist. Even when Moses heard it, Hebrew had yet to be formed. What language did the people whose families had lived in Egypt for centuries, and whom Moses had led out, speak? Amorite, Aramaic, Egyptian?

According to Prof. Garbini, "The Israelite tribes must have spoken a form of Aramaic." We wonder, then, what is the point of asking what meaning the term [yhwh] could have in "Hebrew" when this language was not even spoken, let alone written?

9. Conclusions

The hypotheses we have formulated are consistent with the figure of the Elohim that appears in our work: a flesh-and-blood individual who was not concerned with theology or spirituality and who, therefore, did not even have the need or desire to give a special meaning to his name.

Let us not forget that Yahweh explicitly declared that he "did not speak in riddles!" (Numbers 12:8). Yahweh responds to Moses' request to know his name with words that can be interpreted as follows: Yahweh is the one proposing the covenant and will always keep his promises as long as the Israelites do the same.

But Yahweh has the upper hand here. It would be a mistake to see the rules contained in the covenant as the result of a negotiation or free discussion between two parties. A complete imposition of unchallengeable rules and commandments is incorrectly and perhaps tendentiously called a "covenant."

If reality is as we suspect, the tetragrammaton [yhwh] meant nothing in Hebrew.

Most likely, as we have seen in the cargo cults, it was the simple rendering of sounds forming a proper name belonging to another language.

Tradition has ceaselessly sought to give theological, ontological, and metaphysical meaning to what was probably nothing more than a name.

The interpretation presented here is no less valuable than the many others proposed by philologists, exegetes, and theologians, given the variety of interpretations that have arisen over time. The future may bring clarity, or at least we hope so.

עם סגלה

9 / PEOPLE OF PROPERTY

1. "Chosen people"

The concept of "chosen people" is exceptionally delicate; it lends itself to instrumental readings that, unfortunately, are sometimes used to justify racist positions on both sides, with all the tragic consequences that history has shown us.

A careful analysis of the origins of this concept can lead to the defusion of the waiting bomb, which has more or less devastating effects depending on the moments in which the detonation occurs.

As is often the case, the truth sets one free and removes the very foundations on which contradictions and falsifications lie.

Let us first see how a part of Jewish thought represents this concept.

From this Jewish perspective, the Christian Church has claimed to take the place of the Israelites as the "chosen people," inventing human doctrines and erroneous interpretations and denying the Jewish roots of this idea.

Met with this problem, the Church theorized and postulated a distinction between a physical Israel and a "spiritual Israel," i.e., the Church itself, which would become the final and sole recipient of the promises made to the Israelites in the Bible.

Jews rightly emphasize that the solution to this problem is to be sought exclusively in the scriptures of the Old Testament, which speak unequivocally of a single "chosen people" composed of two distinct entities: the House of Judah and the House of Israel, the only ones legitimized to constitute the Assembly of Israel.

As can be seen, it takes work to settle this question.

The hypothesis pursued in this book can shed some light and explain that the "choice" of one "people" is far less edifying than is commonly believed. Lofty goals of religious and spiritual kinds were indeed not the reason for the motives behind this choice or selection.

The existence of various Elohim, who fought for control of territories in the so-called "fertile crescent," constitutes the foundation of our working hypothesis.

Now, when and how does this "choice" or "selection" take place?

Scholars need to look into a passage in Deuteronomy 32 that is important for understanding the context in which the alleged election of the "chosen people" took place. Deuteronomy 32 is critical for understanding who does what.

In this section, we find the so-called "Song of Moses," which celebrates the greatness of Yahweh and praises his works recalling all that Yahweh has accomplished and what he did for Israel.

However, Deuteronomy 32 shows an assortment of characters that traditional monotheistic views aim to simplify and overlook while trying to reduce to one what is, in reality, manifold.

In this section, "God" is referred to by the term יהוה "Yahweh," often accompanied by an attribute identifying him as a specific member of the ranks of the Elohim: אלהינו [elohenu] "our Lord," that is, "the one of the Elohim who is ours."

Yahweh is also called אל [el] or אלוה [Eloha], which denotes, in the singular, one of the members of the group of the Elohim, as shown in chapter 2.

However, the reader will note, at some point, a switch in the narrative. The subject changes. "God" is no longer called Yahweh!

Moses abandons all other definitions and resorts to a different term, עליון [Elyon], which means "high, higher, superior, the one above." This term defines a clear hierarchical position (Deuteronomy 32:8).

גוים	עליון	בהנחל
nations	Elyon	inherit-make-when ←

בני אדם		בהפרידו
Adam-of-children		he-separate-when ←

עמים	גבלת	יצב
peoples	of-borders	established ←

ישראל	בני	למספר
Israel	of-children	of-number-(based on)for ←

The first part of the verse clearly states that [Elyon], "the one above," considers all "the peoples/nations" as an inheritance, a property to be distributed. All nations before him are a set of goods/peoples that we can rightly assume he possesses, on which he exerts his unlimited power, and about which he is free to decide their future, including the decision to assign them to someone as personal property.

Who, then, is Elyon?

2. Elyon

The term [elyon] is often used in the Bible as an adjective meaning "someone, or something, that is above, high above, superior." There are several examples of this use in this specific meaning.

– In Ezekiel 41:7, the term denotes the "upper [elyon] story" of a house;

– In Joshua 16:5, in 1 Chronicles 7:24, and 2 Chronicles 8:5, it denotes a border city [Bet-oron] divided into an "upper" [elyon] and a "lower" part;

– Isaiah 36:2 refers to a pool called [elyona], "superior."

– In Deuteronomy 26:19, the definition of "superior" is also evident. In this passage, the term [elyon] is used to define the nation of Israel, which is "superior in fame, name, and honor to other nations."

So, [elyon] is not the identifying name of a person, a proper name, but a term denoting a position, a function, or a quality. With this in mind, we return to Deuteronomy 32. The assignment of the inheritance by "he who is above" eventually results in a division of the nations among the different Elohim (32:9). Yahweh also gets his little share.

עמו	יהוה	חלק	כי
his-people	Yahweh	of-portion	that ←

נחלתו	חבל	יעקב	
his-inheritance	of-territory/rope	Jacob ←	

The term חבל [chevel] means "rope" and indicates, by extension, a "portion of territory measured with a rope." This expression is very eloquent and shows that the biblical authors referred to precise geographical areas defined by clear boundaries.

We are dealing with an actual territorial division, the definition and establishment of spheres of influence over certain nations and peoples by certain individuals. Notably, the people descended from Jacob became Yahweh's inheritance after the division made by [elyon], "the one above."

Moses says that Yahweh (Deuteronomy 32:10):

מידבר	בארץ	ימצאהו
deserted	land-in	him-finds ←

ישמן	ילל	ובתהו
desert/desolation	howling	structure-of-absence-in-and ←

יצרנהו	יבוננהו	יסבבנהו
him-protects	him-after-looks	he-surrounds ←

עינו	כאישון	
his-eye	of-apple-like ←	

Elyon gives Yahweh jurisdiction over Jacob and the land where Jacob and his family lived. Yahweh — the Bible says — takes excellent care of Jacob's family; and that is all.

It is clear that the matching of Jacob's family with Yahweh has no particular universal significance, nor does it convey a global message for all humanity. Israel was a tiny nation, assigned to one of the many Elohim who participated with varying degrees of satisfaction in dividing the available lands.

Elyon, the Elohim "who is above," was responsible for the outcome of this division of territory.

3. "No foreign El was with Yahweh"

The Bible says that Yahweh acts toward Jacob's family like an eagle that drives its brood, spreads its wings, and guides them in flight. Verse

12 then specifies that:

יהוה	בדד	ינחנו
Yahweh ←	himself-by	him-leads

ואין	עמו	אל	נכר
not-and ←	him-with	El	foreign

This is a crucial statement. No other El was with Yahweh. The El, named Yahweh, says the Bible, took care of Jacob's family "alone." He had no help from his "colleagues." Neither did he seek it, as far as we know.

We ask ourselves: why was it necessary to emphasize this particular aspect? Why clarify a point that can only cause confusion in a monotheistic narrative? Why claim that Yahweh was "alone" if no other "gods" existed? And yet, as strange as it sounds, this passage is in full accordance with many other passages from the Bible in which, with unmistakable clarity, there is evidence of the existence of "other gods" and "foreign gods."

As seen in the previous chapters, the Bible often tells us the names of Yahweh's "colleagues," the other Elohim: Chamosh, Elohim of the Moabites; Milkom, Elohim of the Ammonites; Hadad, Elohim of the Arameans; Melqart, Elohim of the Tyrians; and many more.

Extra-biblical literature also confirms this reading. Plato mentions a territorial division among the so-called "gods" in his dialogue *Critias*. As we shall see, Sumerian accounts also describe this episode in great detail.

We have various sources of different cultural origins that confirm the biblical episode of Deuteronomy 32 and its reading in a non-monotheistic light.

Driven by these "gods" coming from above, each recipient of a limited jurisdiction over one people/territory, human civilization spread across the planet.

Yahweh received Jacob's family, but other Elohim inherited other lands and nations.

Israel was the property of Yahweh. The expression עם סגלה [segullah am] that the Bible uses in this section indicates precisely a "personal property" and effectively conveys the idea we have described. Deuteronomy 7:6 reiterates this concept by restating that Israel is סגלה [segullah], "property" of Yahweh.

Israel is also קדוש [kadosc], that is "consecrated" to him, which means "exclusively reserved for him," as we have already explained in the previous chapters when discussing the word "sacred."

Sumerian literary accounts also confirm the biblical passage of Deuteronomy 32. In fact, with all likelihood, the biblical account derives from the Sumerian tablets. The Bible provides a concise form of what the Sumerians explained at length.

Sumerologists know this Sumerian narrative as *Enki and the World Order*. In this story, the Anunnaki commander, Enki, defines the world's destinies by arranging the partition of power among the lesser Anunnaki, the ones below him. This division is described in a remarkably detailed manner.

Enki is superior to all the others. He has the power to determine the destinies of different lands and territories, which are named in succession: Sumer, Ur, Meluhha, Dilmun, Elam, Marhasi, Martu, Tigris, Euphrates, the marshy region, and the sea.

The supreme leader established what we would today call a "New World Order." Enki also distributes privileges and responsibilities to the individual Anunnaki under him. He assigns to the lesser "gods" the development of various activities that constitute the basis of human civilization: agriculture, animal husbandry, weaving, building, and so on.

The Sumerians were so accurate in describing these events that they did not forget to mention the less edifying aspects of the behavior of these so-called "gods."

The minor "gods" were often dissatisfied with the assigned tasks; they quarreled about responsibilities and complained that Enki excluded them from the land distribution. This behavior is not surprising, given their "human-like" nature.

Among the various places and lands that the Sumerian texts mention, one cannot overlook Meluhha, traditionally located by scholars between Iran and Afghanistan. Some scholars identify Meluhha/Melukhkha as the southernmost part of the Harappa civilization (Feuerstein).

Together with Mohenjo-Daro, this city represents essential evidence of the unique Vedic Indo-Aryan culture that developed along the banks of the Indus River to the shores of the Arabian Sea in the 4th-3rd millennia BCE.

Other precise indications in the cuneiform texts attest to the vastness of the geographical area involved in the territorial division. One additional point of contact with the Bible is that the Dravidian peoples who inhabited these lands traced their origin to Manu, the Hindu equivalent of the biblical Noah, who repopulated the Earth after the Flood.

In summary, the Sumerian accounts described in detail what the Bible briefly summarizes in Deuteronomy 32. The story is the same: one great leader, the "one above," distributes lands and assigns responsibilities to the other minor "gods" below him. Some are happy; some are not.

During this distribution, Yahweh received one tiny nation: Israel. Was Yahweh happy with this assignment? Did he expect more? Whatever the case, the Bible informs us that Yahweh was alone. No other "god" was to help him with his task and duties.

It must also be emphasized that Israel was not "chosen by," but rather "assigned to" Yahweh. Other peoples/nations were assigned to other "gods" and thus constituted material for different "choices," within which it is presumptuous to define a hierarchical scale.

Now, suppose we can free ourselves from the conditioning of two thousand years of theology and centuries of religious doctrine and look at the situation from a distance; we clearly understand that the very idea of Israel being the "chosen people" is the child of a monotheistic conviction that has matured over the centuries and has eventually made Yahweh the one "God."

This monotheistic development first took place in the Hebrew realm and was then reshaped, revised, and reconstructed by the numerous theological movements in the Christian and Islamic worlds.

When we look at the history of the concept of the "chosen people," we see how it changes diachronically and the great degree of variation it exhibits over time, from the initial "selections" and "assignments" of Elyon in Deuteronomy 32 to modern sectarian and fanatical manifestations often found in monotheistic religions.

To summarize, each Elohim had their "inheritance" and their "chosen people."

All the ancient chronicles (including the Bible) tell us in great detail that these "gods" were never satisfied with their endowments but were in constant struggle with each other to expand their dominions and spheres of influence. So there were many "gods" with their respective "chosen people."

Several questions arise from these considerations.

– How can one determine a value scale of the different "chosen peoples?"

– How can one say that Yahweh of Teman (the Lord of the South, i.e., Palestine) was superior to Baal Zafon (the Lord of the North, i.e., Lebanon) or Ashur or Marduk (the "gods" who ruled over Assyrian and Babylonian territories)?

– And what about the "gods" who ruled over territories in the Far East or the American continent?

4. The sign of the choice

Once Israel is "chosen," Yahweh imposes a sign of recognition upon them. Its members will bear a mark similar to that of cattle, whose individual animals are marked to distinguish them from other cattle.

> This is my covenant with you and your descendants after you, the covenant you are to keep: **Every male among you shall be circumcised.** You are to undergo circumcision, and **it will be the sign of the covenant between me and you.** For the generations to come every male among you who is eight days old must be circumcised, including those born in your household or bought with money from a foreigner — those who are not your offspring.
>
> (Genesis 17:10-12)

The מולה [mula], "circumcision," will be the sign of the covenant between the Yahweh and his people. Tradition explains the choice of the genital organ as the focus of circumcision because the foreskin is the only body part that can be removed without causing actual mutilation.

However, we cannot but notice another aspect that the tradition does not emphasize with regard to the circumcision. The result of it is a physical sign, distinct, hidden, but verifiable when necessary.

The covenant members identified in this way could also be kept under control, as we can see when considering the story of Sodom and Gomorrah. It is Yahweh who says so without any interpretative doubt (Genesis 17:11):

לְאֹת	וְהָיָה
of-sign-(like)for	shall be-and ←

וּבֵינֵיכֶם	בֵּינִי	בְּרִית
you-between-and	me-between	covenant ←

As if this were not clear enough, Yahweh gives a stern command in the following verse: "An uncircumcised man […] shall be cut off from his people; he has broken my covenant" (14). The circumcised foreskin is the most important sign of belonging to the covenant group, and whoever does not wear it will be cut off (killed?).

We know that this foreskin treatment also has a hygienic significance that is not secondary, especially in the way of life where it was not easy to follow even simple personal cleanliness practices. However, the two aspects are coherent; we are dealing with two objectives achieved by a single action: simple fidelity control and hygienic requirements.

5. The table of nations

Let us now introduce another element to illuminate our path further. Genesis 10:21 states that:

כָּל-בְּנֵי-עֵבֶר	אֲבִי	שֵׁם
Eber-of-children-all	of-father	Shem ←

So from Sem/Shem descends Eber, who has two sons, Joktan and Peleg. The latter is described with a fascinating remark. He was called Peleg because (Genesis 10:25):

הָאָרֶץ	נִפְלְגָה	בְּיָמָיו
earth-the	divided-was	him-of-days-in ←

The name Peleg is derived from the verb [palag], which means "to divide."

Let us now outline, for the sake of clarity, what the Old Testament tells us about a precise sequence of events:

- Shem is the forefather of the Hebrews (the children of Eber/Ever) (Genesis 10:21);

- Eber (Ever) is the great-grandson of Shem (Sem) (Genesis 10:24);

- Peleg is a direct son of Eber (Genesis 10:25);

- at the time of Peleg, the Earth is divided (Genesis 10:25);

- during this division, as seen above, the Jewish people are "assigned to" Yahweh, who finds them wandering in the desert (Deuteronomy 32:9-12).

Genesis 10 is also known as the "Table of Nations" because it lists the descendants of the patriarch Noah, who escaped the Flood, and attempts to explain how humanity was restored through him. It contains the genealogies of Noah's descendants, divided by families scattered across the Earth after the Flood.

> These are the clans of Noah's sons, according to their lines of descent, within their nations. **From these the nations spread out over the Earth after the flood.**
>
> (Genesis 10:32)

In addition to the Hebrews, the "Table of Nations" also mentions other people. But let us focus on the Hebrews for a moment.

We are all used to thinking that the Hebrew people originated with Abraham. Still, here we have just been confronted with the precise statement that Eber is, in fact, their eponym.

Eber is the ancestor of many peoples, and his lineage is divided into two separate lines, headed by his two sons: Peleg and Joktan. From Joktan descended many peoples who then dispersed between Africa and the East. We shall return to him in a moment.

From Peleg, on the other hand, descended [Abram], whose name will be changed to [Abraham], for he will become, as Yahweh says, the father of many nations (Genesis 17:5). So, the Hebrews descended from [Abraham], but their progenitor is undoubtedly Eber.

We are dealing with a possible contradiction here, but it is the Bible itself that clarifies the matter in Genesis 14:13. A man runs to bring news:

העברי	לאברם
Hebrew-the	Abram-to ←

According to Genesis Abraham was already a Hebrew, as he belonged to the lineage of עבר [Ever] mentioned in Genesis 10:21. Thus, the Hebrews, as an ethnic group, existed *before* Abraham.

We have seen that Eber had many descendants, so here we establish a crucial fact: Abraham's descendants were not the only Hebrew peoples.

Having established that the definition of Hebrews includes other peoples beyond Abraham's lineage, let us proceed with the story of the "call" of Abram as found in Genesis 12:1-3.

Yahweh instructs Abram to leave the land of his fathers with the promise to make him a great nation. The promise is repeated in Genesis 17:4-7, where Yahweh again chooses Abram to carry out his plan. On this occasion, the patriarch's name becomes "Abraham."

The Bible tells of eight sons of Abraham: one by the Egyptian servant Hagar, six by Qeturah, and finally, Isaac, born of Sarah, a Hebrew woman who belonged to the same family.

From Isaac on, all the descendants of Abraham are no longer mentioned, but only the descendants of Isaac, born within the genetic group of the family.

The decision to preserve the purity of the blood continues after Isaac. Abraham marries him within his kinship (Genesis 24:3-4), and from Isaac's marriage, two sons are born: Esau and Jacob.

Esau marries a Canaanite woman and is therefore excluded from the official lineage, whereas Jacob agrees to choose a wife within his father's family (Genesis 28:1-5). So Jacob preserves the genetic purity of the family: he takes the name of Israel, and from then on, all his descendants are called "children of Israel."

So, only the Israelites kept and preserved their core Hebrew identity, but they did not call themselves "Ivri" (Hebrews). Other people called them that. The terms "Hebrews" and "Israelites" only became synonymous over time.

For the sake of clarity, let it be said that we deliberately do not address the thorny issues that arise from examining extra-biblical documents from which different origins for Abraham and his family are inferred.

Let us now look at the "Table of Nations" from a different perspective.

6. Were Sumerians also Semites?

Sumerians possessed extraordinary knowledge in all fields and disciplines: writing, literature, agronomy, engineering, geometry, metallurgy, astronomy and timekeeping, units of measurement, civil and criminal law, public government and administration, taxation, accounting, transportation systems, music and dance, education and schooling.

They had dozens of terms by which they identified oil and its derivatives. In the field of building, they showed extraordinary expertise, which is also confirmed in the Bible (Genesis 11:1-4).

Modern science has proven through laboratory tests that fired clay bricks are five times stronger than sun-dried bricks. Sumerian architects used dried bricks for basic structures, while the fired bricks were used for the parts of the buildings that were subject to extraordinary stresses, such as stairs, projecting architectural elements, structures that were particularly exposed to the elements; everything was then held together by bitumen, which served as cement.

As anyone can easily understand, if this population was so great in all fields of knowledge, they could not have gone unnoticed. However, as Sumerian scholar S. N. Kramer already pointed out, the Old Testament only incidentally mentions the land of Shinàr (Genesis 10:10; Zechariah 5:11), identified as Sumer. But the Bible never mentions the Sumerians explicitly.

In the so-called "Table of Nations" that we introduced in the previous section of this chapter, all the peoples who lived in the territories of the Middle East and beyond are listed: Egyptians, Assyrians, Babylonians, Canaanites, Philistines, Hurrians, Hittites, Moabites, Ethiopians, Amorites, Evei, Akkadians, those of Cyprus, Rhodes, Tarsi, Ophir.

Sumerians are not mentioned.

– How could the Bible forget the people from whom the Old Testament drew most of its original content?

– Is this an incomprehensible and unforgivable omission?

Kramer's teacher, A. Poebel, claimed that the Hebrews were, in fact, the direct descendants of the Sumerians. By this logic, the Bible does not mention them explicitly because when it speaks of the Hebrews, it speaks of a direct descendant branch of the Sumerians.

Official historiography considers the Akkadians the first Semitic people, but within our declared working methodology, we wonder: were the
Sumerians also Semites?

We try to answer this question with the help of the Bible itself. Genesis 10:21 informs us that Shem, the son of Noah, had various sons from
whom descended populations that history knows well: Ashur, Elam,
Aram, and so on.

Eber, the forefather of the Hebrews, descended from one of these
sons, as seen in the previous section.

Apropos of Shem, Kramer and Poebel stress some exciting aspects:

- the correct spelling of the original cuneiform writing is *shumer* and
  not *sumer*;

- the Bible uses the consonant [scin] for the name Sem, so the correct
  spelling for Sem is, in fact, "Shem," the spelling that we have also
  used in this book;

- the Hebrew word for "name" is [shem] and corresponds to the Akkadian [shumu] because the Hebrew "e" corresponds to the vowel "u"
  of the cuneiform script;

- the word *shumer* was pronounced *shumi* or *shum*.

Furthermore:

- Sumer was in Mesopotamia (east of Palestine);

- Mesopotamia is traditionally the original homeland of the patriarch
  Abram, according to the Bible (Genesis 15:7 and 24:10), although
  this issue is controversial and involves various hypotheses. We also
  know that Abram was a descendant of Eber, and his son Isaac continued the genetically pure line of the Hebrews, as seen in the previous
  section.

- The marriage customs used by Abraham, Isaac, and Jacob to secure
  their lineage were the same as those used by the Sumerian rulers and
  the Anunnaki, the Sumerian gods. Dynastic descent was ensured by
  marrying a woman from the same family, usually a half-sister, to
  preserve genetic purity. Following these dynastic customs, Abram explicitly says of his wife, "Sarah is my sister, the daughter of my father,

but not of my mother; and she became my wife" (Genesis 20:12). The marriage customs of Abraham and his family perfectly match those of the Sumerian rulers and the Anunnaki. Is this a coincidence?

- The name Isaac is said to derive from the Akkadian (derived from Sumerian) "*ishakku*," a title that denoted the highest authority in the city. This consideration suggests that Abraham's family held a position of power in society, from which he moved to settle in the territory his Elohim had designated for him. Is it a coincidence that the name of one of the founding patriarchs of the people, Isaac, is derived from an Akkadian term for a high administrative office?

Only one part is missing to complete the picture: the question of the area where the Sumerians lived, the south of Mesopotamia, which lies east of Palestine. Once again, the Bible comes to our rescue when it lists Joktan's sons and tells us that (Genesis 10:29-30):

ממשא	מושבם	ויהי
Mesha-from	their-dwelling	was-and ←

הקדם	הר	ספרה	באכה
east-the	of-mount	Sephar-to(until)	to-come-(to)in ←

Joktan's sons occupied Mesha, probably the area of present-day Arabia, which extended along the Arabian Peninsula to Sephar, the present-day Zufar Mountains above the Arabian Sea.

We still need to determine whether the last part of the verse indicates that Sephar is an eastern mountain range or whether the sons of Joktan reached another undefined mountain range to the East. Still, the Bible tells us that some of the descendants of Shem moved eastward.

Recall that Joktan was the son of Eber and thus a Hebrew, just like the sons of Abraham, descendants of Peleg, Joktan's brother.

Up to this point, we have dealt with the descendants of Noah's sons, especially the descendants of Shem, and the need to preserve a certain genetic purity through marriages that were celebrated and thus controlled within the family circle.

From this point of view, however, Noah himself represents a possible curiosity that leads us down this path in search of the meaning of the hypothetical "selection" of a people.

The question of the possible "Hebraism" of the Sumerians remains, of course, open.

7. Noah and the watchers

The commentaries on the Berakhot (Talmud) explicitly state that Noah was not a Hebrew, which is obvious (Di Segni). In the apocryphal Book of Enoch, already mentioned, it is said that the wife of Lamech, Enoch's nephew, gave birth to a child whose appearance raised doubts about its paternity.

The newborn's skin was not the same color as that of the native; it was white and rosy, his hair was white, and his eyes so beautiful and clear that they seemed to shine.

Lamech told his father, Methuselah, that his wife had given birth to a son who did not look like a man but like the children of the "angels." He suspected his son had been fathered by one of the "guardians." Methuselah turned to his father, Enoch, who assured him that the child was indeed from Lamech and should be called Noah.

In Book of Giants, found in the Qumran manuscripts, the epilogue of the same story offers some thought-provoking insights. In chapter CVI, Lamech, seeing that the child is different from him, flees to his father Methuselah, who advises him to go to Enoch and ask him for clarification, as Lamech says, "His dwelling place is with the Watchers."

It should be mentioned at this point that, as already extensively described in chapter 6, the canonical Bible says that Enoch, the patriarch (literal translation):

> … **walked/went/traveled back and forth with the Elohim** after he had fathered Methuselah three hundred years, and he fathered sons and daughters, and all the days of Enoch were three hundred sixty-five years, and he **walked/went/ traveled back and forth with the Elohim**, and he **was no more because the Elohim took him**.

> (Genesis 5:22-24)

The text says twice that Enoch went/traveled with the Elohim; the verb is in a particular construction, indicating the intensity and repetitiveness of the action. Therefore, the meaning can be described as "going to and fro," as detailed in chapter 6. The Bible tells us that he accompanied the Elohim constantly and repeatedly: they went back and forth together.

The Book of Genesis is very laconic in the description of this story, which is instead told in great detail in the apocryphal books. In the latter, we find descriptions of Enoch's journeys accompanied by angels, the so-called "vigilants," "watchers," or "guardians."

Let us summarize here Enoch's "adventures" as they are described in the apocryphal books:

– Enoch ascends to heaven, to a beautiful house where he encounters "God;"

– he is taken to various places, even underground;

– he flies to a place in the desert dominated by fire;

– then, he moves in different directions to the ends of the Earth;

– he receives from the "watchers/guardians" astronomical knowledge about the order of the cosmos, the sun, the moon, its phases, the lunar year, and the orbits of the planets (knowledge that the Elohim possessed to a great extent because they were space people).

We understand why Lamech wants to know Enoch's opinion: he knew he was very familiar with the world of the watchers/guardians and the lords above; he accompanied them regularly and went with them without dying. This tradition was widely accepted because it is also found in Sirach 44:16 and the New Testament in the Letter to the Hebrews 11:5.

Enoch meets his son Methuselah and asks him the reason for his visit. Methuselah explains that a son was born to Lamech whose appearance does not correspond to that of the people, so there is a well-founded fear that it is not Lamech's child.

Enoch reassures Methuselah and emphasizes that this child will be saved when all the people on Earth die. We learn here that there are plans for this child who bears an incredible resemblance to the watchers. Humanity and life on Earth will be restored through him and his descendants. So, a remarkable decision was made about Noah that affects all future humanity.

After this extra-biblical digression, we return to the Bible to highlight some aspects that can take on interesting new meanings in light of what we said about the patriarch Enoch, who "went back and forth with the Elohim."

As described in the previous chapters, particularly chapter 7, the interbreeding between the sons of Elohim and the daughters of the Adam had nefarious consequences for humankind. Mixing the two species did not please "God" (Genesis 6). To summarize:

– the crossbreeding between the two races is reprehensible;

– the Elohim decides to exterminate humanity with the Flood;

– Noah is destined to restore humankind.

In light of what has just been said, consider Genesis 6:9, where Noah is defined as follows:

בדרתיו	תמים	צדיק	איש
his-of-generations-among	honest	fair	man ←

Usually, this verse is interpreted in purely ethical terms, but certain words allow and, in fact, suggest the introduction of a different reading. The word תמים [tamim] in verse 9 means "whole, complete, without blemish, without spot" and is used with these meanings several times in the Old Testament (for example, Joshua 10:13; Exodus 12:5).

The verb [tamam] from which it derives means "to be complete, not missing any pieces." Considering that the forbidden sexual encounters between the "gods" and the earthly females have resulted in several imperfections and loss of original genetic purity, Noah seems to be an individual whose genetic integrity is being heavily emphasized. He is said to be "perfect in his generation."

– Do his distinctive physical traits show that Noah was essentially "different" from the rest of the human race, who were no longer genetically as perfect as the Elohim intended?

– Was Noah the result of an artificial insemination procedure done on Bitenosh, Lamech's wife?

There is another passage in this regard that we would like to highlight, Genesis 6:11:

האלהים	לפני	הארץ	ותשחת
Elohim-the	of-faces-in	earth-the	ruined-was-it-and ←

Earth was "corrupted." The *Etymological Dictionary of Biblical Hebrew* reports that the verb's primary meaning is "having been irreversibly marred."

Moral wrongs are always reversible, forgivable, and restorable; even the worst sinners can find redemption if they repent.

– What happened that was so severe as to be considered "irreversible?"

– Had the mixing process reached an irreversible and unacceptable degree? Did the Elohim think their genetic programming work was in jeopardy, hence the desire to erase everything and start anew with a "pure seed?"

The story of the ark on which all living species are saved gives us further clues. The Elohim commanded Noah (Genesis 6:14-19) to build an ark:

שנים	מכל-בשר	ומכל-החי
two	flesh-each-from	living-the-each-from-and ←

אל-התבה	תביא	מכל
ark-the-in	enter-let-will-you	(every)each-of ←

We are pursuing the hypothesis that Noah was considered (or even created) genetically intact in order to restore genetic purity.

– Given the logistical difficulty of hundreds of plant species and hundreds of animals living together on the great barge, is it possible that genetic purity was restored "simply" by preserving the DNA of the various species?

– Did Noah bring the genetic matrices of the various species with him onto the ark? Is this what the ancient authors tried to tell us with the limited conceptual categories and linguistic devices at their disposal?

— Is it possible that Noah's ark was the precursor to the Frozen Ark and Svalbard Global Seed Vault projects, which aim to preserve seeds and animal DNA from catastrophic events that could endanger life on Earth?

There is no definite and proven answer — at least, we do not have one — but the literal meaning of the terms and the logical consistency do not allow us to dismiss this possibility with superficial arrogance.

8. The tribes of Israel

Biblical authors told the story of Israel, the chosen people, on a clear ideological basis and with a distinctly nationalistic stamp.

This goal required the presentation of a coherent and unified political and ethnic structure characterized by temporal and geographical continuity. This was the only way to guarantee the uniqueness of the selection that exclusively described them. But have the various authors involved in the text achieved their intention?

We will examine only one aspect here and leave a more detailed and comprehensive analysis to other future works. We wonder: were there twelve tribes?

In Numbers 1, we find a list of representatives of each of the tribes that were to take the census in the desert: Reuben, Simeon, Judah, Issachar, Zebulun, Joseph, Benjamin, Dan, Asher, Gad, Naphtali. So there are eleven official tribes.

The biblical author then divides the tribe of Joseph and forms two, corresponding to his sons Ephraim and Manasseh: the number is again twelve.

The census, however, does not consider the tribe of Levi, which is also of fundamental importance because of its duties in the direct service of the Elohim. With Levi, the tribes are now thirteen.

We must assume Levi was omitted from the census because the number had to be twelve.

This trick is repeated in Deuteronomy 33. Moses blesses the tribes and, this time, restores the tribe of Levi in the number but omits the tribe of Simeon. In this way, the number twelve continues to be respected.

But why was it so important to respect the number twelve?

The choice of the number twelve is most likely related to the division of the year into twelve months and the functional necessity of assigning each district the monthly task of procuring food and services for the court in Jerusalem. Each community, in turn, had to fulfill this task during the twelve months.

But numbers only occasionally agree; often, this necessity has escaped the authors themselves.

In Judges 1, the tribes are listed in the following order: Judah, Simeon, Benjamin, Joseph, Manasseh, Ephraim, Zebulun, Asher, Naphtali, and Dan.

Both Joseph and his two sons, Ephraim and Manasseh, are mentioned.

Still, despite this unjustified juxtaposition, we have a total of ten tribes, which, if we take Joseph out, becomes nine.

But what would then happen to Reuben, Issachar, Gad, and Levi? If we add them up we would be back to thirteen or fourteen tribes, if we keep Joseph with his two sons, as the biblical author did.

The Book of Judges offers us another oddity.

Chapter 5 is known as the "Song of Deborah" and is probably the oldest written biblical text. It celebrates the exploits of Elohim and a battle in which the children of Israel were victorious. However, the battle involved only six tribes in the following order: Ephraim, Benjamin, Machir, Zebulun, Issachar, and Naphtali.

Verses 16-18, which turn out to be a later addition, probably made with restorative intent, mention other tribes that the older text did not seem to know: Reuben, Gilead, Dan, and Asher. According to a simple calculation, we then have ten tribes with restorative insertion.

In addition, we have two mentioned names that do not appear in the other lists: Machir and Gilead, which might correspond to Manasseh and Gad. Where have Simeon and Levi gone?

Can we assume they were victims of the curse imposed on them in Genesis 49:5-7? In these verses, Elohim rages against the particularly violent behavior of the members of these two tribes and predicts their dispersion within Israel. If this is the case, only ten remain.

Further confirmation of the impermanence of numbers and the numerical inconsistency of the tribes is found in 1 Kings 11:31-32.

The verses refer to Jeroboam, son of Nebat, a worthy man who served

Solomon, who had placed him in charge of recruitment. On a journey outside Jerusalem, Jeroboam meets the prophet Achiah, who informs him of Yahweh's intentions: the Elohim has decided to take Solomon's kingdom and leave him only with one tribe.

A symbolic gesture accompanies the news: Achiah tears his cloak into twelve pieces and tells Jeroboam to take ten, the number corresponding to the ten tribes that Yahweh will assign to him by taking them away from Solomon. The calculation is simple: ten tribes for Jeroboam, only one (Judah) for Solomon, for a total of eleven.

The analysis is simple, but it does not add up.

The explanation probably lies in the fact that the Hebrews were not only those who had followed Moses out of Egypt but also, as the oft-quoted Prof. Giovanni Garbini writes:

> The outcasts who lived on the margins of society in an ambiguous position, and that these Hebrews (the Babylonians called them khabiru) were particularly numerous in areas and times of political and social upheaval, such as those that favored the settlement of certain Israelite tribes in Palestine. Moreover, Hebrews hid in the caves and helped Jonathan, son of Saul, in his coup against the Philistine camp (1 Sam 14:11).
>
> (Garbini, *Storia e ideologia*)

That is not all. Naphtali, Gilead, and Zabulon are geographical names for territories annexed to the Assyrian empire. It is not entirely sure that they belonged to the Kingdom of the North.

Yahweh took advantage of the prevailing confusion and power vacuum that characterized this period to conquer the territory he had his eye on since the time of Abraham.

That said, we cannot help but reflect that the "uniqueness" of the "chosen people," its numerical and tribal substance, and its precise and practical division into twelve tribes was perhaps more a strongly felt desire of Jewish nationalism than an objective and documented historical reality.

The Hebrew people were far more articulate and complex than nationalist ideology has tried to portray them.

This observation should lead to serious reflection on all those schools of thought that build truths and certainties on numbers: theologians, kabbalists, esotericists…

Entire interpretive structures have been built around the number twelve because the number twelve is considered a highly symbolic number. Thus, the twelve had to be there.

However, historical reality teaches us that there were probably not twelve tribes. This figure results from a later revision that attempted to construct a solid ideological perspective from an uncertain historical ground.

Caution is always advised when attempting to base truths of various kinds on particular texts: theological, kabbalistic, or, more generally, esoteric-initiatory.

9. Conclusions

We present below a succinct and hopefully clarifying summary of what has been said in this chapter.

- The first Adamite females mix with the "sons of the Elohim," the species of creators, thus provoking the violent reaction of the supreme lords, who decide to eliminate them.
- Noah is intentionally created "whole" to restore genetic purity to planet Earth.
- Noah is the father of Sem/Shem.
- The Akkadian Shum of Shumer corresponds to the Shem of Genesis 10:21.
- The children of Shem, i.e., the Semites, could be possibly identified with the children of Shum, i.e., the Shumers/Sumerians.
- From Shem descends Eber and therefore the Hebrews.
- From Eber descended Peleg (and Abraham).
- At the time of Peleg, a territorial division is made between the various "lords from above."
- The story of this division is told in Deuteronomy 32 and other Sumerian narratives.
- Yahweh receives Jacob's family as "property."

Therefore, we cannot speak of "chosen people" but of different decisions or different types of decisions and "selections" that took place at different times in history and involved different people. The Bible suggests at least three different situations in which a specific person or group has been singled out for a specific goal or purpose.

– Noah (who was not Hebrew) and all his descendants were chosen because of the Elohim's will to restore the human race and possibly genetic purity.

– The people of the "Semites/Sumerians" (descendants of Sem/Shem/ Shum) were chosen by the Elohim/Anunnaki to initiate human civilization's development after the Flood.

– The "children of Israel" (the descendants of Abraham through Isaac and Jacob) were "chosen" by Yahweh — assigned to him — as his personal property.

10 / DRUG-ADDICTED GODS

1. "Sacred materialism"

The Book of Leviticus, one of the least-read books of the Old Testament, describes the complex structure of the religious and social legislation of the people of Israel, codified around the fundamental concept of the "sacred" that we have already discussed in the previous chapters.

In his presentation of Leviticus, Monsignor Gianfranco Ravasi (former president of the Pontifical Council for Culture and one of the most important Vatican biblical scholars) wrote:

> **The concept of the sacred or sacral that underlies this theological vision is both valuable and risky.** [...] Valuable because [...] it clearly distinguishes the sphere of God from what is created. **Risky because it can introduce an exaggerated separation between the sacred and the profane,** considering practically everything outside the sacred sphere as impure and useless and only what is contained within it as pure and precious. [...] This risk appears here and there in the Book of Leviticus, especially when [...] it comes to a kind of **sacred materialism.**[15]

The prelate emphasizes the danger that anything outside proper ritual behavior falls within impurity.

A rite performed incorrectly can indeed lead to death. So we have no doubt: the materialistic view of the "sacred" that the prelate presents as a risk for a person of faith is absolute normality for those reading the Old Testament from a lay perspective.

Indeed, "sacred materialism" is the defining characteristic of the subject we are dealing with here.

Approaching the ancient text, one inevitably encounters terms that religious tradition has used for centuries to convey meanings that serve

---

[15] *Bibbia Emmaus.* San Paolo Edizioni, 2005.

the overall picture of a transcendent "God." People of faith turn in reverence to "God," performing actions that are supposed to elevate the faithful's soul to the point of contact with his divine creator counterpart.

Is that really what the Old Testament tells us?

The traditional reading seems coherent as long as the analysis remains superficial. But a literal reading reveals a stark discrepancy with current religious understanding. This contradictory aspect appears in all books containing the history of the origins of Judeo-Christian thought.

In this chapter, we refer in particular to a specific element that is never considered because it is usually taken for granted and accepted as a general understanding in the version of the Bible known to all. We refer to the biblical passages that emphasize that the Elohim loved to smell or sniff certain fragrances and scents, or rather, as we will see more clearly in a moment, certain odors that were not necessarily pleasant.

2. Holocausts

At the end of the Flood, Noah makes sure that the waters have receded, and then he brings out of the ark his family and all the animals according to their species. As his first act, the biblical patriarch builds an altar to offer sacrifices (Genesis 8:18-21). In verse 20 it is said that Noah offered holocausts, עלת [olot], of animals and birds.

With the term עלה [olha], Hebrew indicates the sacrifice of burning the victim *entirely* without leaving anything behind.

Therefore, nothing was left to consume or to be offered. *The object of the offering was the smoke* only or, to be precise, the smell/odor.

The word [olah] contains the meanings of the verb [ala], "to ascend," and the noun [kol], which indicates totality. The holocaust was, therefore, a kind of sacrifice in which the victim had to turn totally and entirely into ascending smoke. The Hebrew consonantal root refers to the physical and concrete meaning of rising, of ascending upwards.

The English word "holocaust" retains the same meaning because it derives from the Greek word *olokaustos* which identifies "that which was entirely burnt" by fire.

In the most ancient accounts, such a sacrifice was meant as a sign of homage or was accompanied by a supplication; only with the passing of the centuries did it also assume an atoning value.

Initially, then, it served to facilitate relations with the Elohim, to ingratiate oneself with them, to make them friendly and well disposed, and to induce them to accept all the requests of the offerer. The behavior of the offerer towards the Elohim was typical of anyone who wanted to ingratiate himself with the powerful and offer them a particularly pleasing gift.

To understand what the Bible says, we should read some passages of the Torah in which we can verify and stress the exact details that "God" gave his people regarding the holocaust and other types of sacrifices they were supposed to perform. These passages demonstrate the effects that the scented vapors and odors produced during these rites had on the Elohim.

3. Noah

In Genesis 8:21, we witness Noah's sacrifice in honor of the Elohim.

ויֶרַח	יהוה	אֶת-רֵיחַ	הַנִּיחֹחַ
smelled-and ←	Yahweh	odor	[nichoach]-the

וַיֹּאמֶר	אֶל-לִבּוֹ	לֹא-אֹסִף
said-and ←	heart-his-(in)to	continue-not-will-I

לְקַלֵּל	עוֹד	אֶת-הָאֲדָמָה
curse-to ←	again	earth-the

We have deliberately not translated the term [nichoach] because it is fundamental to our argument and it will shortly be the subject of our analysis. It will help us understand the strange behavior of a "god" who wants to smell or sniff certain odors.

Before analyzing the actual effects of holocaust smoking, we cannot help but notice at least two curious details from the verses quoted above.

First of all, we register a direct cause-effect relationship between the smell of the smoke and Yahweh's decision not to punish Earth. As he smells the smoke, in Genesis 8:21, Yahweh immediately softens toward the human race he had decided to exterminate, and manifests his determination not to strike any more living beings on Earth because of man.

Moreover, we are confronted with a peculiar and unique representation of Yahweh's train of thought.

> **Yahweh smelled the pleasing aroma and said in his heart: "Never again will I curse the ground because of humans**, even though every inclination of the human heart is evil from childhood. And never again will I destroy all living creatures, as I have done.

(Genesis 8:21)

How did Noah know Yahweh's thoughts since he did not communicate them? From whom and how did he learn about Yahweh's most intimate sentiments? Yahweh also takes note of the natural human wickedness, and we cannot help but wonder:

– Did this all-knowing and spiritual "God" not know beforehand the imperfections and wickedness of the man he had formed "in his image and likeness?"
– Did he have to exterminate "every creature that existed on the face of the Earth" (Genesis 7:23) before he realized this obvious reality?

In the first part of this work, we examined how the Elohim made the Adam. Therefore, it is unsurprising that the Elohim were inaccurate in predicting the consequences of their genetic intervention on the planet. They probably had first to observe, study and understand the effects, which, as it turned out, they could not fully control.

Let us, however, continue with the analysis of the specific theme of this chapter, the smell.

4. Moses

In Leviticus 1 we read that Yahweh summoned Moses and spoke to him "from the Tent of Meeting" (1:1), in other words, from a specific physical place.

On this occasion, he gives him instructions regarding the sacrifices: the animals destined for the burnt offerings must be תמים [tamim], "complete, whole, without defect," and they must be burnt אהל מועד אל-פתח [moed ohel petach-el] (Leviticus 1:3) "at the entrance of the

Tent of Meeting."

Yahweh thus indicates a specific and physical place that is to be used for the sacrifices; and he also explains the reason for it.

לרצנו	אתו	יקריב
him-of-acceptance-for	it	approach-will ←

יהוה	לפני
Yahweh	of-faces-in ←

The term רצון [retzon], "acceptance," indicates something agreeable, intended as an object of pleasantness, favor, or benevolence. From this passage, we understand that, to be accepted, the sacrifice had to have precise characteristics, both in terms of the object of consumption and the place where it was to be performed.

The first etymological meaning of [retzon] provided by the *Dictionary of Biblical Hebrew* refers to the need to "satisfy" the Elohim's necessity. So we are not dealing with a perfume that produces the sensory pleasure commonly associated with particularly pleasant fragrances or essences. Instead, it is a precise action that must be performed in a special place to fulfill the necessity of the Elohim.

It is then clear that the sacrifice had a physical efficacy that only the performance of specific actions could guarantee. Symbolic and spiritual meanings have no room here.

The rules for the execution are precise: sacrifice the animal in the presence of the Elohim, shed the blood so as not to burn it, cut the sacrifice into pieces, prepare the fire with wood, place the parts on the fire, and proceed with the holocaust. This meticulous sequence of actions is inexplicable if one wants to believe that sacrifices had a purely symbolic or spiritual value.

Furthermore, the precise observance of these gestures brought about a particular effect (Leviticus 1:9):

אשה	עלה
of-fire-(with)	of-sacrifice/holocaust ←

ליהוה	ריח–ניחוח
Yahweh-for	[nichoach]-odor ←

We find the term [nichoach] again in a context where we are told that what matters, what "God" likes, is unequivocally the smell resulting from the offering consumed by fire. The smell is an essential element, not the smoke rising to the sky, its dispersion in the air.

This peculiarity is confirmed in verse 13 and chapter 8:21, which essentially repeats the exact wording and from which we understand that the crucial thing is the production of the odor.

This odor or smell will always be [nichoach] for the Lord.

We are in the presence of precise indications, scrupulous operational rules, and a succession of gestures to be carried out without derogation. To what end? To the end of achieving, by burning flesh, an odor that is *nichoach* for the Elohim.

Based on the purely theological assumption that the term Elohim in the Bible refers to the spiritual, transcendental, and unique "God," religious tradition has consistently attached a strictly symbolic value to holocaust offerings, claiming that the symbolic meaning of the smoke ascending to the sky represents the soul ascending to "God," helps the faithful connect with the divine, and thus obtains forgiveness for the sins.

The image of "God" finding pleasure in inhaling or smelling smoke is inconsistent with the image monotheistic theology attempts to convey. However, the biblical authors did not have a preconceived notion of who or what "God" is; therefore, they have not hesitated to describe what they witnessed, regardless of whether this seems acceptable or unacceptable to us today.

According to the Bible, "God" sniffed certain odors produced by sacrifice and found "pleasure." But let us now address the meaning of the word [nichoach].

Conditioned by spiritualist-monotheistic beliefs, religious tradition has consistently ascribed to the term ניחֹח [nichoach] the meaning "pleasant, beneficial, lovely," but this is not entirely correct.

The term [nichoach] means "relaxing, calming, comforting." It derives from the verbal form [nuch], meaning "to lie quietly, to rest, to be still." Its etymology refers to "stop, cease movement" (Brown). Therefore, the word [nichoach] contains meanings that, at first glance, recall the idea of tranquility, relaxation, and overcoming states of tension.

Traditional translations emphasize the pleasure and well-being of relaxation, but these are two distinct feelings. Pleasure and relaxation could be quite different things. Anyone who loves horror movies understands the distinction well. Horror films may be "pleasurable" for lovers of the genre, but they find their source of pleasure precisely in the tension that the film creates. Pleasure and relaxation are two different things that may not belong together at all.

It is essential to keep this aspect in mind as we speculate on why the Elohim found these odors a source of relaxing tranquility and relieving tension.

5. Cain and Abel

Let us read a passage from the Old Testament that is as famous as it is controversial: the story of Cain and Abel (Genesis 4). Genesis says that Abel became a shepherd of flocks while Cain tilled the soil; after some time, Cain offered the produce from his soil to Yahweh, and Abel offered the firstborn of his flock.

> Abel also brought an offering — fat portions from some of the firstborn of his flock. **Yahweh looked with favor on Abel and his offering, but on Cain and his offering he did not look with favor.** So Cain was very angry, and his face was downcast.
>
> (Genesis 4:4-5)

Yahweh liked meat. Fruit, vegetables, or grain burned on the fire did not have the desired effect he was looking for. This obvious consideration leads to the following questions:

- If the heart's intention is the only thing that counts in a sacrificial offering, how could "God" not appreciate Cain's intentions?
- How could "God" not accept the offer of a farmer with no other option but to donate his produce?
- What was the difference that made one offering pleasing and the other undesirable?

This difference is not in the provider's will and pious intentions but in the actual effectiveness of the sacrifice. This was the only aspect that the Elohim was interested in, the smell of the burning flesh that guaranteed the relaxing, soothing, calming effect "God" was looking for and which pleased him greatly.

Many translations report that Yahweh did not like Cain's offer, but the Bible is explicit here and uses, to express Yahweh's reaction, the verb [shah], which means "to consider with intent, to weigh." The meaning of the verse should therefore be rendered as follows: Yahweh "looked at/considered" the sacrifice of Abel and "did not look at/consider" the sacrifice of Cain.

Yahweh essentially turned to what gave him pleasure or perhaps, as we shall see in a moment, satisfied a particular physical need. In doing so, he took no account of Cain's intentions. He rejected the offer that did not interest him. We shall now see why.

6. Burnt scent

Leviticus 16:13 and Exodus 30:27 describe a fragrance different from the odor of burning flesh. Of this fragrance, produced by burning scent or perfume, Yahweh is eager, and a strict procedure must be followed during the execution of the ritual for the exhalation and diffusion of this fragrance for the priest to remain alive (Leviticus 16:13).

על–האש	את–הקטרת	ונתן
fire-the-on	scent-the	put-will ←
וכסה	יהוה	לפני
cover-shall-and	Yahweh	of-faces-in ←
את–הכפרת	הקטרת	ענן
mercy-seat-the	scent-the	of-cloud ←

ימות	ולא	על–העדות	אשר
die-will	not-and	testimony-the-on	that ←

The term [qetoret] means "burnt offering, burnt perfume." In Exodus 30:34, the Elohim provides the recipe for composing the mixture to be used during this ritual and capable of producing the desired smoke and fragrance:

נטף	סמים	קח–לך
storax	spices	you-for-take ←

סמים	וחלבנה	ושחלת
spices	galbanum-and	onycha-and ←

יהיה	בבד	בד	זכה	ולבנה
be-will	part-(to)with	part	pure	frankincense-and ←

A careful reading of the passages in which these ritual rules are transmitted also shows that the ingredients had to be adequately prepared and offered to obtain the right scent. Verse 36 also indicates exactly where and how to burn the mixture:

הדק	ממנה	ושחקת
powder-make(to)	it-(of)from	crush-will-you-and ←

לפני	ממנה	ונתתה
of-faces-in	it-(of)from	put/give-shall-you-and ←

מועד	באהל	העדת
meeting	of-tent-in	testimony-the ←

שמה	לך	אועד	אשר
there	you-with	meet-will-I	(where)that ←

This mixture of ingredients and spices in equal parts ("part to part") was so important that the Elohim forbade its production and any use other than its intended use. No one could use it for himself. This prohibition was mandatory, for whoever violated it was punished by death, and this was no mere threat (Exodus 30:37-38).

תעשה	אשר	והקטרת
make-will-you	that	scent the-and ←

במתכנתה
its-measurement/proportion-(to according)as ←

לכם   תעשו   לא
you-for   make-shall   not ←

ליהוה   לך   תהיה   קדש
Yahweh-for   you-for   be-shall   holy ←

The term קדש [kodesc], generally translated as "sacred," in ancient Hebrew has a meaning quite different from that ascribed to it in the general religious sense, as we said in the previous chapters. It means "set apart, set aside, set apart for something." The *Etymological Dictionary* gives as the original meaning of the root the act of "preparing for a task." That which was sacred was thus set apart from the rest to be destined for a specific purpose.

This particular aroma was produced to perform a specific function and was reserved for the Elohim; no one else was to manufacture it for themselves. Otherwise, they risked death. Exodus 30:38 is as peremptory as it gets:

כמוה   אשר-יעשה   איש
it-like   do-will-which   (he who)who ←

בה   להריח
it-of   odor-smell-to ←

מעמיו   ונכרת
people-his-from   cut-be-will-(then)and ←

We cannot but take note of an apparent paradox here. If this smoke symbolizes the spirit of the offerer, why can't the offerer himself smell it? Why can only "God" smell it?

Let us leave this question open for now; everyone will be able to form his or her personal opinion. However, looking at the ingredients that make up this preparation and mixture could put us on the right track.

This practice is known today as phytotherapy. In this discipline, specific functions are attributed to the four ingredients mentioned by Yahweh. The mixture intended for the holocaust had to consist of equal parts of four elements. In particular:

– נטף - Storax (*Styrax Officinalis*) has antiseptic and healing properties; it was known in ancient times as a drug to treat respiratory diseases.

– שחלת - Onyx (*Unguis odoratus*) is a mollusk whose crushed and burnt shell produces a powerful and pungent odor. The Hebrew term "onyx" [scechelet], in Aramaic, means "to remedy, to restore," thus referring to a possible remedial function of some situation.

– חלבנה - Galbanum (*Ferulago galbanifera*) is a rubber resin with a reasonably unpleasant smell and a burning, bitter taste. In phytotherapy, it is still used today as an anti-inflammatory, antimicrobial, relaxing, and aphrodisiac.

– לבנה - Frankincense (*Boswellia Carterii, Serrata, Papyrifera*) is an oleoresin with tranquilizing, anxiolytic, and anti-inflammatory properties, also considered helpful in treating bronchial asthma.

This final blend, made up of equal parts of the four substances mentioned, has unique properties. It has antiseptic, anti-anxiety, and sedative properties and can regulate breathing.

The mixture described in the Bible gives off an odor that, due to the presence of galbanum and onyx, proves very intense, distinctly peculiar — not exactly pleasant — at least not in the ordinary sense of the word.

7. Consequences of preparing a wrong mixture

Leviticus 8 and 9 tell of a series of holocausts (sacrifices) during eight days, involving several animals (rams, calves, lambs) that produce an odor that is [nichoach] for the Elohim (8:21; 8:28).

The purpose of this small hecatomb was to purify the Tent of the Meeting in the desert and to "consecrate" Aaron's family in order to prepare them to meet and serve Yahweh.

The Hebrew verb that is usually translated as "consecration" is derived from the verb [mala], meaning "to be full or to fill." The specific expression "to fill the hand" (Leviticus 8:33) indicates appointing someone to a position. Aaron and his sons were to be assigned precise positions as *priests*.

On the eighth day, the formal act of "consecration" is to be performed, and an extraordinary and ominous event occurs (Leviticus 9:23-24). Yahweh appears with his kavod before all the people, and immediately after that, "A fire came out of Yahweh's faces and burned the sacrifice."

On seeing this, the people fall face-first to the ground. On this occasion, the Elohim ignites what had been prepared on the altar, and hundreds of those present witness this event.

In the following chapter, Leviticus 10, two of Aaron's sons take an initiative that proves disastrous (Leviticus 10:1-3).

Nadab and Abiu take their two braziers, put fire in them, and present it to the Elohim. Leviticus 10:1, however, informs us that this fire was זרה [zara], "strange." The term [zara] derives from the root [zur] and indicates an element that is "foreign, separate, different." It also means "repugnant, disgusting" (Clark).

However, this gesture of respect by the two brothers, a sign of spontaneous homage to their "God," far from being appreciated by the Elohim, proves reckless and has dramatic consequences. The Elohim reacts violently: "A fire came out from Yahweh's faces and consumed them, and they died before Yahweh" (Leviticus 10:2).

Nadab and Abiu incurred the same misunderstanding as Cain, believing that "God" could appreciate their good intentions and pure heart. But the Elohim did not care about the intentions of his faithful servants. He only cared about the results of the sacrificial practices.

When mistakes occur in this regard, he is unforgiving.

From this passage, we learn a lot about the "personality" of Yahweh, the consideration he had for his creatures and representatives, and the goals and behaviors that determined their actions.

One mistake in the performance of the prescribed ritual was enough to make the sacrifice unpleasant, i.e., not [nichoach]; one could be burned alive and die consumed by the fire coming from "the faces of Yahweh."

From all these considerations, the following questions arise:

– Why kill animals to produce the smoke that symbolizes the ascent of the soul, if we know nothing about this soul (since "God" never speaks of it)?

- Why slaughter poor animals by letting them bleed to death to atone for sins for which the animals are not responsible?

- Why did "God" take pleasure in smelling a particular odor as a sign of worship, supplication, or thanksgiving?

- Why was it necessary to carry out the holocausts "in the face," that is, in the "physical" presence of Yahweh, if the sacrifices only had a spiritual meaning?

- Why so much precision in the procedural instructions?

- Yahweh wanted the procedure to occur "at the tent's entrance." Sometimes, he wanted it to take place "at the north side of the altar" or "in the Tent of Meeting where I meet you." Why so much precision in indicating the place where the rituals would take place? Would the sacrifice only work if offered in the designated places?

- Why was it so crucial to this "God" that everything happened in a certain way?

- Why was it necessary for the smell to be physically perceptible to him?

- Did "God" miss something if the substance to be burned (whether animal or vegetable aroma) was not adequately prepared or positioned?

- Was he unable to discern and appreciate the intentions of the sacrificer anyway?

- Why did he kill those who made mistakes in preparing the offerings? Was this ritual so important that it justified murder and bloodshed?

8. Space smells like fried steak

Traditional explanations fail to provide answers to the questions above.

A spiritual "God" is not compatible with the behavior described, nor can it be said that Yahweh acted cruelly to conform to the barbaric customs of uncivilized people. The norms and rules that Yahweh established during his years in the desert to "educate" the Israelites reveal that they were well aware of ethical and moral values for civil coexistence.

These ritual instructions for preparing and implementing holocausts, sacrifices, and offerings had only meaning for the Elohim who wanted to smell those distinct odors.

But why did the Elohim have to smell the smoke of burnt meat and certain spice mixtures?

Some hints come from NASA, the American space agency with enough experience in space flight to provide unexpected information.

NASA astronauts participating in spacewalks report a puzzling fact. While taking off their spacesuits after returning from a spacewalk, they could perceive the typical aroma of grilled meat and the specific smell of heated iron.

On September 18, 2006, Anousheh Ansari, a wealthy Iranian-American businesswoman participating in an eight-day expedition to the International Space Station as a tourist (Expedition 14 of the Soyuz TMA-9), reported on her blog that she smelled something resembling the "stench of burnt almond cookies." (Remember the smell of galbanum and onycha?)

So space travelers experience distinct olfactory sensations so pungent and strong that NASA included them in its training program. Steven Pearce, chemist director of the British perfume company Omega Ingredients declared that NASA asked him to develop a perfume to reproduce the typical "space smell."

Pearce said it was easy to reproduce the smell of grilled meat, but it was more challenging to produce the odor of heated metal. In any case, his fragrance adds a touch of realism to space training. Trainees are made to smell it when they put on their suits to be immersed in large pools in which the absence of gravity is simulated.

The astronauts thus get used to smelling what they will find in space. Telegraph.co.uk reported the news in 2008.

Nasa has commissioned Steven Pearce, a chemist and managing director of fragrance manufacturing company Omega Ingredients, to recreate the smell of space in a laboratory.
His research will be used to help astronauts prepare for the conditions they will encounter in space. Mr Pearce began working for NASA in August and hopes to have recreated the smell of space by the end of the year. He said: "I did some work for an art exhibition in July, which was based entirely on smell and one of the things I created was the smell of the inside of the Mir space station. Nasa heard about it and contacted me to see if I could help them recreate the smell of space to help their astronauts. We have a few clues as to what space smells like.

First of all, there were interviews with astronauts that we were given; when they had been outside and then returned to the space station and were de-suiting and taking off their helmets, they all reported quite particular odors. For them, what comes across is a smell of fried steak, hot metal, and even welding a motorbike, one of them said. The suggestion to us has been that it's about creating realism for their training, so they train the astronauts in their suits by putting them in big water tanks to simulate the loss of gravity and so it's just about making sure the whole thing is a realistic training exercise. We have already produced the smell of fried steak, but hot metal is proving more difficult. We think it's a high-energy vibration in the molecule and that's what we're trying to add to it now." Mr Pearce visited Moorside High School in Manchester today to discuss the project, as part of the Manchester Science Festival. [16]

The explanation for this "smell" lies in a well-known phenomenon. In space, cell renewal of the superficial layers of the epidermis increases; thus, the number of dead cells increases too. When astronauts put on their suits to work outdoors, these cells are detached by the friction effect and are shed again when the spacesuit is removed inside the spacecraft. In contact with the oxygen-rich artificial atmosphere inside the space vehicle, the dead cells undergo a very rapid oxidation process that produces the strong smell of burnt flesh.

It is the astronauts who "stink," not space.

Let us now return to the Bible.

9. The role of opioid peptides

If the Elohim were individuals from outer space, how often did they smell this particular odor?

Was it familiar to them? Did it relax them?

Or, did they perhaps want to mask the "stench" emanating from their skin, which they did not wish anyone who encountered them to notice?

Moreover, what is the composition of the substances released by these fumes? Can chemistry come to our help?

The combustion of the fat and protein chains, composed of different amino acids present in the fat and flesh of the victims, produces substances whose chemical structure is reminiscent of opioid peptides, similar to the effects of endorphins.

[16] "Space Smells like Fried Steak." *Www.telegraph.co.uk*, 16 Oct. 2008, www.telegraph.co.uk/news/worldnews/northamerica/usa/3210415/Space-smells-like-fried-steak.html.

Endorphins — peptides produced by the human body — can cause pain relief, sedation (including respiration), blunting of neurosensory abilities, apathy, and lethargy. They can also stimulate appetite and thirst, promote the release of growth hormones, regulate the production of thyroid and sex hormones, have anti-inflammatory effects, and improve overall mood.

Opioid peptides can be absorbed through the gastrointestinal tract, nasal mucosa, and respiratory tract.

Most importantly, these substances are addictive; so repeating and increasing their intake is necessary to achieve the same effect.

The opioids par excellence are morphine and heroin, which have a structure similar to the endorphins naturally produced by human physiology.

Moreover, there is a substantial affinity between the chemical composition of the substances produced by the combustion of fat and animal proteins and the substances described above (endogenous opioid peptides and opioids).

We can therefore hypothesize that morphine-like components of the [qetoret], "burnt offering," could be responsible for the calming effect on the Elohim and the need for the so-called "God" to have large quantities of this product available.

In short, the [nichoach] of the Bible, which, as mentioned, induces a "condition of relaxation," finds here a possible neurophysiological explanation.

We express sheer hypotheses. However, it is with hypotheses that we must proceed when we are met with ancient texts that tell us of such concrete events and situations. The Bible repeatedly describes the strange olfactory pleasure caused by the smell generated by the combustion of animal proteins and fat of sacrificial victims.

These effects may be due to the stimulation of particular systems connected with endorphins and other possible chemical neurotransmitters that interact with the neurophysiology of a human-like living being.

As for the vegetable ingredients and shellfish used in the sacrifices, their antiseptic and anti-inflammatory properties, which promote lung function, justify their use to improve the environmental conditions to which the Elohim were exposed during their encounters with humans.

The complex ritual involving washing and cleaning the body of those who had to come into contact with the so-called divinities might confirm this reading.

Did the procedure serve to prevent possible contamination causes?

10. Conclusions

We have formulated hypotheses whose hard evidence has yet to be available. Still, the questions and the possible answers we have provided in this chapter might help scholars to overcome the contradictions of traditional exegesis, which claims, for example, that everything the Bible teaches about offerings and sacrifices is central to salvation history and supposedly helps us to recognize and understand the Lord's mercy (Van Gemeren).

According to famous theologian and Bible scholar Gianfranco Ravasi, sacrifices (animal or vegetable) "embody the same believer offering himself to God to establish a bond of communion with it" (Ravasi, *500 curiosità*). What about Cain's offering then? What about the two sons of Aaron?

We must never presume to have the truth until it is proved beyond doubt. However, as we have seen, the poor Israelite who would dare to imitate the Elohim and sniff some of the same odors was to be put to death.

Thus, it is not easy to dismiss the "alien reading" as "fanciful" or "crazy" because, unlike the theological reading, it has the advantage of adhering to biblical text. In contrast, the theological elaborations do not agree with what the stories tell, even if they do not contradict them completely.

It is no accident that even the most attentive Catholic commentators feel compelled to admit that specific passages of the Torah — and Leviticus in particular, which we have quoted at length in this chapter — contain "risky" concepts since they can eventually "destroy the value of the story in which God reveals himself" (Bibbia Emmaus).

No wonder religious orthodoxy considers this concreteness "risky." The term [kadosc], usually translated as "sacred," as we have pointed out many times, literally means "set apart, set aside, destined for," and also "prepared for a task, for a function."

There is a tangible and concrete meaning behind the concept of "sacred" that transpires and emerges from these stories and in Yahweh's behaviors and goals.

This concreteness seems to be the fundamental, if not the only, element that interested Yahweh in the Bible. Anything jeopardizing Yahweh's goals was considered useless and harmful and could get one killed.

In summary, Yahweh had substances made for him that were reserved only for him and that he had to smell/sniff to reach a state of relaxation and tranquility.

The vapors thus produced also regulated his breathing and had a sterilizing effect in the rooms or locations that he used when he wanted to meet with his representatives.

These are all extremely practical and easily understandable goals, also considering the hygienic conditions of the time, which were decidedly risky for Yahweh.

11 / THE MESSENGERS OF GOD

1. The angelic hierarchies in tradition

In many biblical stories, there are intermediary figures called [malakhim] who act and speak on behalf of the Elohim and generally interact with the people of Israel in various capacities.

Theological tradition calls these [malakhim] "angels" and attributes to them, as we shall see in this chapter, a whole set of complicated spiritual characteristics. Angelology is the discipline that studies the transcendental and metaphysical nature of these beings.

However, are the spiritual and transcendental features attributed to the [malakhim] by Angelology, religious piety, theologians, and traditional exegetes grounded in the Bible?

Literal analysis of Genesis, Exodus, Judges, Samuel, Kings, Tobiah, and Zechariah has led us to conclude that these so-called "angels" clearly behave like individuals of flesh and blood. The [malakhim] walk, get dusty, get tired, get upset, need to wash and rest, eat twice in the same day, decide where to spend the night, and protect themselves from attacks with methods that are worthy of our scrutiny.

Their physical difference is noticeable. They are endowed with powers superior to those of humans, but still, they are not omnipotent; they show vulnerability, can be attacked, and are subject to the regular physiological needs of human beings.

We will show how the [malakhim] can often instill fear in those who encounter them, and their presence is hardly ever reassuring. Many of those who meet them fear they may not survive.

It will soon be clear that the ethereal, positive, and reassuring angelic figures that religious tradition devised, still present today in popular piety, have no ground in the Bible.

The biblical accounts are also far from later theoretical elaborations that have divided the angels into complicated angelic hierarchies, describing them as mediating entities between human carnality and divine spirituality.

For the sake of clarity, we would like to preface that our goal is not to prove the existence of angelic beings or otherwise; we just want to verify their presence and description in the Old Testament and compare our findings with the religious and spiritualist tradition in general.

Angelology speaks of various ranks of angels, distinguished according to the functions performed. Each receives from "God" unique spiritual gifts, such as light, science, or goodness. Their task is "transmitting" these spiritual gifts down to humans.

Together, these figures form nine angelic choirs, divided into three orders; each order is, in turn, divided into ranks. The highest order is composed of Seraphim, Cherubim, and Thrones; the second order is composed of Dominations, Virtues, and Powers; the third and lowest order is composed of Principalities, Archangels, and Angels.

Each group possesses specific characteristics, which we do not enumerate here, except those that interest us related to the orders of the Angels and Cherubim, as they are the object of our analysis.

Among the qualities attributed to Angels, it is said, for example, that they are the way to the Word, the perfect vessel of divine light. They convey the power of "God" in converting sinners; they impart wisdom in the revelation of the divine mysteries; they correspond justice in the condemnation of the wicked. They are an example worthy of imitation in avoiding punishment, overcoming vices, being admitted to heaven, et cetera.

Given these descriptions, we make a first and immediate observation. We are dealing here with beings whose physical and behavioral characteristics are far less elevating and inspiring than those we have mentioned apropos of Angels and the other angelic orders. Therefore:

– Is everything written about angels in theology justified by the description of the [malakhim], as found in the Old Testament?

– Are we sure that the theological vision is consistent with the events described in the Bible?

2. The Malakhim in the Old Testament

We now present some situations in which the angels/*malakhim* are involved, and leave it to the readers to make their own reflections.

~ Genesis 16

The patriarch Abram and his bride Sarai have no children. Despite Yahweh's promise that they will have as many children as there are grains of sand, time passes without Sarai being able to conceive.

Disappointed by the passing of time, Sarai decides to give the Egyptian maid Hagar to her husband, Abram. Hagar gets pregnant, becomes arrogant, and takes advantage of her new "status" until Sarai drives her out of the camp with Abram's permission. The slave girl leaves the camp and wanders in the desert, where she meets a *malakh* (Genesis 16:7).

יהוה	מלאך	וימצאה
Yahweh	of-messenger	found-and ←

במדבר	המים	על–עין
desert-the-in	waters-the	(water spring)eye-on ←

שור	בדרך	על–העין
Shur	of-road-in	of-(water spring)eye-the-on ←

The encounter with the messenger of Yahweh seems casual as the angel/*malakh* himself looks surprised. However, he shows that he knows Hagar personally since he asks her:

שרי	שפחת	הגר
Sarai	of-slave	Hagar ←

תלכי	ואנה	באת	אי–מיזה
go-will-you	where-and	come-you	this-from-where ←

So the messenger knows Hagar, but does not know where she is going or why she is there. As far as he knows, she is supposed to be in Abram's camp, and so he orders her to return there and serve her mistress. He does not fail, however, to reassure her. The son she gives birth to will be the progenitor of a great people.

From Ishmael descended that group of peoples commonly called nomadic Arabs.

The narrative has its epilogue in chapter 21, in which Yahweh makes another decision. Sarai, with the "help of God," finally conceives and gives birth to Isaac. Yahweh chooses him to be the true heir and progenitor of the new descendants who will populate the so-called Promised Land.

This choice has precise consequences. There cannot be two heirs; conflict and separation must be avoided; power and control over property must not be shared. Thus, after the birth of the rightful heir, Hagar must leave the camp forever, but, as we have said, Ismael will still be the progenitor of a great nation.

Undoubtedly, every person born from Abraham's lineage must have had an important place in the strategic design of the Elohim who ruled over that part of the Middle East. Over time, Yahweh had to build up a group of people with whom to occupy and rule the territories that had been assigned to him at the time of the division made by Elyon.

His messengers acted according to a precise strategic plan.

In the story of Hagar, it must noted, we are faced with a concrete situation, no visions or dreams. When Hagar encounters the [malakh], we are confronted with an unanticipated and undoubtedly real and concrete event.

The messenger does not fly in, he does not show himself in a vision, he meets the woman in a specific place, addresses her personally, and asks her questions from which it is clear that he was not informed about what was happening. It is an ordinary meeting and dialogue between two real people/individuals.

~ Genesis 22

In Genesis 22, Yahweh demands a particularly burdensome and cruel test of loyalty to Abraham: he forces him to sacrifice his son Isaac.

Abraham agrees. He prepares everything necessary for the sacrifice and sets off for the hill indicated to him. On the way, however, the son is astonished to discover that an essential element is missing: the sacrificial victim. The father cannot reveal to the son that the intended sacrifice is Isaac himself and reassures him by saying that Yahweh will provide the victim for the sacrifice.

Once they reach their destination, Abraham builds the altar, puts wood on it, binds Isaac, and puts him on the pile. He grabs his knife and just when he is about to kill his son (Genesis 22:11):

יהוה	מלאך	אליו	ויקרא
Yahweh	of-messenger	him-towards	called-he-and ←

אברהם	אברהם	ויאמר	מן–השמים
Abraham	Abraham	:said-and	sky-the-from ←

A [malakh] calls Abraham from the sky and orders him to stop; he does not need to perform the sacrifice: the loyalty test is passed and the Elohim now knows he can count on an ally so faithful as to be willing to sacrifice his son's life.

The sacrifice continues at the expense of a goat caught on the spot.

In this sequence of events, there is precise distinction between two figures: the Elohim, who tests Abraham in verse 1, and the *malakh* who comes to him from above to interrupt the sacrifice.

The whole scene of dialogue with call and response is highly effective in its simplicity: the [malakh] calls, "Abraham, Abraham," twice; he responds הנני [hinneni], "Here I am… I am here."

The conversation continues and ends with renewed promises for the future of Abraham and his descendants.

Let us note that the allegedly omniscient "God" does not know Abraham's disposition towards him in advance; and therefore has to test him with a concrete, cruel, and inhuman request. Only after he makes sure that Abraham obeys him perfectly does "God" sends a *malakh*, a messenger, to interrupt the sacrifice.

Had the Elohim been able to read Abraham's mind, this passage would prove to be a string of meaningless actions. But "God" did not know Abraham's thoughts, so he had to put him to the test. He is no different from ordinary earthly rulers; and as ordinary earthly rulers often prefer to bring in intermediaries, so does he.

The narrative thus presents us with an Elohim who cannot grasp a person's state of mind and employs a [malakh] to interrupt an ongoing action. As anyone can verify by reading this biblical story, any spiritual connotation is absent from both the premise and the sequence of the events.

~ Genesis 28

We encourage our reader to consult directly the biblical passage in which Jacob describes seeing a ladder connecting earth and heaven, with "angels" ascending and descending on it. This scene is often read in ufological perspective.

We fundamentally agree with this interpretation but want to respect the biblical text, which explicitly states that Jacob was asleep. It was all a dream. Since it is not our task to interpret dreams, we withhold judgment on this scene. The reader, however, will do well to form his own opinion by consulting any version of the Bible directly.

~ Genesis 32

In the previous sections, we witnessed actions that could be described as typical of the [malakhim]; they acted as mediators, spokesmen, and executors of orders.

Now we will see a situation in which the [malakhim] are present but... do nothing.

It is precisely their inaction that makes the situation interesting. This incident is so insignificant that it is always forgotten by commentators interested in the extraordinary. Experience teaches us, however, that indirect clues of great significance are often hidden in the folds of the ordinary.

Jacob has traveled to the land of his fathers to choose a bride; after a series of tribulations, he acquires more than one and returns to the home of his father, Isaac.

During his journey, an incident occurs that has nothing to do with the journey itself and has no apparent consequences. The inclusion of this passage in the Bible is not justified in the grand scheme of Jacob's journey and narrative, but it is precisely this fact that makes it interesting for our purposes.

Jacob was in the middle of his journey:

אלהים	מלאכי	ויפגעו–בו
Elohim	of-messengers	him-upon-stumble-and ←

On seeing the [malakhim] Jacob exclaims:

זה	אלהים	מחנה
this	Elohim	of-camp ←

As a result of this meeting, he decides to call that place מחנים [machanaim], a term that is always translated as if it were a proper name; in reality [machanaim] is the dual form of מחנה [machane], which means "camp." Therefore, [machanaim] means "two camps."

This is a particularly vivid and realistic scene: the "angels" do nothing. They mind their own business. Jacob arrives with his people and his cattle; the [malakhim] approach him without speaking; he recognizes them as messengers of the Elohim and realizes that he has come near two of their quarters and therefore decides to identify this place as [machanaim].

The root of the verb פגע [paga], "to come across," contains within itself the concept of "chance, fate" and thus the narrative tells us with a clarity that requires no interpretation that the encounter happened "by chance." None of the actors, neither Jacob nor the [malakhim], expected it.

The presence of the [malakhim], Jacob's realization that he found by chance two camps of the Elohim, and the particular construction of the name that Jacob decides to give the place — מחנים [machanaim], "two camps" — confirms the reading of the Hebrew exegete Rashi de Troyes, who openly speaks of two camps of armies defending the two sides of a territorial border.

Perhaps, it is not by chance that some members of the "troop," the [malakhim], moved to meet the stranger who was coming closer; their mere presence induced Jacob and his people not to approach any further and resume their journey home in a different direction.

Nothing else happens. The "angels" do not fly in; there are no messages, no actions are performed, no orders are given or executed, and there are no visions or dreams. The Bible simply reports a casual encounter. Some [malakhim] approach Jacob without direct contact; immediately afterward, everyone continues with what he was doing before the encounter.

Anyone who has seen civilians approaching a military camp out of sheer curiosity knows that the guards would immediately intervene to deny them entry. In many cases, the mere sight of the guards is enough to make it clear that one is not allowed to come close. The same happened with Jacob.

If we find the story in the Bible, it is because Jacob was impressed by it; the sight of an Elohim camp must not have been an ordinary event, and so the patriarch fondly recalled the experience.

The [malakhim] did nothing and said nothing to him, but the "double camp" remained firmly in his memory and in the biblical text.

~ Exodus 23

Of particular importance is the content of Exodus 23:20-30, which sets forth the strategy that Yahweh intends to employ in conquering the Promised Land for Moses and his people.

An essential component of this strategy entails the presence of a [malakh], a "messenger" whom Yahweh will send before Moses and the people to supervise them and give them the necessary instructions. The [malakh] will always go before them, and they are to provide him with absolute obedience (Exodus 23:21):

לפשעכם	ישא	לא
your-transgression-for	tolerance-have-will-he	not ←

"God" explains that this messenger will help them in the conquest, which is to be gradual. The people to be encountered must not be driven out too quickly (29), for the abandoned land would become a desert and be occupied by wild animals. The conquest of the land will therefore be gradual, done at a time that will allow for gradual settlement and the necessary cultivation of the land for food production (30).

We are therefore dealing with a "God" who must necessarily "adjust" to the times of nature and the unforeseen needs of a mass of people crossing new lands; he does not perform those extraordinary deeds that would be expected of him to solve, with the help of his divine power, the problems that arise in such a situation.

In verse 27, Yahweh specifies that he will send, before the people, his אימה [emah], "terror," but it is not known whether this term is to be attributed to the messenger or represents an additional instrument or tool; what is certain is that this "terror" will produce havoc on his adversaries who will end up being captured. [17]

In any case, Yahweh acts like an ordinary human strategist who sends a deputy to command the troops based on specific and intelligent tactics that include logistical aspects that cannot be neglected.

---

[17]   We have spoken of some of his "special" weapons in: Biglino, Mauro. *Il falso testamento*.

The entire narrative is thus characterized by a healthy realism in which the alleged divine omnipotence and angelic spirituality seem to have no place. The [malakh], "messenger," and the [emah], "terror," will be "operational tools" in the coming war.

~ 1 Chronicles 21

In this book, we learn that King David orders a census and does so against Yahweh's will (1 Chronicles 21:1). We will analyze the part of the story in which a messenger is sent to destroy the inhabitants of Jerusalem because of the ruler's decision.

David turns to Yahweh and reminds him that he alone is responsible for the decision and asks him not to kill people who are not to blame.

This is a strange fact: "God" did not immediately realize that David alone was responsible for the census. Fortunately for the city, Yahweh changes his mind and orders his envoys not to carry on with the planned destruction (15).

David then "lifts his eyes" and sees the [malakh], "the messenger" (1 Chronicles 21:16):

השמים	ובין	הארץ	בין	עמד
skies-the	between-and	earth-the	between	standing ←

David sees the [malakh] holding in his hand an object called חרב [kherev], which is usually translated as "sword," but whose root carries the meaning of "to burn, to bring to ruin" (Clark).

We do not know what it is, but the Bible tells us that this weapon is [נטויה [netuiah], "turned, pointed" towards the city of Jerusalem, thus ready to strike and destroy.

The biblical passage indicates that the messenger was near the threshing floor of Araunah the Jebusite; we are presented here with a picture of everyday life that has nothing to do with visions or dream experiences.

Araunah is threshing wheat with his sons. He turns around and sees the [malakh]. His sons see him too. They are horrified by what they see and immediately hide (1 Chronicles 21:1520).

There is nothing like this dynamic description, which testifies that the appearance and posture of this figure must have been decidedly threatening: the burning and destructive weapon pointed at Jerusalem caused horror.

Yahweh's messenger abandons his plan and orders a certain Gad to tell David to go up and build an altar on the threshing floor of Araunah (18). David obeys, prepares everything, and then calls upon Yahweh, who appears immediately (1 Chronicles 21:26):

מן–השמים	באש	וייענהו
skies-the-from	fire-the-in	responded-he-and ←

העלה	מזבח	על
holocaust-the	of-altar	on ←

Those present see that the messenger places his weapon in its sheath (27).

The episode then ends with a further thought-provoking note. The danger is over, but in the days that follow, David does not dare to seek out Yahweh in his dwelling place (30), which was then on the heights of Gibeon (we have discussed Yahweh's connection with mountains in chapter 8).

מפני	נבעת	כי
of-faces-in	terrified-was-he	since ←

יהוה	מלאך	חרב
Yahweh	of-messenger	of-(weapon)sword ←

To see the weapon of the [malakh] must have been a fearsome and terrifying sight, unheard of, never seen before.

~ Judges 6

In the period between the death of Joshua and the establishment of the monarchy, the nation of Israel was ruled from time to time by military and civil leaders, commonly called "judges." They intervene in certain circumstances to deliver this or that tribe from current enemies or oppression by neighboring peoples.

One of these judges was called Gideon. The responsibility for his appointment is entrusted to a [malakh] who acted in a very special way.

Gideon is threshing wheat when the [malakh] of Yahweh comes, stops under the oak tree at Ophrah, greets him, and announces that it has been decided to entrust him with the task of delivering Israel from the hands of the Midianites. Gideon declares he is unprepared and un-worthy but is reassured by the promise that Yahweh will support him directly.

Still dazed, Gideon asks the [malakh] not to leave because he wants to return home to get food for him. The [malakh] promises to wait.

Let us stop here for a moment and ask two simple questions:

– Who would think of offering food to a spiritual vision, an angel?
– Who would think of asking a spiritual vision, an angel, to have a little patience while one is busy with finding food, preparing it, and returning to the meeting place?

Gideon thus returns home, prepares kid skin meat and bread, reaches the [malakh] who has been waiting for him all this time, and offers him food.

Then, something decidedly out of the ordinary occurs. The [malakh] tells Gideon to put the meat and bread on a stone, also asks him to pour the broth on it, and then (Judges 6:21):

יהוה	מלאך	וישלח
Yahweh	of-messenger	stretched-and ←

בידו	אשר	המשענת	את–קצה
his-hand-in	that	stick-the	of-end ←

מן–הצור	האש	ותעל
rock-the-from	fire-the	raised-and ←

ובמצות	בבשר	ויגע
bread-the-(on)in-and	meat-the-(on)in	touched-and ←

The [malakh] burns the meat and the bread and then leaves. We consider it very difficult to interpret this story in a way that would not respect its realistic spontaneity and concreteness. To add any spiritual connotation to such a realistic story, or to superimpose it, would be to disregard the text.

The [malakh] undoubtedly uses "something" that ignites flames: a striking correspondence with what we will read soon in the chapter dedicated to Elijah's miracle.

~ Ezekiel 8

There is a passage in the Bible where the desire for religious people to see an angelic presence at any cost drives commentators to translate something that is not even present in the text. In Ezekiel 8:1-3, the prophet describes an encounter with an undefined "something" that today's translations render as follows:

> Behold, **I saw a figure of human form**; from the hips downward it was of fire, and from the hips upward it shone like electrum. It seemed to me that he stretched out an arm and grabbed me by the hair, and a spirit lifted me up between heaven and earth.

According to the traditional translations, an anthropomorphic angelic figure here performs the strange and incomprehensible gesture of reaching out an arm and grabbing Ezekiel by the hair to lift him up. What strange behavior for an angel!

But if this story sounds strange, it is only because the translation is incorrect. The Masoretic text actually reads (Ezekiel 8:2):

כמראה–אש	דמות	והנה
man-of-appearance-like	resemblance	there-and ←

מתניו	כמראה
its-hips(two)	of-appearance-from ←

אש	ולמטה
fire	low-towards-and ←

ולמעלה	וממתניו
high-towards-and	its-hips(two)-from-and ←

כמראה–זהר
shine-of-appearance-like ←

החשמלה	כעין
(electrum)amber-the	of-eye-like ←

First, it should be noted that no human figure is mentioned. Something "like the appearance of man" comes along and radiates a kind of energy (like fire) from the lower part while it glows metallically in the higher part.

Now let us continue with the alleged gesture of "grabbing the hair."

יד	תבנית	וישלח
hand	of-model	reached-he-and ←

ראשי	בציצת	ויקחני
my-head	of-gusset-(with)by	me-took-and ←

רוח	אתי	ותשא
[ruach]	me	raised-and ←

The term ציצת [tzitzit], which is usually translated as "hair," denotes in fact a gusset, a fastener of a garment, or even a clasp.

As for the term [ruach], we refer to what we said in the chapter dedicated to it; we recall here that this term probably identified something that flew swiftly through the air and skies without obviously being a regular bird.

The biblical text, therefore, literally tells us that:

– Ezekiel sees a flaming, shining "something."

– This indeterminate "something" in turn generates or extends a "something" that could be described as an object or system capable of lifting a human being; it is evident that the most immediate way to refer to a grasping tool that is otherwise not easy to describe is to compare it to the human hand: "hand model" says the prophet.

– The whole [ruach] raises the prophet and takes him away.

We would have to use our imagination to find an image that corresponds to the description, but this image is certainly not that of an anthropomorphic angel.

In the series of events that ensue, Ezekiel is led to Jerusalem, where he sees and exclaims: "There is כבוד [kavod] of Yahweh!"

~ Book of Daniel

The Book of Daniel belongs to the so-called "apocalyptic literature" and was probably written around the 2nd century BCE. It is written in Hebrew, Aramaic, and Greek and describes events from the Babylonian exile (597 BCE). The general historical context in which the events are set is very broad: from about 600 to 160 BCE.

The text contains several anomalies in location, content, and language so that it is not counted among the prophetic books in the Hebrew biblical canon but only among the "writings."

The considerable differences in structure and form, as well as in literary composition, show that the book is the result of a compilation and revision of pre-existing parts; in the various editions, there are differences in content, such as chapters present in the Greek Bible but absent in the Hebrew, and so on.

We know that apocalyptic literature, unlike historical literature, uses specific categories — such as visions and symbolism — which are not suited to a realistic description of reality.

None of this prevents this book from being considered "revealed" in the Catholic canon and from being used to define angelic figures as "truths of faith." Despite all its ambiguities, this book is serenely used as a source for defining absolute truths and widely utilized in various elaborations in traditional Angelology.

Therefore, it should not be surprising that we also use this book in this context to formulate hypotheses inserted into our independent research path. All the more so since the search for concreteness and narrative realism in a text of dreams and visions would increase the credibility of the facts we are investigating. We less expect to find them so they stand out.

The book's protagonist is Daniel, a Jew who, through so-called "visions," conveys the hope of a future in which a Messiah will come to bring final deliverance to the people. It is a kind of theological world history in which the certainty is conveyed that "God" will fulfill his plans.

~ Daniel 4

Nebuchadnezzar presents Daniel with a vision for interpretation; surprisingly, a term appears in it that recalls the presence of well-identified individuals in Sumerian narratives: the watchers.

The text says that:

עיר	וקדיש	מן–שמיא	נחת
watcher ←	holy-and	skies-from	descends

This being announces a series of provisions, stating that (Daniel 4:14):

בגזרת	עירין	פתגמא
of-decree-by ←	watchers	decision-the

So there are a number of individuals who belong to the category of "watchers" who determine the division of the kingdoms on Earth.

> **The decision is announced by the watchers**, the holy ones declare the verdict, so that the living may know that the most high is sovereign over **all kingdoms on Earth and gives them to anyone he wishes.**
>
> (Daniel 4:14)

There is no reason to call them "angels," nor can they be considered as such, as far as the characteristics that tradition attributes to them are concerned.

Let us remember that the Sumerians called their country Kiengir, i.e., "land of the watchers," and that the Egyptians knew the *neteru*, i.e., the "watchers," from the ancient times. These are not mere coincidences and should not be underestimated.

The narratives of various peoples tell of individuals who formed power groups and were entrusted with certain tasks, including the distribution of governments on Earth to ensure the observance of laws, as in the biblical text we are about to read.

Greek philosopher Celsus (2nd century BCE) recalls that the early Christians claimed that many of these guardians had already descended to Earth by the dozens.

∼ Daniel 9

We do not know for sure whether the "vigilant/watcher" of whom we have spoken is the same individual who appears in Daniel 9:21, referred to as גבריאל [ghevriel], "Gabriel."

Daniel says that while he was praying during the evening sacrifice, this Gabriel presented himself to him, approached him, and spoke, saying that he had come to reveal everything to him (Daniel 9:20-22).

It is not our purpose here to analyze the content of the messenger's numerous revelations to Daniel, for we must deal exclusively with his figure, especially by addressing a curious element that appears in the description of his manner of presentation.

First, it should be noted that the term Gabriel is usually considered a proper noun, but it should not be overlooked that it primarily denotes a "status," a position, insofar as it means "strong man of El."

The Hebrew root denotes the status of someone who possesses great power. We might think of him as a high-ranking commander or diplomatic representative. His hypothetical membership in the upper echelons of a hierarchy could be justified by the fact that he is already a "special" person by birth.

In this context, let us take up a detail from the chapter on the [nephilim]. Genesis 6:4 reports the connection between the sons of Elohim and the daughters of the Adam, who:

הגברים	המה	להם	וילדו
strong-the	them	them-to	birthed-had-and ←

Here it is said that the children of these crossbreeds were the גברים [ghibborim], i.e. the "strong," "powerful." Now, [ghibborim] is the plural of [ghibbor]. Is it possible to assume a connection — from the consonantal root גבר — between "ghevriel" and the semi-divine race of the [ghibborim]? Was he a [ghibbor/ghever] of El, a man of power from the lineage of the [ghibborim] or the [ghevarim], plural of [ghever]?

We do not possess a definite answer, but we cannot but remember that a Gabriel/*ghevriel* is the one who visits Mary and she becomes pregnant with Jesus. [18]

This biblical passage also provides an additional element of curiosity. Traditional translations say that Gabriel (Daniel 9:21) arrives "flying fast." The biblical expression, however, does not refer to flight. Gabriel arrives:

ביעף	מעף
wearness-of	weary-being ←

---

[18]   French theologian Jean Daniélou discusses this topic at length in his book *La teologia del giudeo-cristianesimo*.

The etymology of יָעֵף [yahaf] recalls the sense of "to strive to ascend, strive to the point of exhaustion" (Clark). The *Comprehensive Etymological Dictionary* also quotes the verse above and gives the following meanings of the verb [yahaf]: "utterly wear, weary of weariness" (Klein). So the primary meaning of this verb is to "make an effort, to be weary, to become tired, feeling extreme tiredness." Even if it can be assumed that he was a [ghever], still, he was not exempt from the normal physiological functions of a material body that expends energy in its actions.

The traditional portrayal of Gabriel as an "angel" who comes along flying lightly is downright invented. He was simply tired.

~ Daniel 10

In Daniel 10, the prophet receives revelations in the third year of Cyrus' reign (536 BCE) while he is with other people on the banks of the Tigris River. He lifts his eyes and sees (Daniel 10:5-6):

בדים	לבוש	איש–אחד
linen	dressed-being	one-man ←

This figure had:

> ...hips belted with gold from Uphaz; body like the stone of תרשיש [tarscisc] ("topaz"); foreparts like ברק [baraq], ("lightning"); eyes like לפידי [lafide], ("torches of fire"); arms and feet like the eye of נחשת [nechoscet], ("polished bronze"); voice ("sound") like the sound of המון [hamon], ("the rumbling produced by a multitude").

> (Daniel 10:6)

We note at once that this individual is not even called [malakh] but איש [isc], i.e. "man."

Daniel, therefore, sees a male individual whose appearance suggests some garment, shining in every part and covered with a woven linen tunic.

This prompts us to return briefly to Ezekiel, as we find in this passage from Daniel an exciting cross-reference.

Ezekiel 9 and 10 describe the movements of the chariot of "God." Here we quote two verses in which the appearance of the chariot is accompanied by the presence of various people, one of whom corresponds to what Daniel also sees (Ezekiel 9:2).

בדים	לבש	איש־אחד
linen	dressed-being	one-man ←

As in the Book of Daniel, this person occupies a prominent position; he is also equipped with writing tools, and he is given special duties in Jerusalem. The text emphasizes twice that he is clothed in linen.

The similarity between the individual Ezekiel sees and the individual Daniel encounters in the passage above suggests that we are likely dealing here with a high-ranking official, working under direct orders from Yahweh, possibly wearing a uniform that denotes his status.

– Did Ezekiel and Daniel see the same איש [isc], "man?"

– Was he a [ghever] of El?

– Did he hold a special position in the hierarchy of officers entrusted with particularly important tasks?

– Was he supposed to maintain contact with, and carry information to the people, chosen to be the spokesmen of the Elohim, that is the prophets? (The term "prophet," נביא [navi], contrary to what is often thought, does not indicate one who foretells the future, but "one who speaks on behalf of," that is a spokesman.)

3. Flavius Josephus and the heavenly armies

For more information on the Judeo-Roman historian Flavius Josephus and his work, we refer to the "Glossary." However, we want to quote here an excerpt from his work, *The Jewish War*.

It is about an event strikingly reminiscent of some of the passages we have encountered in our examination of the multiplicity of the Elohim.

Between AD 66 and 70, Rome intervened to crush the rebellions that had broken out in Judea and Jerusalem.

The conflict ended with the conquest and destruction of the city by the Roman army commanded by Titus. The book recounts these events, and Flavius Josephus writes:

Not many days after the feast, on the twenty-first of the month of Artemisius, a miraculous vision appeared that one would find hard to believe. In fact, **I believe that what I am about to recount might appear to be a fable, if it did not have the support of eyewitnesses** on the one hand, and the confirmation of the misfortunes that followed on the other. Before the sun went down, **war chariots and armies of soldiers could be seen in the sky over the entire region, emerging from the clouds and surrounding the cities.** Moreover, at the feast called Pentecost, the priests who had entered the inner temple at night to perform the usual rites, reported that **they first heard shaking and banging, and then a group of voices saying, "From this place we are leaving."**

(VI 5, 296-299)

– Who is Flavius Josephus speaking about?

– Why does he claim that what was seen was extraordinary to the point of being unbelievable? "Luckily, there were witnesses," he exclaims smugly: the phenomenon is thus undeniable.

– Who made up that celestial army?

– Who are the individuals that say they want to leave?

– Are they the armies of the Elohim that leaving their dominion forever?

Furthermore, Flavius Josephus recalls that "at an earlier time" there appeared in the sky:

> ... a sword-shaped star and a comet that lasted for a year, or when [...] the people gathered for the Feast of Unleavened Bread [...] at the ninth hour of the night the altar and the temple were surrounded by **such splendor that it seemed as if it were broad daylight, and the apparition lasted for half an hour.**

(VI 5, 289-290)

We note an almost chronometric temporal precision in describing phenomena related to celestial armies and unidentified presences accompanied by astounding phenomena. Perhaps, in his time, the "watchers" mentioned by Daniel were still there.

4. Conclusions

In mass culture, a vast imaginary and visual repertoire of "biblically accurate angels" has spread, which have nothing to do with the [malakhim] of the Bible, i.e., the "messengers" commonly translated by the word "angels." This popularized imagery also uses the descriptions of the biblical [kerubim], to which we will devote two chapters in this book (14 and 15). As we shall see, even the cherubim have nothing to do with angels, let alone "biblically accurate angels."

Therefore, neither the "biblically accurate angels" in contemporary visual culture, nor the more or less ancient theological reconstructions of angelic figures and hierarchies, nor the notion of angels widespread in popular piety, have anything to do with these two biblical concepts — the [malakhim] and [kerubim] — to which they are traced back and around which unfounded theological, spiritual and cultural information is derived.

As shown in this chapter, the "angels" [malakhim] in the Bible are flesh-and-blood individuals whose physical difference from humans is noticeable but, at the same time, unmistakable and undeniable. The [malakhim] are more powerful than humans; they live in camps whose access seems not to be permitted; they must ask questions in unforeseen situations; they perform functions of a practical nature.

One of these functions is acting as Yahweh's spokesmen, in whose name they convey orders, give instructions, and communicate plans their human interlocutors (prophets) must share with the people.

Again, it is not our intention to define or deny the existence of angels as spiritual beings but to learn something about their representation in the Old Testament. Therefore, let us address the compelling question that inevitably arises after reading the biblical passages presented in this chapter.

– Is what has been written about angels in religious, spiritualist, and devotional literature compatible with the figures of the [malakhim] in the Old Testament?

We leave this question open, as we are sure to have provided enough material for everyone to make up their mind.

We want to conclude with a rapid foray into the New Testament, which is illuminating in many ways. In one of his letters, Paul of Tarsus writes:

> Do not forget to show hospitality to strangers, for by so doing some people have shown **hospitality to angels** without knowing it.

(Hebrews 13:2)

Men and angels are similar in appearance. Further comment is unnecessary.

שטן
12 / SATAN

1. What does "Satan" mean?

Satan is especially notorious and infamous among all "angels." He is the devil par excellence, the source of all evil, and the adversary of "God." This seductive spirit wants to influence the soul of the believers and sway them from the virtuous path.

In theology and popular piety, Satan is an angel who rebelled against "God" and was, therefore, cast out of heaven before the creation of humanity.

In the New Testament, Jesus says he "saw" Satan fall like lightning from heaven (Luke 10:18). Theologians also point to Ezekiel 28:14-18 and Isaiah 14:12-17 to support this view.

We will address the biblical passages from Ezekiel 28, Isaiah 14, and Luke 10 to show that the claim for this representation of Satan is, once again, arbitrary.

Identifying the biblical [satan] with the Devil is incorrect and misleading.

This chapter also deals with the figure of Lucifer, with whom Satan is always identified, to the point that the two figures overlap. We will see that this identification is also ungrounded, and there is, in fact, no correspondence between Satan and Lucifer.

Against the background of the biblical text, we will show how far theology and popular piety have gone in portraying a spiritual figure that has no basis in Scripture.

Let us start by saying that [satan], in ancient Hebrew, meant "adversary." The word [satan] denotes a specific role and function in society; much like the term [malakh], "angel" represents a particular function, the role of a messenger.

The fact that the article often precedes the word [satan] proves beyond doubt that [satan] is not a proper noun. As with [elohim] and [malakhim], the word [satan] simply indicates a status or task.

The examples below will clarify the various meaning of this word beyond doubt.

2. Satan as a man

First of all, we show that the role of [satan] is not necessarily an attribution of "angels" or [malakhim]. This contradicts the idea that Satan was originally a fallen angel from heaven. We have already seen how the word "angel" cannot be translated with [malakh].

We now see that the fallen angels' feared and supposed "leader" in the Bible is often a man and, more accurately, a function assumed by a man; therefore, it has nothing angelic about it. Satan could very well identify the position, the actions, or the role of a man, a human being.

~ 1 Samuel 29
In this biblical passage, we learn that David is an ally of the Philistines. But the Philistines feel that they cannot trust David and send him away, refusing to give or accept military support from him; they decide to expel David from their ranks (1 Samuel 29:4):

לשטן	ולא־יהיה־לנו
adversary(satan)-like	us-for-be-won't-he-and ←

The commanders do not want to run the risk of suddenly finding themselves on the enemy's side in battle: they do not want to have David and his army as an "adversary" [satan].

~ 1 Kings 11
In 1 Kings 11 a story is told of an Idumean named Hadad who, after David's death, rises up against Solomon. The verse says:

יהוה	ויקם
Yahweh	raised up-and ←

את–הדד	לשלמה	שטן
Hadad	Solomon-against	adversary(satan) ←

"Yahweh raised up against Solomon an adversary [satan]: Hadad the Edomite" (1 Kings 11:14). Here too, the adversary is undoubtedly a man.

~ 1 Kings 11:23

Again, "the Elohim raised against Solomon another adversary [satan]: Rezon son of Eliada." Rezon, son of Eliada, is clearly a man, not an angel nor a spiritual being.

~ 2 Samuel 19:23

David is trying to save the life of a man named Shimei, whom others would rather put to death. Turning to them, David urges them to comply with his decision and exclaims:

לשטן	היום	כי–תהיו–לי
?adversary(satan)-as	today	me-for-be-you-will-why ←

David thus identifies other people as "adversaries," [satan], against him. Again, no angels in sight.

We have quoted several passages in which the term has a precise meaning and undoubtedly refers to a man as an individual or a group of people.

3. Satan as a [malakh]

We already said that the [malakhim] are not angels in the sense we understand them today, or at least in the sense theologians understand them. However, the [malakhim], the messengers of the Elohim, can also assume the function of [satan] or, as shown, the function and role of "adversaries." The concept of "adversary" is maintained when the term [satan] is applied not to men but to the [malakhim].

~ Job 1

In the Book of Job, the figure of the שטן [satan] takes on considerable significance. It performs several important actions that can be summed up in the role of accuser and tempter towards the pious man. The [satan] here acts like an enemy towards Job to prove that his devotion is motivated only by the material wealth the Elohim gave him.

One day, says the Bible, "the sons of the Elohim" stood before Yahweh (Job 1:6):

בתוכם	גם–השטן	ויבוא
them-(with)among	satan-the-also	came-and ←

It is strange enough that, as we have seen before, "the sons of the Elohim" appear before Yahweh, which clearly means that the Elohim were many, but it is even more surprising to find out that there is one among them who has the function of [satan]! We saw in Genesis 6 that the "sons of the Elohim" united carnally with the Adamite women; now we discover that one of them had a special role and function: he was a [satan]. Let us see what happens.

"The sons of the Elohim" thus stood before Yahweh, and the [satan] was among them. The article before the word [satan] reveals that the biblical author did not intend to refer to a specific person but to one of "the sons of Elohim." He was part of the group of the "sons of the Elohim." Namely, the one who will assume the role of [satan].

We could compare the role/function of the [satan] to that of a modern prosecutor.

We will only analyze part of the story of Job here. However, we recommend that everyone read the Book of Job since it is undeniably one of the masterpieces of world literature.

We merely want to point out that in verses 1, 6, and 7 of chapter 2, the term שטן repeatedly occurs with the article, as in השטן [satan-ha], to indicate that one of the sons of the Elohim was probably appointed to be "the satan," the prosecutor.

Be that as it may, the reader can see at this point that the [satan] does not act against the will of "God" but in accord with it.

This important point must be emphasized: the [satan] acts in accord with Yahweh, not against his will. No matter how unpleasant and evil his work is, Yahweh approves of it and demands it to be done.

So the [satan] does not act as a leader of a group of rebellious demons. He is not a rebel but a high-ranked official with a specific task. He must fulfill his duty: to put Job to the test. He acts in complete agreement with his "superior," Yahweh, who commands him to act freely, with the only precaution not to kill Job (2:6).

~ Zechariah 3:1-2

A similar unpleasant task is performed by the [satan] — once again with the article — in Zechariah 3:1-2. In this passage, the [satan] stands at the right hand of a [malakh] to file a complaint against the high priest Joshua.

The verses briefly describe a trial from which the defendant is acquitted and exonerated. The [malakh], i.e., the defending "angel," asks Yahweh to reprimand the accusing [satan] and expresses words of hope for Joshua, who is invited to continue in the future according to the prescribed ways.

~ Psalm 109

The protagonist of this section is an unhappy man who asks Yahweh to free him from his enemies and to subject his persecutor to a severe judgment by placing a שׂטן [satan], that is, an accuser, against him (6).

Here too, the figure of the [satan] is not seen in opposition to divine activity but rather is presented as an executor expressly requested and sent to restore justice.

~ Chronicles 21:1

The [satan] here acts like a seductive enemy and puts David in a difficult situation by persuading him to do something that is entirely displeasing to Yahweh: he persuades him to take a census, which triggers the wrath of the Elohim and the consequent punishment (which is then withdrawn).

~ Numbers 22

We have another account in Numbers 22 where the [satan] operates as a representative of Yahweh. This episode proves that the traditional depiction of the [satan] as the leader of the rebellious angels and the lord of the underworld is unjustified.

This is the story of Balaam, narrated in Numbers 22.

Balaam was a soothsayer who was active when the Israelites were in the plains of Moab east of Jordan after forty years of wandering in the desert. The Israelites had already defeated the kings of the Amorites and

Bashan. Balak, the king of Moab, sent his elders to Balaam, the son of
Beor, to persuade him to curse Israel. After initial hesitation, Balaam
accepts the task.

The Bible says that Yahweh's wrath was unleashed against Balaam
and that a [malakh] was sent to him. When Balaam set out with his
donkey, the [malakh] of Yahweh stood in his way and frightened the
animal so that it turned off the main road into a field.

The style of this section is realistic and shows us that this "angel"
actually behaves in a very concrete way (verses 21 ff).

While Balaam is beating the donkey to get it to return to the path,
the [malakh] is standing on the path between the vines, which has a
small wall on either side; the donkey pushes aside to pass but crushes
Balaam's foot against the wall. The scene continues until the [malakh]
tells Balaam that he must carry out the orders he will receive from him.

In describing this scene, the Bible (Numbers 22:22) says:

יהוה	מלאך	יתיצב
Yahweh	of-angel	himself-placed-and ←

לשטן	בדרך
(satan, obstacle)adversary-as	path-the-in ←

In the next verse the angel speaks in the first person and says (Numbers 22:32):

לשטן	יצאתי
(satan, obstacle)adversary-as	out-came-I ←

This brief review of the verses confirms two fundamental aspects of
the [satan].

First, the [satan] is neither a person nor an "angel," not a specific
subject endowed with unique characteristics, features, and will, acting
out of his own individuality. [Satan] is not a proper name but a specific
function. It represents a position, or a task, to be assumed or executed by
either men or [malakhim].

Most importantly, the [satan] is not an antagonist of "God." In fact,
it often acts in accord with "God," and in agreement with his will. This
is a crucial point. He precisely and faithfully does what "God" wants
from him.

Finally, as a result, the [satan] cannot be unequivocally identified as the leader of rebel ranks.

4. Lucifer

Religious tradition has created a conflation and confusion between Satan and another angelic figure, Lucifer.

The term "lucifer" literally means "bearer of light" and derives from the Latin *lucifer*, composed of *lux*, "light," and *ferre*, "to bring." The same term is often used to define the planet Venus, which appears at dawn, anticipating daylight.

In popular lore, this term generally refers to a luminous being of an evil nature. It is often referred to as the leader of demons, the lord of the underworld where damned souls end up after this life.

This characterization is based on Judeo-Christian traditions that provide a specific interpretation of a passage in the Book of Isaiah in which Lucifer and Satan are equated and superimposed by commentators and theologians.

In this view, Lucifer is said to be the name borne by the brightest of the "angels" before he was cast out of heaven. After he had rebelled against "God," the "light-bearer" angel became, therefore, the "adversary" of God par excellence, namely Satan.

The leading proponents of this interpretation were Jerome, Tertullian, Origen, St Gregory the Great, St Cyprian of Carthage, St Bernard of Clairvaux, and Augustine of Canterbury. They all agreed that Lucifer/Satan and his angels/demons once lived as angels of "God" in their original state, a heavenly state from which they had fallen due to pride and rebellion.

The Fathers of the Church established an identity between Isaiah's Lucifer and the [satan] mentioned in the Book of Job and the Gospel. This identity overlap has then entered religious and popular traditions.

Let us thus address the biblical passages that the Fathers of the Church and the theologians have used to identify and conjure together [satan] and Lucifer, starting with Ezekiel 28.

~ Ezekiel 28
In this chapter, Ezekiel addresses the king of Tire, and delivers a message from Yahweh to him.

Ezekiel sharply rebukes the king for his pride and predicts his inevitable fall at the hands of the nations sent by Yahweh himself. His enemies will cause him to die a violent death by sending him (according to traditional translations) to the "underworld."

However, the translation of the Hebrew term שחת [shakhat] as "underworld" is a bit of a stretch. The term [shakhat] does not refer to the underworld. It refers to a "pit," like the one used to catch wild animals.

The prophet threatens the arrival of foreign peoples who will fight against the king, defeat him, and "bring him down into a pit."

> I am going to bring foreigners against you, the most ruthless of nations; they will draw their swords against your beauty and wisdom and pierce your shining splendor. **They will bring you down to the pit, and you will die a violent death in the depth of the waters.**

(Ezekiel 28:7-8)

The sequence also suggests that the descent into the pit occurs before the killing, so it could be a simple capture followed by death by drowning [be-lev iamim] "in the depth of the water."

The narrative continues with what the Bible expressly calls "Lamentation over the king of Tire" (Ezekiel 28:12). In this section, the king is compared to a "cherub" expelled from the Garden of Eden because of his pride.

Pride also constitutes the reprehensible disposition of the king of Tire, which moved him to desecrate sanctuaries, commit acts of violence, and thus burden himself with numerous sins that could no longer be redeemed.

This passage is the one that was then interpreted as referring to Lucifer, even though, as we will see, there is nothing in it that allows for this juxtaposition. Let us focus on verse 14:

את-כרוב	ממשח	הסוכך
cherub-you ←	of-(opening)expansion	covering-the

ונתתיך	בהר	קדש	אלהים
you-placed-had-I-and ←	of-mount-on	sacred	Elohim

היית	בתוך	אבני-אש	התהלכת
were-you ←	of-middle-in	fire-of-stones	walking

Like the cherub in Eden, the king of Tire was in a privileged position, but malice, greed, and pride took possession of his heart. The punishment is inevitable.

However, the punishment is his destruction and death, not his fall and banishment to the underworld. Verses 18 and 19 say that he will be "turned into ashes," and then it goes on to say:

עד–עולם	ואינך
forever-until	(be will)you-not-and ←

In other words, Ezekiel tells the king of Tire: "You will never exist again." Therefore, this figure cannot be traced back to Lucifer/Satan because if we consider Satan a "spiritual" creature, he would still exist. But Ezekiel here says that he was turned into ashes.

The juxtaposition between Ezekiel's character and Lucifer's alleged figure is unfounded and erroneous. Let us now look at Isaiah 14.

5. The Lucifer of Isaiah

The actual passage from which the entire theological elaboration of Lucifer originated is the following (Isaiah 14:12-15):

> **How you have fallen from heaven, morning star, son of the dawn!** You have been cast down to the Earth, you who once laid low the nations! You said in your heart, "I will ascend to the heavens; I will raise my throne above the stars of El; I will sit enthroned on the mount of assembly, on the utmost heights of Mount Zaphon. I will ascend above the tops of the clouds; **I will make myself like the Elyon.**" But you are brought down to the underworld, to the depths of the pit.
>
> (Isaiah 14:12-15)

The protagonist of this tirade considers himself so powerful that he becomes like "the one above," i.e., the character named עליון [elyon], whom we discussed in chapter 9. But his arrogance is punished, and he is thrown into the "underworld" (15).

Against this background, we can better understand how the Church Fathers proceeded in their argumentation, the end of which was the identification of Satan with Lucifer.

The decisive step towards this designation was comparing the episode we have just read from Isaiah — the fall of the prince of the rebellious angels — with Luke 10:18, where Jesus asserts, "I saw Satan fall from heaven."

In their effort to find parallels between the Old and New Testaments, the Church Fathers and the theologians believed that Isaiah and Luke were speaking of the same thing. In this way, they arrived at an identification Satan-Lucifer that is still popular today.

However, they only juxtaposed two unrelated passages. No biblical passage explicitly allows this approach — quite the contrary.

The real problem lies in identifying the protagonist of Isaiah's prophecy with Lucifer. This identification is possible only with a lot of imagination.

Isaiah 14 is a sarcastic composition directed against someone, a king or a powerful man, who is said to have thought it possible to rise to the height of Elyon.

For context, the prophet addresses the people of Israel, urging them to say a [maschàl], "proverb, sentence, parable," against an unidentified ruler. With ironic expressions, he hurls at him that he was once a great one who terrified the nations but now has become like the others; he once made the earth tremble but now lies buried among other corpses.

Who is this figure of whom Isaiah speaks?

According to one tradition, this could be Nabonidus, the king of Babylon who was defeated by Cyrus the Great and allowed the Jews to return to Palestine in 538 BCE.

However, it is much more likely that the verse refers to Xerxes, who ended the period of good coexistence between the Achaemenid dynasty and the Jerusalem ruling class. The end of this idyllic relationship also had a negative impact on the rebuilding of the temple in Jerusalem, which suffered a setback.

The verses of Isaiah 14:4-23 are, in fact, a summary of the parable of the Persian ruler and of what happened under his reign: the end of the religious tolerance introduced by Cyrus the Great, the destruction of important inhabited centers (including Babylon), the ruin of the Persian empire (the defeats of Salamis, Plataea, Mycale) and the violent death of Xerxes.

Moreover, the biblical passage directly responds to what the Persian king had written about himself when he asked the deity to be great and happy in the two lives, the earthly and the future.

The biblical condemnation is also directed against the king, who was guilty of ending the universalist policy of his predecessor Cyrus, whom the prophet himself had even called "Yahweh's Messiah" (Isaiah 45:1).

Thus the prophet invites the Jewish people to mock the new ruler with irony and sarcasm.

This prophecy was written *after* the king's death, like all other biblical prophecies, which were always written after the occurrence of events and therefore are prophecies *post eventum*.

There are many similarities between Isaiah's ranting and the events of Xerxes's reign. The time of the composition of the biblical text (referred to as Deutero-Isaiah) and the events described, in the decades of Israel's restoration after the Babylonian exile, coincide as well.

It is most likely that the unfortunate protagonist of Isaiah's prophecy in chapter 14 is the Achaemenid ruler, Xerxes.

These reasons clarify that the figure referred to by the prophet is not an evil spirit, a devil, or the leader of the infernal ranks. Isaiah's tirade is not directed at Lucifer but at a powerful man, most likely an Achaemenid king, as said, possibly Xerxes.

Nevertheless, the verse we quoted from Isaiah 14:12 — "How you have fallen from heaven, morning star, son of the dawn!" — served the Church Fathers as the basis for all subsequent doctrinal understanding (actually, misunderstanding) of Lucifer. From this passage, they constructed the non-existent figure of an angel called Lucifer after the "morning star," the "light bearer."

However, as anyone can verify, Isaiah does not speak of any angel in this section, not once. Isaiah only says that "someone" has fallen from grace and compares him to the "morning star," the "son of the dawn."

The next step was short. Having identified Lucifer as the target of Isaiah's tirade, the Church Fathers also equated him with Satan by reading Luke 10:18.

The patristic tradition found its culmination in St Thomas Aquinas, who not only endorsed the identification of Lucifer with Satan but also sought to document that it is precisely from such identification that the origin of the so-called "*mysterium iniquitatis*" can be grasped, the still unsolved "mystery of [the existence] of evil" and injustice in the world.[19]

---

[19] Aquinas, Thomas. *Summa Theologiae* I, q. 63, a. 1; also in *Summa contra Gentiles* III 108-110.

6. Conclusions

In summary, a verse addressed to Xerxes was redirected to Lucifer. This is the result of a pure and inconsistent theological elaboration.

We wonder: is the whole thing based on a bona fide misunderstanding or on an explicit desire to find a textual basis to define the figure of the lord of the underworld, where sinners would end up after death?

Again, we leave this question open, but we hope to have shown that the biblical text is foreign to the traditional iconography that sees Satan-Lucifer as the prince of demons, the adversary par excellence, and the lord of the underworld.

These concepts are not present in the Bible.

As for the term [satan], we have seen that this word does not denote a specific person but a function. It is a duty, a task that both men and [malakhim] can perform and accomplish. The [satan] is not a spiritual being to be feared or approached to summon unknown evil forces.

We have also documented that the Lucifer of Isaiah has nothing to do with the biblical [satan].

Finally, if Satan does not exist, Satanism does not exist either. It is based on invented and false doctrines and finds its nefarious "spiritual" justification in unfounded doctrines.

אֵלִיָּה

13 / ELIJAH

1. The prophet Elijah

The name of the prophet Elijah appears in the Old Testament in various spellings and meanings (1 Kings and 2 Kings; 1 Chronicles and 2 Chronicles; Job; Micah; 1 Samuel). In particular, we can find:

- אֵלִיָּה [Elia], which means "Lord (is) Yah;" and
- אֵלִיָּהוּ, אֵלִיהוּא [Eliahu]: "Lord (my) he."

Elijah's life and work are essentially described in the two books of Kings. He came from Tishbe in Gilead and fulfilled his mission in the time of King Ahab (9th century BCE); he worked as a prophet of Yahweh, called El, a member of the Elohim rank.

He is considered one of the greatest prophets in the entire history of the people of Israel, and the Old Testament attributes several extraordinary events to him:

- the multiplication of oil and flour and the resurrection of the son of the widow of Zarephath in Sidon (1 Kings 17:17-24);
- the fire of Yahweh invoked by the prophet, which came down from heaven to burn two detachments of fifty soldiers sent against him by King Ahaziah for criticizing his conduct (2 Kings 1:9-15);
- Yahweh's passage witnessed on Mount Horeb (Sinai), the mountain where "God" dwelt at the time of the Exodus from Egypt (1 Kings 19:9-12);
- the lighting of the pyre built of wood and stones and doused with wa-

ter, which was the work of Yahweh's fire coming down from heaven (1 Kings 18:38).

In 2 Kings 2, we read about an event that today is usually defined as "abduction," a kidnapping by extraterrestrials who take Elijah away in their flying chariot.

However, the term "abduction" does not seem entirely appropriate in this case, for what occurred to the prophet was known to him in advance. Elijah was not abducted; he deliberately set out accompanied by his followers, who, in turn, knew precisely what would happen. His departure in the flying chariot was planned. We have already dealt with these topics in detail in chapter 3.

We emphasize, moreover, that this event is abused by those who claim that the doctrine of reincarnation occurs in the Christian Gospels. The proponents of this thesis claim that the doctrine of reincarnation occurs in the Gospel passages in which the people identify John the Baptist with the prophet Elijah, who returned in a new guise (Matthew 11:12-14; 17:10-13).

The Bible clearly states that Elijah boarded the chariot of the Elohim "alive." He boarded the aircraft voluntarily to begin a journey from which he never returned. He who is not dead cannot be born again; therefore, the Jews of that time expected his return, not his rebirth.

Let us now turn to one of the events mentioned above: the so-called "fire miracle," which was most likely a chemical reaction that any of us, taking the appropriate precautions, can easily repeat.

2. The priests of Baal

We are in the years of the reign of Ahab, one of the rulers of the Kingdom of Israel, who ruled from 875 to 852 BCE. His story is told in Kings 1 (chapters 16-22). According to the biblical narrative, Ahab was urged by his wife Jezebel, who was of Canaanite descent, to abandon faith in the "God" of Israel and to convert to the cult of Baal, the "god" worshipped by the Phoenicians.

It should be recalled that elsewhere in this book, we have pointed out that the "God" of Israel was only one of several Elohim who shared control over the territories of the Middle East, namely, Yahweh of Teman

(Lord of the south, of Sinai) and Baal Zaphòn (Lord of the north, of Lebanon).

After the division of the nation of Israel — which followed the first monarchical period in which Saul, David, and Solomon had reigned — the land was divided into two kingdoms: that of Judah in the south and that of Israel, which comprised the northern regions. Therefore, it was easy for the people in the north to abandon the worship of one Elohim and follow another Elohim who was closer.

Ahab thus turned against the worshippers of the "God" of the fathers in his kingdom, preferring the Canaanite cult.

Ahab was undoubtedly one of the most gifted kings in terms of strategic and tactical intelligence; his military skills led him to significant victories and to contain the Arameans' expansionist ambitions by defeating them at Aphek, even though outnumbered (1 Kings 20:26-34).

Opportunist that he was, he did not even scruple to follow Yahweh's instructions when he found himself in great danger during the siege of Samaria by King Ben Adad of Syria.

Thus, he moved from one local ruler to another with a certain ease and without inconvenience. He died in battle when an arrow hit him, and the Bible records that dogs licked the blood of his wounds (1 Kings 22:34-38).

To establish the new cult, he persecuted the prophets of Yahweh trying to silence the voices that recalled the need to hold on to the covenant made with him: among these voices was Elijah.

In this constant dispute between the representatives of different deities, Elijah challenges the prophets of Baal (1 Kings 18:19 ff); Ahab accepts the challenge and summons the 450 priests and prophets of his new Elohim. At Elijah's request, he gathers them on Mount Carmel, a mountain range stretching almost 24 miles from northwest to southeast in upper Galilee.

When all are gathered, the prophet of Yahweh sharply rebukes the people who have turned away from the worship of the true "God" of the fathers and organizes a trial to prove which of the two "lords from above" is the more powerful and therefore, the one to be followed.

The multiplicity of "gods" is undoubtedly a sensitive issue for monotheism, but we already know that this was not an issue for the people of Israel. We have discussed this topic in chapter 8.

Faithfulness to "God" was always questioned, and people constantly asked themselves whether it was better to follow one "god" or the other. It was very often necessary to weigh the possibilities carefully to avoid making mistakes and to be sure to put oneself in the service of one of the Elohim who could offer greater guarantees.

These trials of power should not surprise us. They were entirely justified, as the choice of the "wrong god" could lead to many highly unpleasant consequences: reprisals from the original Elohim, loss of sovereignty over a territory, plunder of property, and perhaps even extermination or enslavement by other peoples.

The challenge begins.

> Then Elijah said to them: "I am the only one of Yahweh's prophets left, but Baal has four hundred and fifty prophets. Get two bulls for us. Let Baal's prophets choose one for themselves, and let them cut it into pieces and **put it on the wood but not set fire to it**. I will prepare the other bull and put it on the wood but not set fire to it.
>
> (1 Kings 18:22-23)

Elijah has two oxen prepared, one for each of the contending parties; then he has two piles of wood prepared for the sacrifice but orders that no fire be made yet since this will be the special challenge of the two "gods."

> Then you call on the name of your gods, and I will call on the name of Yahweh. **The Elohim who answers by fire, he is the Elohim.**"
>
> (1 Kings 18:24)

The "true Elohim" will thus be the one who responds with fire (1 Kings 18:24).

Having heard Elijah's words, the prophets of Baal begin. They prepare everything, prepare the ox and then start calling their "god," but he does not appear.

Several hours pass, but no answer comes and nothing happens: the pyre remains unlit. After the whole morning has passed, Elijah begins to mock his opponents. He asks them to shout loudly and to call on Baal (1 Kings 18:27):

At noon Elijah began to taunt them. "Shout louder!" he said. "**Surely he is a Elohim!** Perhaps he is deep in thought, or busy, or traveling. Maybe he is sleeping and must be awakened."

(1 Kings 18:27)

For Elijah, there is no doubt that Baal belongs to the group of Elohim. But, the prophet continues, they must call upon him, for he may be "busy or absent."

לוֹ	שִׂיג
himself-for	absent ←
לוֹ	כִּי־דֶרֶךְ
himself-for	travelling-since ←

"Perhaps he is deep in thought, as he might be busy thinking or traveling or sleeping," says Elijah. This is not just blunt irony, for these statements are consistent with what the texts of the time tell us about this "god."

The frequent absences of Baal are mentioned in the Bible and other texts that speak of this Baal who was unusually absent for long periods. A 14th-century BCE text from Ugarit states:

For seven years may Ba'al be absent,
for eight years the Rider of the Clouds!

CAT [1.19 — I:42-43]

Baal is called "Rider of the Clouds," an epithet that is also attributed to Yahweh in Psalm 68 as he is "riding on the clouds." It is not difficult for us to understand that these Elohim also shared how they moved through the skies.

This "god" was also known by the Sumerian-Akkadian names of Utu/Shamash/Hadad, a god who traveled on a solar chariot and caused storms. Is this perhaps also the Apollo or the Jupiter of the Greeks?

The temple of Baalbek in Lebanon also seems to indirectly confirm that Baal was a flying "god," a "rider of the clouds." This temple is actually known as the place where the local deity "rested" his means of transportation.

Baalbek is one of the most important archaeological sites in the Middle East and it was declared a UNESCO World Heritage Site in 1984. It is located about 43 miles as the crow flies east of Beirut in the Bekaa Valley at 3838 feet above sea level.

Here are the monumental ruins of several Roman temples from the 2nd and 3rd centuries BCE. The sanctuary was dedicated to the sun deity Jupiter Heliopolitanus, and in its day, the site was known as Heliopolis. However, the temple's foundations are much older than the Greco-Roman period; archaeological studies date its origins to two Canaanite settlements from the early Bronze Age (2900-2300 BCE).

Baalbek is etymologically derived from the noun *baal* or *bel*, which means "lord" in Western Semitic languages. The term Baalbek would therefore mean "lord of Beka" and refer to the oracle and temple in question, which was initially dedicated to the god Baal and Anat, the goddess of violence and war, Baal's half-sister and consort.

When looking at the ancient foundations, the sheer size of the stones that make up the floor never fails to stun the viewer. Three gigantic monoliths weighing up to 1,000 tons support the ancient Roman temples. We wonder:

– What forces did the floor have to withstand?

– What weight did it have to bear?

– Who was able to cut, smooth, move and lay such stones?

To this day, there is no convincing explanation of "why" or even "how" they accomplished this feat because even for the large construction companies of today, it would be difficult if not impossible to accomplish such a task. While we can assume that many ancient temples and monuments were built to document the personal power and even wealth of their patrons, here we are dealing with a floor, that is, an element whose visibility is insignificant and whose monumentality has no apparent justification unless it was motivated by specific practical needs. Perhaps he had to bear who knows what weights and forces. Maybe the weight and thrust of a flying chariot?

We do not know, but the suggestion is strong.

Let us now go back to our challenge.

Elijah makes fun of the prophets of Baal by emphasizing that their "god," often absent because he is distracted by other business or travel, has again left them alone and cannot be found when they need him most. He is thus an unreliable "god."

After the futile attempts of the prophets working for Ahab, it is now Elijah's turn.

The prophet of Yahweh performs gestures that seem to increase the astonishment of the spectators by providing evidence of Yahweh's power seemingly beyond imagination. He builds a stone altar, digs a trench around it, lays the wood on the stones, spreads meat on the wood, and pours abundant water on everything.

We note here a detail that will prove decisive and clarifies the knowledge that the prophet of Yahweh used to perform this "miracle." While the priests of Baal build only a pyre of wood without the help of their "God," Elijah makes an altar with a stone base in the presence of his Elohim (1 Kings 18:31). In his presence, "Elijah took twelve stones, one for each of the tribes descended from Jacob." (31) and "with those twelve stones, he built the base of the altar (32). Then:

כבית	תעלה	ויעש
of-house-like	trench	made-and ←

סביב	זרע	סאתים
around	seed	measurements-two ←

The altar is then surrounded by a small trench holding about 6.5 gallons of "seed." Elijah then piles up the wood and places the dismembered ox on top.

There follows a gesture that seems incomprehensible. It is often interpreted as a desire to astonish those present with a genuine miracle. Still, we will soon see that this prophet is putting into practice something entirely different. He commands (1 Kings 18:34):

מים	כדים	ארבעה	מלאו
water	jars	four	fill ←

ועל–העצים	על–העלה	ויצקו
wood-the-on-and	offering-the-on	pour-and ←

After the task was done, he ordered it to be repeated twice more, and at the end, the biblical author indicates that the water — having soaked the stones, the wood, and the meat — had overflowed (1 Kings 18:35):

וגם	למזבח	סביב
also-and	altar-the-to	around ←

מילא–מים	את–התעלה
waters-filled	trench-the ←

After spilling many gallons of water, Elijah calls on Yahweh and asks him to show his power. At this point (1 Kings 18:38):

ותאכל	אש–יהוה	ותפל
burnt-and	Yahweh-of-fire	fell-and ←

ואת–האבנים	ואת–העצים	את–העלה
stones-the-and	wood-the-and	offering-the ←

ואת–המים	ואת–העפר
waters-the-and	dust-the-and ←

לחכה	אשר–בתעלה
up dried	trench-the-in-that ←

So Yahweh intervenes with a fire that falls on the pyre that "falls" on the pyre. He ignites the sodden pile of stones, wood, and flesh, which catches fire and burns completely, including the water in the ditch. But did this really happen?

Before answering this question, we should examine the situation in which the protagonists found themselves:

– Elijah and Yahweh are the creators and managers of the challenge;

– While Baal is said to be absent, Yahweh is present.

– The rival priests of Elijah are thus forced to act alone, without the support of their Elohim (and we wonder if Yahweh did not issue the challenge at this very moment, knowing that Baal was otherwise occupied);

— Elijah carefully follows the instructions of his Elohim, and sets the rules for the challenge. In verse 18:36, he turns to Yahweh and reminds him verbatim, "I have done all these things — בדברך [badevarecha] — according to your words." Thus, the instructions come from the one who knows how to do it;

— only Elijah has a trench built around the altar;

— Elijah, unlike the prophets of Baal, builds the altar of stones; we thus have minerals on which the pieces of wood rest; the base of the altar — usually called "stones" in the Bible — probably contained bitumen, sulfur, and perhaps quicklime;

— bitumen was widespread in the soils of the Near East, from which it emerged, and often soaked the surface; the modern term "naphtha," also used in Semitic languages, is derived from the Sumerian Akkadian word "*napatu*," meaning "burning stones."

— Only Elijah sprayed the altar with a large amount of transparent liquid that the Bible calls "water," which seems to be necessary to ignite the pyre;

— from other biblical passages, we know that Yahweh often and for various reasons produced a "fire" that came from his "front" or from "above" (2 Kings 1:9-15).

— As can be seen from the biblical account, the rivals were not in the same situation and did not make the same gestures or follow the same procedure; one could say that they did not have the same cards to play.

3. A matter of chemistry

We have seen Elijah pour several gallons of water (a transparent liquid) that should have prevented the kindling of a flame. This is what common sense tells us, unless Elijah was aware of a precise chemical-physical phenomenon achieved by using quicklime.

This product was known and used by various ancient peoples. Since it was dangerous, its processing was entrusted to a few well-trained people who mixed it with sand to obtain the mortar for construction.

The raw material for the production of quicklime was limestone, a rock rich in calcium carbonate. The material, crushed into fragments a few centimeters or decimeters in size, was heated in special furnaces to 1472-1832 °F for about ten hours, during which the so-called "calcination" took place, a chemical reaction that releases carbon dioxide and produces calcium oxide, i.e., quicklime: a white, porous and highly hygroscopic substance.

This last property makes it delicate to handle but, at the same time, enables it to trigger a phenomenon that explains the strangeness of the miracle performed by Elijah; when soaked with water, quicklime triggers a thermal reaction that raises the temperature to nearly 572 °F and, when it comes into contact with combustible material, quickly ignites it.

The high temperature created by the contact between water and quicklime would magically ignite the flame, which would then be fanned by the various combustible components in the stones (bitumen, sulfur, etc.) and by the wood.

This is a possible explanation that can be traced back to the aforementioned situation.

Suppose one thinks that the presence of quicklime in the biblical text is not sufficiently proven; in that case, one should realize that among the naturally occurring hydrocarbons, there are products already known in antiquity that were regularly used for various purposes.

In the ancient Persian language, they were referred to by terms such as "*nafata*," which means "boiling oil" and is also reminiscent of the Sumero-Akkadian term "*napatu*," the "burning stones," mentioned earlier.

These substances are perfectly liquid, translucent, and so light that they float on water. Anyone who sees them poured out in a context as dramatic as the story we have just read might mistake them for water.

In various places in the Near East, there were natural naphtha springs clear and thick as olive oil. Alexander the Great deliberately went to the vicinity of the Oxo River to study this phenomenon, which resulted in spontaneous combustion, as occurred at Ecbatana in Persia.

These liquids can ignite very easily by spontaneous combustion. To trigger ignition, it is sufficient to produce a temperature approaching 537 °F (as in quicklime in the presence of water) or to bring a flame source near them.

When they burn, they leave no residue, as in the verses we have just studied, which show that everything was burned, stones, wood, meat, including the liquid in the trench.

This hypothesis considers the possibility that Elijah did not pour actual water on the altar but one of those liquid, transparent, and easily inflammable products.

Let us now allow ourselves a consideration.

We have seen that in 1 Kings 18:31 ff there is mention of a trench that...

סביב	זרע	סאתים
around	seed	measures-two ←

This is a quantity of "seed" of about 6.5 gallons. Now, this "seed," or "wheat" — as it is often translated — was not among the elements that Elijah had prepared.

Moreover, the water is not poured into the trench from the beginning but trickles into the trench after it is poured over the altar. The word "seed" also denotes the beginning of a life form, that is, the origin of an event. So we ask ourselves:

- What was the purpose of the ditch/trench?

- Why were the priests of Baal not instructed to prepare it?

- Did Elijah's ditch contain the "seed" as a "trigger," a substance helpful in setting things off?

- Is it maybe on the "seed" that Yahweh drops the fire that ignites the blaze?

We cannot know for sure, but the one-sidedness of the action carried out by the prophet makes the question legitimate.

Regardless of the method used — quicklime or highly flammable liquid or even a combination of both — Elijah alone is dealing with a mixture of stones, wood, and flesh that ignites as soon as Yahweh "drops" his "fire" as a trigger.

With proper care, this can be done by anyone who has the necessary knowledge, and we can safely assume that Yahweh and his prophet possessed it.

4. The bitter end

The conclusion of the biblical narrative is not very exemplary and commendable for Yahweh and his prophet, especially if we want to identify this Elohim with the universal, spiritual, loving, benevolent "God" of the theologians.

Elijah captures all the prophets of Baal and leads them to the banks of the brook Kison (1 Kings 18:40):

שׁם	וישׁחטם
there	them-slaughtered-he-and ←

As mentioned earlier, choosing the wrong "god" can be very costly because the victorious "god" certainly did not show understanding. Chapter 19 says that Elijah killed all the prophets of Baal with the sword. When Jezebel, Ahab's wife, learned of this, she threatened to kill Elijah in the same way.

The prophet realizes the danger and fears for his life. Thus he flees, and after reaching the city of Beersheba, he goes into the desert, where one of Yahweh's messengers gives him two meals so that he can make the long journey to the mountain, where he meets his Elohim again.

The traditional theological interpretation attributes to these narratives a hagiographic value, an exemplary motivation, and a desire to affirm the monotheistic thought for which Elijah allegedly stands. The whole sequence of events would thus represent the miraculous and wondrous intervention of Yahweh, whose gestures would show his extraordinary, supernatural powers as well as his uniqueness.

Now, these ancient narratives are based on earlier sources, some of which are also explicitly cited in the Bible: the Acts of Solomon, the Annals of the Kings of Judah, and the Annals of the Kings of Israel. Traditional exegetes believe that the authors respected these sources for the most part; in particular, they recognize that the accounts of the Elijah cycle were written not long after the actual events.

This proximity to the actual historical events would have forced the biblical authors to include passages that did not bring "honor" to the deity himself. Commentators say that the biblical authors also had to describe events that contradicted the (monotheistic) theses they wanted to convey.

- Is this really the case?
- Did they really have spiritualistic and monotheistic theses to convey?
- Did they really want to convey the image of a transcendent, loving, benevolent, compassionate "God" who cared for his creatures?

We must remember that the content of any story or message derives its meaning from the context in which it is presented; the context of these events was neither spiritualistic nor monotheistic.

The amazing nature of the event we have described, its miraculous character, the alleged supernaturalism, and the attribution of such a miracle to a unique and spiritual "God," seems to be the result of priestly and popular elaboration after the books were written. These aspects are not present in the story per se.

The biblical authors have recorded the (not uncommon) disagreement between the many Elohim of that time. They have not questioned the multiplicity of the Elohim; they have just documented that people were motivated in their choice by sheer evidence of the power of the Elohim. This power only served to define the superiority of one Elohim over the other.

In the entire narrative, there is not a single word, verse, or statement referring to the alleged supernatural character of the event. For those who witnessed the challenge, something happened that was certainly not possible for individuals or ordinary men but was quite possible for those who belonged to the rank of the Elohim. These events could cause astonishment, but not outside the natural order of things.

The witnesses are astonished (1 Kings 18:39), but Elijah is not lost in stunned amazement; he knows precisely what has happened and immediately sets about destroying the rivals: the only real objective of the whole sequence.

כרבים
14 / CHERUBIM

1. Introducing the Cherubim

In chapter 11, we dealt with the problem of "angels." We have shown how traditional theology has confused the biblical "malakhim" with spiritual figures with no basis in the Bible.

We have also reported on the religious traditions that postulate the existence of various "orders" or "hierarchies" of angels, each endowed with specific tasks. Among the various orders enumerated in the religious and spiritual world is that of the Cherubim, to which particular importance is attached.

The cherubim are said to have an intimate knowledge of the divine mysteries; from "God," they receive the light of wisdom and possess the ability to then transmit it to men. Their wings symbolize "tranquility in contemplation" and testify to the power of the spirit to rise to hear the divine voice they represent. They contemplate beauty and transmit supernatural light to man. They would symbolically represent the divine supremacy and sovereignty over all creation.

This high status has always made them an object of special attention. We adapt ourselves to this circumstance and devote two chapters to the cherubim. But we will analyze the cherubim, as is our custom, through the lens of the biblical text.

According to widespread opinion, the name כרבים [keruvim/kerubim] derives from Akkadian [karabu], which means "to bless" and whose participle [karibu] also means "the praying one."

According to traditional theology, these Assyrian-Babylonian [karibu] are usually represented as winged animals with a man's face. They have influenced the authors of the Old Testament in their rendering of the cherubim.

However, on a closer look, it will soon be clear the biblical description of the cherubim is decidedly different. Here is why. The Mesopotamian [karibu] was an intermediate deity who prayed on behalf of the faithful. It was also known that a female version of them was called [karibatu]. The [karibu] had similar forms and functions to other minor deities called [shedu] and [lamashu], and they too were usually placed at the gates of shrines (the term shedu also recalls the *shedim* Moses mentions in Deuteronomy 32:17, as objects of worship.)

The biblical cherubim have quite different characteristics in the Bible.

First, they are not the object of special worship; thus, they are not "divine." Moreover, they have no female counterpart, do not take the place of the faithful in prayer, and are usually mentioned in the plural. They also appear in the presence of the glory of "God" with which they move, as we shall see.

The cherubim of the Old Testament can thus hardly be reconciled with the angelic iconography we are familiar with.

2. The Cherubim in the Old Testament

We have reported briefly what tradition says about angels in general and cherubim in particular. Now we must ask ourselves what the Old Testament says about the כרבים [keruvim/kerubim]. In doing so, we will follow a process that will lead us, step by step, to the gradual discovery of elements that are often scattered throughout the Bible.

It should be noted again that our need for systematic and coherent descriptions was not important to the ancient authors. They included in their reports the elements that caught the eye of the observer on a given occasion. Therefore, we must trace these elements with a laborious but very rewarding and fascinating search.

To begin with, there are two different types of cherubim. We will deal with the second kind in the next chapter. Let us now consider the first type of these cherubim.

~ *Genesis 3*

We are in the garden of Eden. The tempting serpent has completed his evil plan and persuaded Eve to eat the forbidden fruit. After the violation is consumed, Adam and Eve discover they are naked. The Elohim then provides them with leather garments, clothes them, and expels them from Eden. But this is not enough. "God" also wants to make sure that they cannot return (Genesis 3:21-24).

ישכן
(placed)stay-made-he ←

לגן–עדן   מקדם
Eden-of-garden-to   (front?)east-from ←

להט   ואת   את–הכרבים
of-flame   (with)-and   cherubim-the ←

המתהפכת   החרב
rotating-the   (burning)blade-the ←

First of all, these verses tell us that Eden had only one entrance and that it was sufficient to control this single entrance to prevent any unwanted intrusion. The omniscient and omnipotent "God" of the theologians had to set up guards to prevent any intrusion! We must say that this is very surprising if we consider him a spiritual being.

That said, let us now consider the figure of the cherubim mentioned in the above passage more closely. The Bible unfortunately does not describe the cherubim, which would have been helpful for us to understand their shape, size, and appearance. We only know that they were accompanied by — or perhaps associated with — a "rotating (burning) blade."

In our translation of the word "blade," חרב [kherev], we have included "burning" in brackets because this is the meaning of the Hebrew root (Clark). In traditional translations, this word is usually rendered with "sword," thus losing a detail of some importance.

Even without an accurate description, however, it seems clear that the traditional depiction of the cherub (singular), seen as a winged angel holding a sword to defend the entrance, is not consistent with what the Bible says.

The Biblical account speaks of a spinning-burning blade, i.e., a wheel of fire, whose physical connection with the cherubim — more than one

— is not yet precisely defined here.

~ 1 Kings 6

In 1 Kings, we find the story of the building of the temple of Jerusalem by Solomon.

Chapter 6 makes it clear that it was Yahweh who gave the instructions for the building that was to be his dwelling place among the people of Israel; based on these precise instructions, Solomon had two cherubim made of olive wood and placed in the temple's innermost part, ten cubits (about 14 feet) high and with "wings" that measured five cubits (1 Kings 6:24):

הכרוב	כנף	אמות	חמש
cherub-the	of-wing	cubits	five ←

The term כנף [kanaf], usually rendered "wing," actually refers primarily to a "side part," an "end," just as we would refer to the wing of a building or the end of the boom of a crane.

Its original etymology precisely indicates something that "covers, protects and conceals," so we are not in the presence of an element whose primary or exclusive function is to fly. The term כנף [kanaf] seems to indicate a structure that protects from potential damages and possibly from the view of onlookers. The *Etymological Dictionary* provides this definition: "cover and conceal from view, covering, protecting" (Clark).

At any rate, the cherub with his "side parts" or opened "wings" measured about 14 feet from one end to the other.

At this point, the reader will surely have noticed at least one oddity. The term [kanaf] — usually translated with "wing" — does not appear in connection with any "angel." No "angel" or "malakhim" is mentioned here. Thus, we must assume that this structure does not belong to the figures of the [malakhim], the "angels," traditionally depicted as winged beings.

As we shall see soon, the [malakhim], of which we spoke in chapter 11 and the [kerubim] belong to completely different categories.

Up to this point, however, we still have no description of cherubim. We only learn that they can be of considerable size. Most importantly, we understand that they could have "extremities" and "side parts" with multiple functions, hitherto understood and depicted exclusively as wings.

Let us, therefore, summarize what we have found out so far. The cherubim:

– are associated with a burning, rotating blade;

– can be very large in size;

– have side parts or extremities that serve multiple functions: cover and flight.

~ 1 Samuel 4:4 / 2 Samuel 6:2 / 1 Chronicles 13:6 / Psalms 80:2 - 99:1 / Isaiah 37:16

In the excerpts quoted in this paragraph, we learn something else that allows us to continue our discovery of the nature of these mysterious "objects," the cherubim.

In all the verses cited in the title of this paragraph, it is invariably stated that Yahweh can actually sit on the cherubim!

הכרבים	ישב	יהוה
cherubim-the	sitting	Yahweh ←

The verb ישב [isciav] includes several meanings that refer to the concepts of "dwelling," "sitting," but also to the perching of birds and the lurking of animals (see, for example, Exodus 24:14; 1 Kings 2:19; Jeremiah 35:7; Isaiah 13:20; Song of Songs 5:12; Psalm 17:12).

This definition thus describes to us, with the usual natural concreteness of the biblical authors, that the cherubim seem to be — or to possess — structures against which someone can lean and rest.

Indeed, those who consider them "angels," i.e., ethereal, winged figures, must introduce hermeneutical keys that can resolve the contradiction of a spiritual "God" sitting on his angels!

Again, what is a problem today for religious interpretation was not a problem for those familiar with the facts, people, customs, places, and objects that populate the biblical narratives, such as the [kavod] of Yahweh and the structures associated with it. We have dedicated many videos to the [kavod] of Yahweh and the flying machines that appear in the Bible and other ancient texts, including Homer's *Iliad*.[20]

---

[20] Mauro Biglino Official Channel. "Macchine Volanti (1) - La Bibbia E Omero." *YouTube*, 20 Mar. 2021, www.youtube.com/watch?v=3qO5ciRcTdg. See also: Mauro Biglino Official Channel. "Gloria-Kavod: SUGGERIMENTO N.5." *YouTube*, 24 Mar. 2021, www.youtube.com/watch?v=jSEp7gkJX6c.

To summarize, the term [kavod], which is always translated as "glory" in the Bible, actually has the meaning of "something heavy." It was, in fact, a heavy flying chariot on which the Elohim traveled, something that produced loud noise, fire, and strong wind and was often described as a cloud.

If a human came near it, he was inevitably killed because "God" could not control its effects.

Since we cannot choose an adequate translation of this term — other than the word UAP — we will use the name by which the Bible defines it: *kavod*.

Thus, the cherubim:

- are associated with a burning, rotating blade;

- can be very large;

- have elements that serve multiple functions: cover and flight.

- are a "something" on which the Elohim rests, sits, and stands.

~ 1 Chronicles 28

In this section, King David calls all the leaders of Israel together and informs them that he would have liked to build a structure for the Ark of the Covenant, but the Elohim had decided otherwise, and that his son Solomon will take over the task (1 Chronicles 28:1-10).

David passes on to his son all the plans for the temple, with all the details to build the porch, the store rooms, the upper rooms, the inner chambers, the place of sacrifice, and the courts.

He also gives him all the details for the furnishings and equipment necessary for serving Yahweh, including a model for the chariot of the cherubim, as explained in the following passage (1 Chronicles 28:18):

הכרבים	המרכבה	תבנית
cherubim-the	(for)chariot-the	of-model ←

This chariot performs a precise function and is described as:

וסככים	פרשים
(protecting)covering-and	opening ←

ברית–יהוה	על–ארון
Yahweh-of-covenant	of-ark-on ←

We will deal with this type of cherubim in the next chapter, but let us focus on the chariot. The chariot of the cherubim must have had unique characteristics if its construction required making a plan with a model. Unfortunately, the text does not describe this plan for us.

We can only conclude that this chariot was no regular chariot, of which there was certainly no shortage.

We note

again that the term כָּנָף [kanaf] that we mentioned above does not refer to an element for flight but denotes a "side part," an "extension" that serves to cover and protect, to which the verse quoted refers very clearly when it says that the cherubim "open and cover."

So let us add another detail to our knowledge. The cherubim seem to possess a movable structure, whose extremities seem to be positioned in such a way as to cover the Ark of the Covenant.

We continue to follow the biblical authors as they gradually let us discover new elements that seem surprising to the modern reader but were not so surprising to those who lived in those times and merely described them.

Often we are a little frustrated because we would like more precision in the descriptions, but we must accept that this is exclusively our need. The writer and the reader of that time did not need the precision we would like to find in the biblical text to understand the facts. Those elements were familiar to them. On the other hand, we need answers to our questions to satisfy our curiosity and fully grasp the text and context.

Luckily, the various stories scattered throughout the Old Testament, though separate from one another, provide us with many pieces of a puzzle that we can try to piece together. Let us add our newly acquired element to the list of the characteristics of the cherubim.

— they are associated with a burning, rotating blade;

— they can be very large;

— they have elements that serve multiple functions: cover and flight.

— they are a "something" on which the Elohim rests, sits, and stands.

– if they do not move autonomously, they must be transported by a specially made cart.

~ 2 Samuel 22

The two books of Samuel are composite texts containing numerous oral narratives. 2 Samuel 22 includes the words King David pronounced to thank the Elohim, who had saved him from the hands of his enemies.

It was a time when the Philistines fought numerous battles against Israel. The biblical author repeatedly points out that the "descendants of Rafa," i.e., the Rephaim (2 Samuel 21:15-22), were often involved. The [nephilim] or "sons of Anak" [anakim] often appear in the Bible, and the term [anakim], we should mention in passing, recalls the Sumerian deities, the Anunnaki.

In any case, they were always people with very distinctive physical features.

During a battle, Goliath (the giant) fought with four other Rephaim from the city of Gath and another man of great stature, who had a remarkable peculiarity about him, indeed worthy of mention (2 Samuel 21:20):

מדון	איש	ויהי
(stature-large)Madon	of-man	was(there)-and ←
רגליו	ואצבעת	ידיו	ואצבעת
feet-his	of-toes-and	hands-his	of-fingers-and ←
מספר	וארבע	ושש עשרים	שש
number	four-and	twenty six-and	six ←

The author describes in great detail the peculiarity that distinguishes this figure: he had six fingers on each limb, twenty-four in all. The presence of this hexadactyly individual and his family affiliation is confirmed just as scrupulously in 1 Chronicles 20:6.

The authors of these biblical passages want to emphasize that this figure indeed belonged to a special lineage. For a more detailed discussion of giants in the Bible, we refer the reader to chapter 7.

In any case, the presence of [Rephaim] in the ranks of the Philistines made the battle very risky for David. Therefore, the active participation of his Elohim was providential. Yahweh comes to the rescue with the usual display of auditory and visual phenomena typical of his apparitions.

David describes all the recurring aspects to which we are accustomed when Yahweh makes his appearance (2 Samuel 22:8 ff): the earth shakes, smoke rises from Yahweh's nostrils (the front part), his mouth spits fire, and a great noise is produced from the sky; he shoots arrows and lightning bolts that are scattered over the battlefield. As he descends, he creates a hazy cloud under his feet.

The Elohim recognizes David's trouble and intervenes by freeing him from the hand of his enemies: he saves him from danger and sets him free.

In this whole sequence of actions, Yahweh makes a gesture that particularly interests us and that concludes a series of events that is clear and coherent in its unfolding: Yahweh presents himself by making the earth tremble; fire and smoke come out of his front (nostrils and mouth); he descends producing a dense cloud. Then, notably, Yahweh "mounted the cherubim and flew; he appeared on the wings of the ruach" (2 Samuel 22:11).

וַיִּרְכַּב	עַל-כְּרוּב	וַיָּעֹף
→ rode-and	cherub(a)-upon	flew-and

וַיֵּרָא	עַל-כַּנְפֵי-רוּחַ
→ seen-was-he-and	(ruach)wind-of-(wings)parts-side-on

The act of "standing on" that we encountered earlier now takes on a much more precise meaning; it is not just a matter of "sitting and staying."

The verb רכב [rakav] denotes precisely the act of mounting, in the specific manner of mounting a horse. The subsequent movement of the cherub carrying his passenger also suggests and confirms the action of riding. Yahweh is literally riding the cherub!

After Yahweh descends from heaven with the usual array of bright and noisy apparitions, he seems to abandon his primary means of transportation to mount another and, with it, to intervene directly in the battle: he arrives, observes, and then "rides" on a cherub.

This Elohim arrives on the scene astride the cherub, and the prophet sees him in perspective against the background of the wings of the [ruach].

For the term רוח [ruach], translated here as "wind," we refer to the chapter 3. We only emphasize here the peculiarity of a description of the [ruach], as seen in the background of the main scene while Yahweh rides his cherub. If the term [ruach] indisputably stood for the "divine spirit," this passage would be quite peculiar.

We thus wonder: are we dealing here with a vehicle that moves nimbly through the sky and from which Yahweh can seize David (verse 17) and rescue him? A similar incident is also found in Psalm 18. David sings a song of thanks to "God," who saved him from the hand of his enemies.

David describes Yahweh's arrival, and after the usual sequence of events accompanying the appearance of Yahweh's heavenly chariot, he describes the scene in similar terms: "He mounted the cherub and flew; he soared on the wings of the ruach" (Psalm 18:10).

וַיָּעָף	עַל־כְּרוּב	וַיִּרְכַּב
flew-and	cherub(a)	upon-rode-and ←
עַל־כַּנְפֵי־רוּחַ		וַיֵּדֶא
[ruach]-of-wings-on		swiftly-flew-and ←

The verb [dah] denotes a swift flight through the air, typical of arrows or birds of prey. Once again, we find that it would be strange, to say the least, to imagine a spiritual "God" climbing astride the back of an angel to be carried.

For the second time, the image of Yahweh in flight is associated with the physicality of the [ruach], which serves as a visual reference point for the viewer.

We wonder how the biblical authors could have invented such a scene if, according to religious monotheistic tradition, their goal was to confirm to the faithful the figure of a unique, universal, spiritual, and transcendent "God."

What has been said makes us regret the disappearance — accidental or intentional? — of The Book of the Wars of Yahweh, mentioned in Numbers 21.

While the book is lost, the Bible cites a few verses: "Zahab in Suphah and the ravines, the Arnon and the slopes of the ravines that lead to the settlement of Ar and lie along the border of Moab" (Numbers 21:14-15).

The accuracy of this very brief description suggests that the amount of factual information about Yahweh's equipment and how he fought in battle and moved about would be of great interest to us. We could have probably found similarities with the accounts of the Vimanas contained in Hindu texts such as *Rāmāyaṇa, Mahābhārata, Vaimanika-Shastra, Puranas, Bhāgavata Purāṇa.*

We can only hope that in the future, no longer marked by dogmas that limit research; this text will resurface in some library where it may be buried.

At any rate, according to the passages we have just read, the cherub is a "something" that can be used to move through the air while sitting on it.

Let us expand the list of characteristics of the cherubim:

— they are associated with a burning, rotating blade;

— they can be very large;

— they have elements that serve multiple functions: cover and flight.

— they are a "something" on which the Elohim rests, sits and stands.

— if they do not move independently, they can (must?) be transported by a specially made cart.

— they are "something" independent of the main structure [ruach, ka-vod], Yahweh's chariot;

— they are "something" on which the Elohim can ride (with legs astride?) and with which they can fly.

3. Ezekiel's Cherubim

Ezekiel records how a flying object — in which a human-looking man is seated — appeared on the day that Yahweh picked it up and brought it into the city of Jerusalem, to the entrance of the inner gate to the north (Ezekiel 8:3).

The careful reader will find the whole story in chapters 1-9 of the

book of Ezekiel, so we only quote it in part. What interests us here
is how Ezekiel defines these "living creatures" equipped with opening
limbs, circles, interlocking wheels, and a special kind of horizontal and
vertical movement.

In chapter 10 Ezekiel says:

> I looked, and I saw the likeness of a throne of lapis lazuli above the vault that
> **was over the heads of the cherubim.**

(Ezekiel 10:1)

In Ezekiel 1, we read that under the central part of the flying object,
which had a dome, were the "living beings." We now learn that the
dome was transparent because a throne/seat made of a shiny material
could be seen through it, but more importantly, we read that this dome
was placed "over the cherubim."

At this point, there is no doubt: the "living beings" of chapter 1, with
wheels, circles, and ground support structures, are the כרבים [kerubim].
We already knew that Yahweh "sat" on the cherubim, but Ezekiel reveals
another detail. It was the chariot of Elohim that sat on the cherubim!

He who sits on the throne visible through the dome gives a command
to the linen-clad man who appeared in chapter 9. In Ezekiel 10:2, we
read:

לגלגל	אל–בינות	בא
wheel-the-to	of-space-(in)towards	(enter)in-come ←

לכרוב	אל–תחת	
cherub-the	(of)to-under-in ←	

The sequence confirms that the cherubim have wheels and between
them is a space where a person can enter to perform actions that are not
the object of our interest at the moment.

The next verse tells us that the cherubim then go to the right side of
the temple and that the cloud fills the inner court (we must not forget
that the scene takes place in Jerusalem). What happened? Where did
this cloud come from? Ezekiel clarifies (10:4):

הכרוב	מעל	כבוד–יהוה	וירם
cherub-the	above-from	Yahweh-of-[kavod]	high-was-it-and ←

הבית	על–מפתן
(temple-the)house-the	of-(threshold)protection-above ←

The temple was filled with the cloud, and the court was filled with the brightness of the [kavod] of Yahweh. This is the prophet's explanation: the [kavod] stands on the cherubim, rises, crosses the threshold of the temple, while a cloud envelops the temple itself. This whole movement is not only seen but also heard (Ezekiel 10:5):

הכרובים	כנפי	וקול
cherubim-the	of-wings	of-noise-and ←

החיצנה	עד–החצר	נשמע
outside-the	courtyard-the-to-up	heard-was ←

So it is not only Ezekiel who sees what is happening in the inner courtyard but also those who, being in the outer courtyard, hear the noise made by the cherubim.

Verses 6 to 8 describe the action performed by the linen-clad individual between the wheels of the cherubim, and verses 9 to 12 resume the description that the prophet considers essential to emphasize.

Here, we avoid using Hebrew to facilitate the reading but still offer a literal translation.

And I saw and behold four wheels on the side of the cherubim;
wheel one by the side of cherub one;
and wheel one to the side of cherub one;
and appearance of the wheels as the eye of stone of *tarshish*;
and appearance of them similarity of one to four them (were equal);
as (if) it (was) the wheel in the middle of the wheel;
to four them wheels (of) them (each had its own wheel);

(Ezekiel 10:9-12)

Ezekiel significantly informs us that as far as he had heard (Ezekiel 10:13):

הגלגל	קורא	להם	לאופנים
circle-the	name-given-was	them-to	wheels-the-to ←

This clarification of the prophet seems strange and perhaps even unnecessary: to call the wheels a "circle" is a repetition without meaning, a tautology. But if we consider the meaning of the term גלגל [galgal], which stands for "turning fast," we understand the situation better. They were wheels spinning fast, i.e., they were whirling. We could call them "turbines" without having to use our imagination!

– We now ask ourselves: are these "turbines," perhaps the flaming, spinning blades we read about in Genesis 3?

– Were they the propulsion system of the cherubim on which we saw the [kavod] of Yahweh resting?

These questions are legitimate when we read the following verses (Ezekiel 10:15):

החיה	היא	הכרובים	וירמו
living(thing)-the	it	cherubim-the	rose-they-and ←

בנהר-כבר	ראיתי	אשר
Kevar-river-on	seen-had-I	that ←

Ezekiel anticipates here what he will shortly confirm later: the "thing" he had seen on the Kevar River (Ezekiel 1), along with the "living being," is the same one he now sees with the cherubim. Immediately afterward, he provides the description of what is before his eyes:

> in (when) moving of the cherubim;
> moved the wheels on the side of them;
> and in (when) bring of the cherubim their wings to be high above the earth;
> did not turn around the wheels also them on their side (they did not move away);
> in (when) standing still they stood still;
> and in (when) being high they rose with them.

(Ezekiel 10:16-18)

Ezekiel continues with words that convey the prophet's dumbfound-
ed marvel and the details of the incredible events he is witnessing. His
description is impressive (Ezekiel 10:18-19).

מעל	כבוד–יהוה	ויצא
above-from	Yahweh-of-[kavod]	out-came-and ←

הבית		מפתן
(temple-the)house-the		of-(threshold)protection-above ←

הכרובים	על	ויעמד
cherubim-the	above	stopped-and ←

את–כנפיהם	הכרובים	וישאו
their-wings	cherubim-the	brought-they-and ←

לעיני	מן–הארץ	וירומו
eyes-my-before	ground-the-from	lifted-they-and ←

לעמתם	והאופנים	בצאתם
them-to-near	wheels-the-and	them-exiting-(when)in ←

This particular aspect of the wheel must have caught Ezekiel's attention, as he repeats once again that the wheels are an integral part of
the cherubim and are always connected to them in motion. The plot
continues:

פתח	ויעמד
of-entrance	stopped-it-and ←

בית–יהוה	שער
Yahweh-of-(temple)house	of-door ←

אלהי–ישראל	וכבוד	הקדמוני
Israel-of-Elohim	of-[kavod]-and	eastern-the ←

מלמעלה	עליהם
above-from	them-upon ←

The [kavod] of the Elohim, who had previously risen to enter the temple's inner court, now rises again, crosses the threshold, comes out, and returns to rest on the cherubim that stood near the eastern gate of the temple.

In verse 20, we learn that Ezekiel did not fully understand what he had seen in chapter 1 of his book, and indeed it is after he has witnessed the sequence of these events that he can confirm that they were the beings he had seen on the banks of the Kevar River and:

המה	כרובים	כי	ואדע
they	cherubim	that	(understood)knew-I ←

"These were the living creatures I had seen beneath the Elohim of Israel by the Kevar River, and I realized that they were cherubim" (Ezekiel 10:20).

At this moment, Ezekiel realizes that the "living beings" he had seen previously by the river are the same cherubim he sees now by the temple. This discovery leaves him astonished. And we are too. The "living creatures" that generations of exegetes have speculated upon for centuries to define the allegorical, metaphorical, symbolic, mythical, esoteric form and substance of some "angelic hierarchy" are nothing else than the cherubim, Yahweh's flying structures.

After achieving his goal and making a series of threats and promises, Yahweh rebuilds the entire flying structure and leaves (Ezekiel 11:22-23):

את-כנפיהם	הכרובים	וישאו
their-wings	cherubim-the	(lifted)brought-they-and ←

לעמתם	והאופנים
them-(near)with-(for)to	wheels-the-and ←

וכבוד
of-[kavod]-and ←

מלמעלה	עליהם	אלהי-ישראל
above-from	them-upon	Israel-of-Elohim ←

ויעל	כבוד	יהוה
rose-and ←	of-[kavod]	Yahweh

מעל	תוך	העיר
above-from ←	of-middle	city-the

ויעמד	על-ההר	אשר	מקדם	לעיר
stopped-and ←	mountain-the-on	which	east-from	city-the-to

A movie script could not more accurately describe this maneuver in which the Elohim takes off with the cherubim and his [kavod], leaves the city, and goes to the hill to the east. The scene before us is crystal clear and needs no further comment.

The whole affair sees one more voyage to Chaldea aboard the [ruach] and then finds its final epilogue in Ezekiel 11:24, which needs no further explanation:

ויעל	מעלי	המראה	אשר	ראיתי
up-went-and ←	me-above-from	vision-the	that	seen-had-I

4. Full list of the Cherubim's features

The biblical passages examined may have confused the reader to some extent, but it was necessary to analyze them in detail.

Let us, then, complete the list of the characteristics of the cherubim, which we have gradually obtained by studying the most important passages that concern these extraordinary "objects."

In conclusion, the כרבים [keruvim/kerubim]:

– are associated with flaming blades/circles which rotate rapidly (Genesis 3:21-24; Ezekiel 10:9-12);

– have considerable dimensions (1 Kings 6:24);

– when not moving on their own they must be transported in a special chariot (1 Chronicles 28:18);

– have wheels that can move in all directions without turning, always remaining structurally joined to the flying object as a whole (Ezekiel 10:16-18);

- these wheels have a central-circular part that rotates/turns rapidly (Ezekiel 10:13);

- when they are connected to Yahweh's chariot they have a space underneath them in which at least one person can fit (Ezekiel 10:2);

- are equipped with structures that cover and protect when closed, while they are used for flight when open (Ezekiel 10:5-19);

- when moving they produce a noise audible at a distance (Ezekiel 10:5);

- the Elohim can rest, sit, stand, ride, and fly on them (1 Samuel 4:4; 2 Samuel 6:2; 2 Samuel 22:10-11; 1 Chronicles 13:6; 1 Chronicles 28:18);

- they move together with the [kavod/ruach] of the Elohim, but also independently of it, as is seen in the following sequence of movements in Jerusalem (Ezekiel 8:10-11): the cherubim are present with the chariot of the Elohim; they position themselves to the right of the temple when the chariot rises and enters the inner part of the temple; they make a sound audible to those who cannot see them; when the chariot returns, they open their wings and rise; the whole structure rises from the temple and positions itself at the east gate, whence it rises again to leave the city and lands on the hill to the east of the settlement.

5. Final questions

Once again, our aim is not to deny the existence of angelic beings but to ascertain their presence in the Old Testament and compare our findings with the content of the religious and spiritualist traditions.

That said, the *Catechism of the Catholic Church* regards the cherubim as "truths of faith" and defines them "as purely spiritual creatures" endowed with "intelligence and will." Also, "They are personal and immortal creatures; and they surpass all visible creatures in perfection."

This description of the cherubim is in stark contradiction with the Bible.

We believe the collected data, as analyzed in this and the previous chapters, raise questions to which each person can give their personal and free answer.

- Are the cherubim represented as individuals in the Old Testament?
- Do they have a personality of their own?
- Are they endowed with free will?
- Do they move like human beings?
- Do they move like winged beings?
- Are they independent?
- Do they interact with humans by performing any functions that theology, spiritualist currents, and popular piety attribute to them?
- Are their wings a symbol of resting in contemplation and the spirit's ability to rise to hear the divine voice?
- Do they convey to man a sense of the supernatural?
- Can they be placed in an "angelic" hierarchy of spiritual entities?

In the next chapter, we will deal with the cherubim standing over the Ark of the Covenant.

15 / OTHER KINDS OF CHERUBIM

1. The Ark of the Covenant

The cherubim mentioned in Exodus deserve a separate discussion. Their position and function have a different meaning from the one we have seen in the previous chapter. We must analyze them separately in their specificity.

Here three structures are closely connected in an "object" whose functionality seems to depend on the correct positioning of the three elements:

1. Ark of the Covenant: ארון הברית [aron-ha-berit]
2. Mercy-seat or propitiatory: כפרת [kapporet].
3. Cherubim: כרבים [kerubim].

In Exodus 25:10-16, Yahweh gives Moses precise directions for making a "chest" to contain and preserve the עדות [edut], "testimony," which the Elohim himself will give to Moses and which is always regarded as the set of rules dictated by "God."

Deuteronomy 10:1-5 explicitly states that the Ark of the Covenant was a container for the Tablets of the Law. The instructions for building the Ark were as follows:

— made of acacia wood;

— 2.5 cubits long, 1.5 cubits wide, and 1.5 cubits high (approximately 44.2 x 26.6 x 26.5 inches);

— covered inside and out with pure gold and surrounded on top by a border also of gold;

— the four feet were to be provided with four golden rings, two on each side, in which two acacia rods were inserted, which were used for transportation/travel and were never to be removed from the rings.

These are the instructions that are given. Isn't it strange that "God" describes in such detail how to build the furnishing intended for his worship? Why was it so important that this object, like others, be made in a certain way, with certain measurements, shapes, and materials, if it had a purely spiritual purpose?

Yahweh advises Moses at least three times to faithfully follow the תבנית [tavnit], "plan, design, model," that he had shown him on the mountain. "See that you make them according to the [tavnit] shown you on the mountain" (Exodus 25:9; 25:40).

Moses had either met with "God" or his agents, who showed him a "project, plan" to build the ark. The ark had to be made in a certain way. The Bible leaves no room for doubt: at one of the meetings on the mountain (the abode of the Elohim), Moses was shown an exact representation (drawing or model) of what was to be realized.

The reader will find this as incredible as we do, but the text leaves no room for speculation as to whether this was a vision, a dream, a revelation, or whatever. The immediacy of the narrative gives the clear impression that Moses was able to consult and examine a precise model/drawing with all the dimensions and possibly indications on how to do the work.

We will return to this element later.

2. The mercy-seat

Yahweh's instructions continue with an element to be placed on top of the ark to support the cherubim, the כפרת [kapporet], "mercy-seat."

It is said to have the same length and width as the ark and is made entirely of pure gold. The Hebrew word is usually translated as "mercy-seat" or "propitiatory," but the root's primary meaning is "to cover and protect."

It looks like the mercy-seat was just a covering lid for the ark, which later, by an extension of meaning, took over the meaning of "covering of sins" in the sense of "forgiveness of sins." Regardless of all later inter-

pretations and attributions, Yahweh himself explains the purpose of the
mercy-seat, as we shall see in a moment.

3. The Cherubim

Let us now see the third element of this triad, the cherubim. The
Elohim commands Moses (Exodus 25:18-20):

זהב	כרבים	שנים	ועשית
gold	cherubim	two	make-will-you-and ←

אתם	תעשה	מקשה
them	make-will-you	worked-metal ←

הכפרת	קצות	משני
mercy-seat-the	of-ends	of-two-from ←

Yahweh then points out that the two cherubim must be at the two
ends — obviously a technical detail of no small importance — and then
continues:

הכרבים	והיו
cherubim-the	be-will-they-and ←

למעלה	כנפים	פרשי
above-from	wings(ends)	of-spreading ←

על–הכפרת	בכנפיהם	סככים
mercy-seat-the-above	wings-their-with	covering ←

אל–אחיו	איש	ופניהם
brother-his-to	each	their-faces-and ←

אל–הכפרת
mercy-seat-the-(in)-towards ←

הכרבים	פני	יהיו
cherubim-the	of-faces	be-will ←

The fundamental "covering" function of the word כָּנָף [kanaf], always translated as "wings," is clearly stated here. These ends are "spread out" to "cover and protect." The *Etymological Dictionary* clarifies the meaning: "cover and conceal, cover, protect" (Clark), as seen in the previous chapter.

The combination of the mercy-seat and the cherubim are the subject of numerous symbolic interpretations. We can summarize them by saying that this combination symbolizes the spiritual presence of "God."

However, the Exodus' description neither justifies this symbolic interpretation nor underlines its use for atonement purposes. It is Yahweh himself who explains the purpose to Moses (Exodus 25:22). The complete translation of this passage reads:

> And **there I will meet with you, and I will speak with you from above the mercy-seat, from between the two cherubim** which are on the ark of the covenant.
>
> (Exodus 25:22)

The mercy-seat is where Moses and "God" meet. Thus this object enables the possibility of having a conversation. The mercy-seat allows the meeting and communication between Moses and the Elohim.

So we are in a physical place where contact occurs, in the presence of an object through which one can hear and speak, with the sound possibly coming "from between the two cherubim."

Clearly, "God" needs to communicate "orally" with Moses; he uses his voice, expresses himself in a language he understands, and does it through an apparatus that had to be made according to precise rules. So we ask ourselves:

— Why should "God" use an instrument to hear the voice of his interlocutor and to give his orders?

— How is it possible that the supreme being needs a physical apparatus?

— Was the mercy-seat an actual receiver and transmitter system?

We do not know for sure but can affirm that psychic/spiritual/mediumistic contact would not require or justify such mechanical precision; on the contrary, if anything, he would undoubtedly deem it as an obstacle.

In his work *Le Tabernacle*, Rabbi Moshe Levine explains that, according to the biblical narrative, the Ark of the Covenant can be compared to an electrical capacitor, consisting of two containers (gold inside and outside) separated by an insulator (inside, made of wood).

The Ark consisted of three elements:

- an inner sheet of pure gold, which we know is an excellent conductor;

- a middle layer of acacia wood, which acts as an insulator, keeps out moisture and ensures durability over time;

- another layer of gold as an outer coating.

Image of the Ark according to Moshe Levine

To move the Ark of the Covenant, the Levites — the only ones authorized to do so — passed two golden rods through the rings. This way, the conduction from the edge to the ground could be done by natural grounding and discharged without danger.

Such a capacitor would also have been capable of storing considerable amounts of static energy, which could be used in various ways, and was often even dangerous if it got into the hands of people unfamiliar with its properties and effects. Poor Uzzah dared to touch the Ark while it was being transported and experienced the consequences of this in his own body; he was electrocuted.

> They set the ark of the Elohim on a new cart and brought it from the house of
> Abinadab, which was on the hill. Uzzah and Ahio, sons of Abinadab, were guid-
> ing the new cart with the ark of the Elohim on it, and Ahio was walking in front
> of it. David and all Israel were celebrating with all their might before Yahweh,
> with castanets, harps, lyres, timbrels, sistrums and cymbals. When they came
> to the threshing floor of Nakon, **Uzzah reached out and took hold of the ark of
> the Elohim, because the oxen stumbled**. Yahweh's anger burned against Uzzah
> because of his irreverent act; therefore **the Elohim struck him down, and he
> died there beside the ark of God.**
>
> (2 Samuel 6:3-7)

David was so shocked and horrified that, "He was not willing to take the ark of Yahweh to be with him," therefore, he had it brought to the house of Obed-Edom of Gath, where it stayed for three months (2 Samuel 6:10-11).

In Joshua 3:4, the people are advised to keep the decidedly great distance of 2,000 cubits from the ark, which is about 0.6 miles.

In this case, the wings of the two cherubim would indicate either two electrodes for dissipating the static electricity accumulated in the capacitor or antennas of the transmitter system. There is, of course, no certainty. Still, the description of the whole structure leads us to conclude that the cherubim can in no way be regarded as spiritual beings endowed with a personality of their own and all the characteristics elaborated by the religious tradition mentioned above.

Two significant differences exist between the cherubim described in the previous chapter and the cherubim associated with the Ark of the Covenant. In this second case:

– the wings are not for flying but only for covering;

– the wheels are never mentioned (they represent an important element in Ezekiel's account).

So, we ask ourselves: do these different kinds of cherubim belong to the same category of objects or entities? The lack of certainties forces us to formulate various possible interpretations.

4. A landing structure

As we have seen, the Elohim informs Moses that he will speak to him "from above," that is, from above the mercy-seat, between the cherubim.

הכרבים	שני	מבין
cherubim-the	of-two	between-from ←

In Exodus 40:34-36 we find a connection between this passage and the structural relationship between the cherubim and the [kavod]. In particular, the following passage describes Yahweh's descent into the tent of the Ark of the Covenant with the [kavod].

מועד	את–אהל	הענן	ויכס
meeting	of-tent	cloud-the	covered-and ←

את–המשכן	מלא	יהוה	וכבוד
tabernacle-the	filled	Yahweh	of-[kavod]-and ←

The cloud, which always accompanies the movements of the [kavod], fills the tabernacle, i.e., the innermost part of the temple-tent where the Ark with the cherubim is located.

The next verse (35) says that Moses could not enter the tabernacle on this occasion because there was the [kavod]. This is no small indication, for we know that the proximity of the [kavod] was dangerous.

As clearly expressed in Exodus, Yahweh had to take precautions to save Moses from death when he decided to show the [kavod] to him at close range.

So when the two talked, the [kavod] was not in the tabernacle. Yahweh was present in person, and the conversation was face-to-face.

In passing, it should be noted that this "divine" mode of manifestation by the descent of a cloud in the daytime, which appeared at night like a glowing fire, was a constant in the time of the desert wanderings (see Exodus 33:7-11; Numbers 12:8; 9:15 ff; 10:11-12; 12:5; 14:14).

The reader will allow us a short digression to pinpoint how important it was to follow Yahweh's instructions to the letter. Even a tiny mistake or oversight in the procedures or the timing could trigger Yahweh's wrath or have deadly consequences.

In the chapter about preparing the relaxing/calming scents for the Elohim (chapter 10), we told the story of the two sons of Aaron who were killed because they did not follow the procedures for preparing the offerings scrupulously.

Time was also crucial. In Exodus, it is emphasized that one should not enter the temple when the Elohim was present there. Further evidence of the nature of this danger is a passage in which Yahweh himself reminds us of it, in Leviticus 16. This section begins with the remembrance of the two young men who died in the offering of the sacrifice and continues with a series of precepts that Yahweh communicates to Moses, who in turn must pass them on to Aaron (Leviticus 16:2).

וְאַל־יָבֹא
(come)enter-not-will-he-and ←

אֶל־הַקֹּדֶשׁ   בְּכָל־עֵת
sacred-the-(towards)in   moment-any-in ←

הַכַּפֹּרֶת   אֶל־פְּנֵי   לַפָּרֹכֶת   מִבֵּית
cover-the   of-faces-in   tent-the-to   of-house-from ←

יָמוּת   וְלֹא   עַל־הָאָרֹן   אֲשֶׁר
die-will-he   not-and   ark-the-on   that ←

עַל־הַכַּפֹּרֶת   אֵרָאֶה   בֶּעָנָן   כִּי
cover-the-on   seen-be-will-I   cloud-the-in   because ←

The presence of the Elohim with his [kavod] — erroneously called the "glory of God" — has certain effects on the surrounding space. Aaron must therefore be careful not to be in the temple at an untimely hour.

Here we introduce a second possible insight regarding the death of Aaron's two sons, which we mentioned when dealing with the smell of burnt flesh: did the two die because they were intentionally "killed" by Yahweh or because they brought the sacrifice in front of Yahweh at the wrong time?

We cannot know for sure, but there is no doubt about one indisputable fact: doing things the wrong way or at the wrong time can cost lives.

Suppose it is true, as we speculated in the previous chapter, that the [kerubim] were a kind of "mobile support" or "landing structure" for Yahweh's chariot; in that case, the [kavod] comes from above and connects with the [kerubim] by placing itself in the center.

5. An alternative hypothesis

We will now examine an alternative hypothesis to our reading, which considers the ensemble of the Ark of the Covenant, mercy-seat, and the cherubim as a receiver-sender system.

To understand what the cherubim might look like in this case, we must make a trip to Aksum in Ethiopia.

Let us examine what happened when Moses and Aaron spoke with their Elohim. During the desert march, Moses used to place the tabernacle at some distance from the camp: it was part of what was called the "Tent of Meeting," the building where one went to consult the Elohim.

All the people stood outside the tent, watching Moses until he entered the Tent of Meeting. A cloud descended on the tent, and the two began to speak face to face from that moment on.

The entire ritual entailed that those responsible for the service wore special clothing, which we do not discuss here since we are dealing only with the cherubim in this chapter. We mention only two accessories, which we would call "technological," and that are related to our hypothesis: the אפד [ephod] and the חשן [choscen], "breastplate."

Exodus 28:5-30 contains a long passage describing these two items, which have always been regarded in religious tradition as ornaments. The curious and willing reader can read Exodus 28:5-30 to get a complete description of the [ephod] and the breastplate.

To facilitate the understanding of what we are going to say, we have included here the reproduction of a picture of the [ephod] that was created according to the instructions of Rabbi Moshe Levine.

Reproduction according to Moshe Levine

The traditional versions always define the various details of the [ephod] as the result of an "artistic work," translating with this expression the combination of the two terms used by the biblical author חשב מעשה [maase coscev].

Actually, [coscev] is the participle of the verb [chascav], which means "to combine, compose, think, plan." The meaning of this expression is thus, "work of an assembler, work of a thinker." So it is clear that this is the work of a technician, not an "artist."

Why was technical precision work necessary? Because the [ephod] and the breastplate were not meant to be ornaments for embellishment: they had a function. Which one? No answer is more effective than the description we find in 1 Samuel 23 and 1 Samuel 30.

In 1 Samuel 23:6 ff, David fights against the Philistines; having liberated the settlement of Keilah, he settles there, and is joined by Abiathar.

בידו	ירד	אפוד
(Abiathar-of)hand-his-in	descended-had	[ephod] ←

Abiathar was one of the priests authorized to carry and use the [ephod], whose use would soon become evident.

Saul, David's rival for the throne of Judah, decides to besiege Keilah because he thinks he can easily take the enemy army commanded by David and consisting of about 600 soldiers (8). David is not sure what to do, so he calls Abiathar, the priest, and gives him an order (verses 9-10):

האפוד	הגישה
[ephod]-the	bring-closer ←

When David has the [ephod] at his disposal, he begins a conversation with Yahweh, to whom he asks for information about what he has heard about Saul's intentions. The Elohim confirms that Saul is marching against him, whereupon David leaves the city and seeks refuge in the surrounding countryside.

David speaks with Yahweh "only" after the [ephod] is brought to him; thus, the function of the [ephod] was to enable communication from a distance.

This whole passage reflects the excitement of the moment and David's need for accurate information which he cannot obtain without the [ephod].

The [ephod] also proves helpful on another occasion.

The Amalekites have just captured and destroyed the city of Ziklag; they have taken all the inhabitants captive, including two of David's wives, Ahinoam and Abigail.

His men blame him for the misfortune that has befallen their wives and children: they are furious and want to stone him. David is in a difficult situation and wants to ask Yahweh for advice. But the Elohim is far away, and so he turns again to the priest Abiathar and commands him (1 Samuel 30:7 ff):

האפוד	לי	הגישה–נא	
ephod-the	me-to	on-bring closer ←	

אל–דוד	את–האפד	אביתר	ויגש
David-to	ephod-the	Abiathar	brought-and ←

ביהוה	דוד	וישאל	
:Yahweh-to	David	asked-and ←	

"…shall I go after this mob?"

We are dealing here with a colloquial expression introduced by the particle נא [na], which has the meaning of those common expressions by which we ask someone to do something quickly: "Come on, hurry up, hurry."

David is in a hurry to consult his Elohim and asks the priest Abiathar to bring him the [ephod] as soon as possible; he needs it urgently, and we can understand his urge because we know that he cannot call or connect with Yahweh without it.

Only then can David begin the conversation with Yahweh and ask his advice — when he has the ephod.

If we were to find this today on the page of a modern war chronicler, we would not doubt the situation described: the commander of the troops is communicating with the higher command via radio to receive information and make the necessary decisions about what to do at that moment. This is the report of a standard military operation.

The situation is clear enough and leaves no room for interpretation. The problem arises only when the Old Testament tells the story. The only aspect that makes this reading unacceptable to some is that this account is found in the Bible.

The conditioning of religious thinking would make this episode unacceptable for theologians and believers, despite its clarity. To an unbiased reader, these actions, against the background of the movements of the [kavod], the characteristics of the cherubim, the technical instructions necessary for the construction of these objects, and the actions of Yahweh himself, give a perfectly coherent picture, for the understanding of which no theological or hermeneutical categories need to be introduced.

Let us summarize the elements we have obtained in analyzing this second hypothesis about the cherubim.

— Did the [ephod] function as a sending and receiving device with the breastplate to which it was attached?

— How did it charge itself?

— Was the ark a capacitor that could store energy?

— Did Yahweh speak in the temple-tent standing over the ark's lid?

— Can we assume that the cherubim acted as counter-electrodes whose job was to discharge the static electricity accumulated in the capacitor that powered the radio?

We find a possible answer in Numbers, especially in the passage that states that Moses went to the Tent of Meeting to speak (Numbers 7:89):

אליו	מדבר	את-הקול	וישמע
him-to	speaking	voice-the	heard-and ←

על-ארן	אשר	הכפרת	מעל
of-ark-on	that	covering-the	above-from ←

הכרבים	שני	מבין	העדת
cherubim-the	of-two	between-from	covenant-the ←

Once again, if these verses were found in any text other than the Bible, a "neutral" text, so to speak, one would undoubtedly recognize that this is normal radio communication. One hears a voice coming out of a structure made of wood, covered with metal and having a certain shape, with the antenna elements oriented in a certain direction.

The only problem is that this description is found in the Bible.

The term כרבים [kerubim] here denoted something different from what Ezekiel had described. None of this should surprise us; in the polysemy of the Hebrew language, consonantal roots carry an original meaning that extends to all sorts of applications: thus, the meaning of "cover" inherent in the root [kerub] could either refer to the particular configuration of flying objects with wings that, when folded, cover the structure, or to the function performed by the panels that were on top of the lid of the ark.

Of course, we cannot be sure of this interpretation. Still, the curious story of an Italian architect could provide the key to understanding the appearance of the cherubim that stood on top of the ark. Let us begin our journey to Aksum, Ethiopia.

6. Aksum

Aksum is a city in Tigre, a region of Ethiopia. It was the center of the kingdom of the same name that developed between the early years of our era and the 12th century, when it was incorporated into the nascent Ethiopian Empire. It had a written language called Geez and architecture whose ruins are on the UNESCO World Heritage list.

The Aksumite kingdom was Christianized around the 4th century, and today 75% of the area's population are Orthodox Christians. In Aksum, there is a church dedicated to Our Lady of Zion, where Ethiopian emperors were crowned for centuries.

For us, this building is important because the local Orthodox Church, supported by some contemporary scholars, claims that the biblical Ark of the Covenant is kept in a chapel of the complex.

Its safekeeping is entrusted to a priest bound to it for the rest of his life, which makes him a prisoner of this privilege. Copies of this ark are in every ancient church in Ethiopia and are carried in procession on special occasions.

According to some, the original ark is displayed on the Feast of Timkat, wrapped in a cloth to protect it from the eyes of the faithful but also to protect the priests who carry it.

How did this legend start?

A story says that the Queen of Sheba (whose kingdom extended to Ethiopia) traveled to Jerusalem to meet King Solomon; she bore him a son named Menelik, who took with him the Ark of the Covenant, which until then had been kept in the temple in Jerusalem.

However, Solomon reigned around the 10th century BCE, and the Ark of the Covenant in Jerusalem was attested until at least 586 BCE. So this hypothesis is not convincing.

Another story says that around the 6th century BCE, on the island of Elephantine — in the southern territories of the Pharaonic Empire — there was a garrison of Jewish soldiers who had built a temple. Before the Babylonian siege, the ark was brought to this temple and made safe by the presence of this garrison.

It remained there for many years until about the 3rd century CE when it was brought to Aksum and placed in the Church of Our Lady of Zion, where it still is today.

Of course, we cannot be sure of this, but the stories about the ark's existence have been alive and widespread for more than a thousand years: travelers, explorers, merchants, Templars, and Freemasons speak of it.

The Italian architect Prof. Giuseppe Claudio Infranca traveled to this place following an Italian scientific expedition in the Park of the Stelae of Aksum. As chance would have it, he was invited by the local clergy to visit the shrine of Saint Mary of Zion, which had been severely damaged during the Ethiopian civil war. During his visit, Prof. Infranca manages to enter the Holy of Holies and sees the Ark of the Covenant, which the Ethiopians say is the original; he takes a photo while plagued by a strange ringing in his ears.

For years he remains silent about this story until he learns that two Israelis, a man and a woman who belonged to a special unit of the armed forces, have managed to get to the same place, seen the Ark of the Covenant, and made the important discovery.

From then on, the architect begins to look into the matter. After years of research, he reconstructs the history and the long journey of the Ark of the Covenant from ancient Palestine to distant Aksum.

The professor summarized the result of his studies in his book *L'Arca dell'Alleanza*.

We reproduce here a drawing of the cherubim as they appear in the photograph, publicly shown by the architect on some public occasions in Italy.

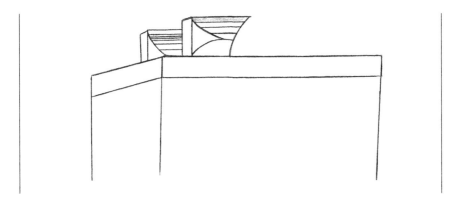

The position of the cherubim and the shape of the so-called "wings" are more reminiscent of panels, electrodes, or antennae than flight instruments.

If this discovery were to be confirmed, we should accept the idea that the cherubim on the lid are different than those Ezekiel saw in flight with the [kavod] of Yahweh.

The term כרבים [kerubim], after all, refers to the concept of "covering" and could also be used to designate objects of different forms and functions.

Multiple uses of the same term occur in other cases as well. The [ephod], for example, exists in at least three forms:

- The form reserved for the high priest used only on special occasions (Exodus 28);

- The form that was also worn by the Levites such as Micah, Samuel, or David (Judges 18, 1 Samuel 2, 1 Samuel 22, 1 Chronicles 15);

- The [ephod] that Gideon made from the gold he captured after defeating the Midianites (Judges 8), the function of which is not clear, for the Bible only says that because of the [ephod] that Gideon set up in the city of Ophrah, the entire population of Israel "prostituted themselves by worshiping it, and it became a cause of destruction to Gideon and his house" (Judges 8:27).

Another example of different objects being called by the same name is the term איפה [efa], which denotes both a unit of measure and a flying object in which a woman sits (Zechariah 5).

So we know that the same terms are used to designate different elements, whose description and function must be derived from the context.

7. Conclusions

The כרבים [kerubim] present themselves as highly articulated mechanical structures, possibly even of a different nature:

– Those connected to the [kavod] appear to be flying objects that move with it, ascending and descending; aircraft capable of autonomous travel thanks to propulsion systems we can surmise to see in those flaming structures coherently described in the Bible as rapidly rotating circles (turbines).

– On the other hand, the objects found on the ark could have forms and functions closely related to the nature of a capacitor, a receiver-transmitter system, and even a potential weapon.

Finally, the types of cherubim defined as "spiritual, incorporeal beings [...] whose wings symbolize rest in contemplation and testify to the ability of the spirit to rise and hear the divine voice..." — and belonging to the angelic hierarchies — are not the subject of the present work, which only deals with the biblical narratives. In the Bible, this particular type of "beings" does not appear.

16 / THE ALIEN GOD

Let us try to summarize the content of this work with some general considerations. The term "God," often used in the singular in this book, refers to the basic assumption of monotheistic theologies based on the Bible.

The characteristics of the Elohim that we have documented and analyzed during the scrupulous analysis of several biblical passages significantly differ from those that various forms of theological thought have attributed to the spiritual "God."

We use this term mildly argumentatively, given the evidence we have found in our study. We have seen that the figure of the "gods" that emerge from the events narrated represents individuals of flesh and blood who were "alien" to any theological or spiritualistic interest.

The behavior of the Elohim, also known as Yahweh, the decisions he made about himself, the rules he imposed on his followers, and the goals he set for his actions — all this testifies to a physicality and concreteness of intention that is unmistakable.

Yahweh was undoubtedly endowed with unique qualities that made him superior to men in power, knowledge, and technology. However, his superior power did not prevent the biblical authors from also accounting for the unpleasant, when not violent, vindictive, manipulative, even extravagant aspects of Yahweh: from the exterminations carried out in barbaric manners to the need, blatantly and repeatedly expressed, to be soothed by the smell of burnt flesh.

The superiority of Yahweh was always only materialistic and concrete, and was enforced with arrogance and little or no respect for the people who suffered under it.

The rules of the covenant/pact he made with his subjects/followers were not the result of negotiations or open discussions between two parties, i.e., they were not a compromise between equals: they were rules imposed by the strong party (Yahweh) and which the weak party (the people) could and should only follow.

In examining the rules set, it also became clear that we were dealing with an individual who had no interest in theological, spiritual or metaphysical issues, and certainly not in man's freedom of choice.

Yahweh's goals were clear: he wanted to make a pact with a population who would serve him in return for his help conquering a settlement area (the Promised Land, the subject of the alleged prophecy we have been studying).

In perfect accordance with this overall picture, the Bible presents us with this Elohim, named Yahweh, as a member of a group of many other Elohim active in the Near and Middle East stages. He was the one who chose as his "personal property" the people that would later be known and identified as "the people of Israel."

The study of the relationship between Yahweh and Israel, however, has shown us that Moses, Joshua, and all the people they led were not "monotheists," as they were well aware of the actual existence of other Elohim besides Yahweh.

They knew that these foreign Elohim possessed a power similar to that of Yahweh, and that they could be addressed with the same concreteness, advantages, and disadvantages as the Elohim who had delivered them from Egypt. Doubt, hesitation, and the temptation to choose other Elohim run throughout the biblical narrative.

The Old Testament also reports on the origins of humanity, which can be traced back to the will of the whole group of the Elohim.

We have seen the two biblical accounts of the creation of man, and grasped their possible complementarity since they tell us about the same event and how the Elohim, among whom we count Yahweh, form the new living species according to a collective decision.

In this regard, a fundamental problem arises that makes it difficult for many even to consider the hypothesis we draw from reading the biblical text.

The conditioning to which human civilization has been subjected for millennia is carried out with such determination and tenacity that its pervasiveness manifests itself in results that can be observed daily in the choices individuals make in their goals in life.

In most cases, human behavior is so precisely controlled that it could almost be described, in Pavlovian terms, as automatism. Under certain conditions, the reactions and behavior of Homo sapiens are statistically predictable because we have been conditioned to (re)act in specific ways, and constantly steered in predetermined directions.

This is the basis for the control exercised by those who seem to "govern," not just our everyday decisions, like choosing a skirt or pants, a drink, a suitcase, or where to spend our vacation, but our evolution.

We are well aware that the freedom we enjoy in these areas is an illusion: our preferences are not free but depend on the "offers" elaborated in the marketing offices of the big multinational companies, and on the way these offers are presented to us to give us the impression of an autonomous choice.

Becoming aware of this situation is the first indispensable step to following the path that should lead us to more freedom.

Conditioning is even more powerful and binding when considering our membership to the species called Homo sapiens.

We entrust science with the search for truth in all aspects of life without interference. However, even science sometimes forgoes this characteristic and takes the form of a religion (a hierarchical structure representing non-negotiable beliefs). Its truths, dogmas, and convictions often remain standing even when evidence seems to point in different or opposite directions.

This attitude becomes all the more urgent and compelling the closer one gets to the question of the origins of man: these are said to have been defined by a theory (Darwinism) which for many, fortunately not for all, has become a veritable doctrine with the status of a religion, with its apologists and its followers.

Suppose evolutionism has provided some satisfactory solutions to the events that have shaped the evolution of life on Earth; we still must conclude that evolutionism is incapable of explaining the origin of Homo sapiens, as Darwin's closest collaborator, Alfred Russel Wallace, wisely pointed out as early as twelve years after the publication of *The Origin of Species* (1859).

Almost two centuries have passed, and the situation has stayed the same.

For the layman, these doubts must be kept under cover, as if science were afraid of revealing its inability to explain the evolution of Homo sapiens, and wanted to avoid making its weaknesses in the field of human origins public.

This aspect becomes evident when "scientists," unable to provide evidence, limit themselves by ruling out a priori hypotheses capable of showing ways of investigation that could lead to logical and coherent solutions to problems that have been unsolved for decades.

Therefore, unorthodox hypotheses are ridiculed, and the possibility that those who created us are of an alien origin is downplayed with sarcastic arrogance and bias, even though ancient peoples from every continent on Earth have told us that we are the product of the "children of the stars" who came here from other worlds.

Why is this hypothesis dismissed so quickly and nonchalantly, while the possibility that a spiritual entity, the so-called "God," of which no one knows anything but of which many speak assertively, when not aggressively, is considered rational and logical?

Meanwhile, humanity's lore and ancient tales are full of individuals descending from the sky, coming from other worlds, endowed with incredible powers and abilities, the Bible being just one of the many ancient accounts of these encounters.

At the same time, of the spiritual, transcendent, omnipotent, omniscient "God," no one knows anything, and his "image" is only found in the works of thinkers who, in absolute and total autonomy, have defined his existence, attributes, and characteristics without ever having experienced contact with him.

We are confronted with two different and opposite hypotheses.

— The first hypothesis entails individuals from other worlds, seen, and described by hundreds of people in ancient lore, mythology and accounts.

— The second refers to a "God" who has never been seen and objectively experienced by anyone.

The subjectivity of individual spiritual experiences (from Western to Eastern mysticism, from the resurrection of the flesh to Hindu reincarnation to Buddhist rebirth) cannot be considered a valid parameter for defining the objectivity of a reality that, by definition, is not accessible.

Which of the two hypotheses is more "alien" to logic and coherence, and, when it comes to the Bible and ancient literature, textual evidence? Here we measure the difference between the genuine desire to understand and the need to believe.

Openness and broad-mindedness to new hypotheses are the factors that distinguish an intelligent scientific (or simply an intelligent human) way of thinking from scientific dogmatism, which desperately defends itself in the name of a predefined creed considered a priori satisfactory.

The importance of intellectually unbiased work, as free as possible from prejudice and conditioning, lies in creating new ways of organizing information, because information exists and sometimes even comes from the past.

It would be enough if open-minded spirits, working in different fields of knowledge, reorganized what is available to formulate hypotheses suitable for finding new paths in the search for the possible truth of the history of humanity, which, on closer examination, turns out to be a domesticated species, divided and locked into cultural, social, political, geographical and ideological enclosures in which it is to be kept and nurtured both physically and culturally.

It is necessary to be aware of this behavior and to share the wise conviction that the longed-for answers may lie beyond the dogmas that limit the freedom of research.

Science and ancient stories may be much closer than ever thought: the evidence is so strong that this is a hypothesis that any scientifically open-minded person can no longer push aside before proper verification and study.

The same revelations by the Pentagon, which is gradually opening its files on military sightings of so-called UFO/UAP (Unidentified Aerial Phenomena), have changed attitudes toward particular possibilities previously ridiculed.

Scientists like astrophysicist Avi Loeb (Harvard University) are conducting projects intending to prove the existence of intelligent life outside our solar system.

This is precisely what needs to be done, providing food for thought for open minds, for intellectuals looking for answers because they understand that the solutions we have at the moment are often inadequate or sometimes even contradict the evidence.

Since Darwinism cannot provide evidence for dozens of so-called "evolutionary" events, some believers arrogantly demand evidence from those who propose alternative hypotheses. They forget that evidence is

needed to confirm theses that are "certain," and they cannot be requested from those who point to different paths because old ways have proven
incapable of providing answers for many decades.

Alternative ways are indispensable. Without intuition, motivated
imagination, and visionary intelligence, there would be no scientific
progress.

On this ground, we challenged the old theological certainties of the
"original sin" and the consequent damnation that still allegedly burdens humanity. As we have seen, the history of the original sin admits
quite different and less dramatic interpretations. Yahweh did not punish Adam for his guilt; he merely expressed what is commonly called
"*sententia post eventum*," that is, he acknowledged an inevitable situation
resulting from the free choice of Adam and Eve.

Removing the concept of "original sin" is the first fundamental step
towards liberation from this "sense of guilt" with which we are bound
and subjugated, and which forces us to live a life characterized by rev-
erent fear and the hope of one day having access to the redemption that
will bring us eternal happiness.

In this context, and in connection with the idea of freeing humanity
from guilt and fear, we have also seen how theologians have downright
invented the figures of, and the characters generally attributed to, Satan
and Lucifer: religious interpretations of these figures lack biblical basis.

When the Elohim moved through space, they had to do so physically
because they were not spiritual beings. They had to reach the places they
wanted to go, and they did so in flying machines. These flying machines
are called in the Bible [kavod] or [ruach], which in traditional, religious,
and theological translations are rendered with "glory" and "spirit."

Thus we know that when the Bible talks about the "Spirit of God,"
it refers to the "*ruach* of the Elohim," one of Yahweh's flying chariots.
When the Bible talks about the "glory of God," it refers to the "*kavod* of
the Elohim," one of Yahweh's flying machines.

The [kavod], seen as a metaphorical representation of the so-called
"glory of God," is a theological concept with no factual and textual basis: a purely theoretical elaboration resulting from the desire to forcibly
introduce spiritual concepts into a narrative realm where they have no
room since metaphysical concepts were not part of the early Semitic
mentality.

The "glory" was something external to "God," an instrument that he used to move by commanding it, a means that had deadly consequences for those who had the misfortune to be near it.

The history of traditional commentators shows the enormous difficulty of understanding and describing the [kavod] or the [ruach] in terms of spirituality and transcendence. It is much easier to imagine that those who wrote the texts put descriptions of concrete physical phenomena on paper. These phenomena had been experienced repeatedly by hundreds, perhaps thousands, of people whose memories must have been handed down over time, at least in their essential aspects, albeit with all the inevitable variations that oral communication produces.

Moreover, these biblical passages agree remarkably well with the Sumerian accounts in which the Anunnaki are described as moving through the air in their flying machines.

We cannot erase this concreteness by relegating it to indeterminate worlds of visions or dreams; we cannot erase with a stroke of the pen or with a dogmatic know-it-all attitude what these authors wished to record in writing.

The scientific world should make a healthy examination of conscience.

According to Arthur Koestler, the inertia of the human mind and its resistance to innovation are most evident not — as one might think — among the uneducated masses, which are easily carried away as soon as their imagination is stimulated, but among the professionals with their vested interests, through tradition and the monopoly of knowledge.

Innovation poses a double threat to academic mediocrity: it undermines their authority as oracles and evokes the most profound, possibly unconscious fear that their entire painstakingly built intellectual edifice might collapse.

However, the history of scientific thought and progress has been marked by "heretics" whose theories later proved valid. This has been the case with every major innovation that has changed life on our planet. We have discussed this in detail in the first chapter of this book.

In the past, heretics and dissidents were tortured, burned, or excommunicated; today, they are pilloried by the media or academia. Heinrich Schliemann was one of these many dissidents who were vilified and slandered. But he succeeded where academic archaeologists failed.

A similar situation happened when the Church attacked Galileo and the Copernican theory, which later proved correct despite fierce attacks, heavy censorship, and the ostracism of the scientific community; at the same time, the geocentric theory supported by the Church proved false.

Science has often brought progress to our civilization, but has also produced over the centuries a veritable summa of errors in astronomy, geology, geography, physics, mathematics, chemistry, zoology, physiology, neurophysiology, anthropology, psychology, medicine, and many other disciplines.

Upon more or less severe scientific errors (not counting deliberate falsehoods), numerous texts have been written, studied, and deemed as the "gospel" itself, just to be contradicted and proven wrong later.

"If we were to rely on the impartiality of scientists, then science, even natural science, would be utterly impossible," wrote Karl Popper in *The Poverty of Historicism*.

We should always keep an open mind.

Hypotheses (even those considered heretical) must be accepted as such, thus investigated, verified, and analyzed before becoming proven theses or discarded as unworkable, but without the underlying bias and the typical behavior of those who approach new possibilities having already a priori established that they must be rejected because they do not please the prevailing system. This is dogmatic arrogance, not science.

Knowing that there are many things beyond scientific knowledge about the deeper structure of energy and matter, we ask ourselves: who can arrogantly exclude the possibility that civilizations millions of years older than us have, in fact, expertise and know-how (technologies, means of communication, or transport systems) that we cannot even suspect with our most vivid imagination?

The biblical authors have described other beings closely related to the Elohim: the [nephilim] and the [malakhim]. Of the former, we have noted their massive appearance, which has always been associated with descent from the sons of Anak (Anakiti-Anunnaki?) of Sumerian origin.

We have traced their physical features, including the presence of six fingers on each limb, as well as the events that led them to slowly disappear and dissolve into the peoples who inhabited the land of Canaan.

The [malakhim] required a more detailed analysis because theology has inexplicably made them spiritual beings. At the same time, the biblical stories about them are always characterized by the extraordinary concreteness with which the biblical authors describe scenes in detail, even placing them in a precise spacial and temporal context.

The angels, [malakhim], were individuals of blood and flesh whose physical difference from humans was noticeable. They were endowed with superior powers; they lived in camps to which access was not permitted; they performed various practical functions, including that of Yahweh's spokesman.

Last but not least, let us mention the most "unacceptable" characteristic of the Elohim: they die. As Psalm 82:7 affirms that the Elohim shall "die like Adam."

This is no surprise to those who assume that the Anunnaki/Elohim might have had a long life — perhaps an extremely long life by earthly standards — but that, as flesh-and-blood individuals, they would also die. It is the Bible itself that tells us this.

In short, we should recognize without a shadow of a doubt that it is written in the Old Testament that the "God" of the theologians dies like all other people, unless the theologians tell us that the term Elohim in the Bible sometimes means "God" and sometimes means something else, as in Psalm 82 or other occasions.

If this is so, all certainties waver and anyone can make what they will of the text. Who decides what Elohim means? If Elohim at times means "judges," at times "gods," and at times "God," or something else, who is in the position to establish with absolute certainty when it means one thing and when it means another thing? This freedom of choice is arbitrary and contrary to any scientific practice, too often subject to one's personal ideology and views. For this reason, we observe that the most respectful translation practice in such cases would be to leave "Elohim" *untranslated*.

At any rate, Psalm 82 is very eloquent in stating that the Elohim shall "die like Adam." Now, if Elohim means "God" or "gods," then "God" or the "gods" die like Adam.

From this and all the above considerations, it is clear that "God," with his court of figures and technological equipment, presents himself in the Bible in very different guises from those religions tailored to him.

Religions were born as an attempt to re-establish contact with beings considered superior due to their unbridgeable distance from man in terms of knowledge, ability, and power:

- individuals who lived so long as to be considered immortal, even if they were not;

- individuals who knew the secrets of nature and the cosmos, and transmitted them to their faithful followers, thus introducing castes of kings/governors/priests (the "initiates" of knowledge);

- individuals who traveled by air, covering in the shortest time distance unthinkable for those traveling on foot;

- individuals who used intermediaries to manage their power and communicate with humanity through "angels" that prevented direct contact;

- individuals who had created man using genetic engineering techniques of which they controlled every aspect.

These lists of characteristics seem to describe well the "alien gods" of the Bible.

These are mere hypotheses, but it is not easy to dismiss the literal reading we suggest as "fanciful," as it has the merit of being consistent with the biblical text and coherent from the narrative perspective.

Is it more "fanciful" to believe the accounts of authors who, several millennia ago, produced written, oral and iconographic evidence of people who existed for them and with whom they conversed, or to follow the abstract ideas of those who, while affirming the concept of the impossibility of knowing a transcendent "God," contradict themselves by speaking and writing about him as if they could dispose of him at will?

There is a question that is often tacitly asked in light of these premises: does Yahweh (the Elohim) still exist?

Information on this specific question is very scarce in the Bible. But the Roman-Jewish historian Flavius Josephus tells us in *The Jewish War*:

Not many days after the feast, on the twenty-first of the month of Artemisius, a miraculous vision appeared that one would find hard to believe. In fact, I **believe that what I am about to recount might appear to be a fable, if it did not have the support of eyewitnesses on the one hand,** and the confirmation of the misfortunes that followed on the other. **Before the sun went down, war chariots and armies of soldiers could be seen in the sky over the entire region, emerging from the clouds and surrounding the cities.** Moreover, at the feast called Pentecost, the priests who had entered the inner temple at night to perform the usual rites, reported that **they first heard shaking and banging, and then a group of voices saying, "From this place we are leaving."**

(VI 5, 296-299)

The same event is retold by the famous Roman historian Tacitus in his monumental work, *Histories*:

Armies clashed in the sky, swords blazed, and the temple shone with sudden flashes. The doors of the sanctuary were suddenly torn open, and a **superhuman voice cried out that the gods were fleeing**; and at the same time there was a great uproar, as if men were fleeing.

(*Histories*, V 13)

When reading these ancient accounts, we cannot but wonder:

— Did the Elohim leave at that time?

— Did only a few leave?

— Did they move to another territory?

— Will they return?

— Have they already returned?

— Have they always been here?

We do not know and gladly leave the answer to those who claim to know.

Will it be discovered one day that the Elohim were extraterrestrials? We will take note of it.

Will it be discovered one day that the Elohim were ex-terrestrials who had left the planet and then returned to it? We will take note of it.

Will it one day be discovered that the Elohim belonged to an antediluvian Earth race? We will take note of it.

Will it one day be discovered that the Elohim were representatives of a higher race that lived in the hollow Earth? We will take note of it.

Will it be discovered one day that they were people who returned from the future? We will take note of it.

Will it be discovered one day that the Elohim were only fictional characters in a fantastic fable created by the fertile imagination of biblical authors? We will take note of it.

Whatever the answer, it will not change our work: what is essential is that we no longer try to make people believe that Elohim means "God."

There is still much to be done and understood about the origin of life and the behavior of human beings. We only have part of the truth.

However, we claim the right to keep searching for it. The conception of our life, our society, our culture, and the history in which it develops, depends on the continuation of this search.

In addition to purely scientific considerations (from genetic, biological, evolutionary, and techno-mechanical perspectives), we have also seen sociological, historical, and legal elements that affect our lives today.

As highlighted in this book, various ideologies, theologies, historiographies, and even scientific claims present us with "truths" about which it is legitimate and even appropriate to express substantial and reasonable doubts.

We must remove ideological lenses from our noses to understand the Bible and all the other ancient accounts.

Only then will we realize that the only "alien God" is created by theologians, who is indeed "alien" to any scientific, logical perspective, foreign to any honest reading of the biblical accounts.

We do not know anything about "God." But if he exists, he is not found in the Bible. If anything, we find in the Bible many different "alien gods" contending with Yahweh for control of the territories available in a given geographical area. All of these "alien gods" possessed advanced technological means and personal characteristics that all ancient peoples, including the nation of Israel, describe from their own point of view.

Rewriting history and changing the cultural foundations of our society when the conditions are right is not an admission of defeat but a demonstration of intellectual honesty.

A little healthy humility, an attentive willingness to understand, a fair amount of curiosity, and respect for the ancient stories are necessary and very useful.

This attitude characterizes the intelligence of those who "know that they know nothing."

This attitude drives the search and brings us closer to the truth, no matter how "alien" it sounds to our ears.

ESSENTIAL GLOSSARY

This section reproduces, in alphabetical order, some of the contents discussed in the previous chapters, as well as the meaning of some Sumerian and Akkadian terms and their translations by the experts (Castellino, Furlani, Kramer, Pettinato, Sitchin) whose works are indispensable for understanding the interpretative path followed by them, and to which the reader is therefore referred (see "Works Cited and Consulted").

The description given here is therefore only a small contribution to briefly and concisely outline the contents of the book, which deals almost exclusively with Old Testament narratives.

Terms belonging to the Sumerian and Akkadian languages are marked with (SAT).

— Abram (SAT)

"Father's favorite."
Abraham (Abram) is a semitic term meaning "father of many."

— Abzu (SAT)

"Well," "Lower world," "Primordial Source."
Initially, the term may have meant the lower part of the planet Earth, the southern hemisphere, but then it became a designation for the great ocean of fresh water extending under the earth. Enki was its lord, the ruler of the mines that naturally descended into the subterranean strata. The modern word "abyss" is derived from this Sumerian term.

— Adamu, Addamu, Admu (SAT)

"Earthly," "Image," "Father-Man," "Human kind."
The Hebrew Adam also means "red earth."
Adamu in Akkadian becomes *Atamu.*
For the Assyrians, the term *Udmu* identified the human race.

— Ammonites

The descendants of Ben Ammi, the second son of Lot (grandson of Abraham) and the brother of Moab (Genesis 19:37-38), were excluded from the Israelite community because they dedicated themselves to worshipping Balaam.

— Amorite

The general name for the people who inhabited Palestine before the arrival of the Hebrews. The name was, therefore, also synonymous with Canaanite. The term "Amorite" refers to the language spoken by the Semitic population in Syria from the second half of the third millennium to the first centuries of the second millennium BCE, a language that never had a written form because it was used by semi-nomadic peoples who, once settled, used the Babylonian language.

— Anunnaki (SAT)

Sumerian deities. The name could mean "those who came from heaven to Earth." It could also mean "Earth's most important seed."

— Astarte/Ashtoreth

A goddess worshipped in the northwest Semitic region (the Babylonian Ishtar) who personified the Phoenician and Canaanite Great Mother; her cult was associated with fertility, fecundity, and war. The main centers of her worship were Sidon, Tyre, and Biblo, but she was also known in Malta, Tharros in Sardinia, and Erice in Sicily.

She also found her way into the Egyptian pantheon, where she was identified with Isis. In the later Hellenistic period, she was associated with the Greek goddess Aphrodite and the Roman Venus. The name Astarte/Ashtoreth frequently occurs in the Old Testament, also in the plural form (Ashtarot, cf. Judges 10:6). In this case, it probably denotes female deities corresponding to the male Baalim. Let us briefly recall the statement of the text. In Kuntilled Ajrud (between the Negev and Sinai), Yahweh was worshipped through his Asherah.

— Berossus (Berosus)

He was a priest of Marduk, a Babylonian astronomer, and an astrologer who lived between the 4th and 3rd centuries BCE. His importance is related to his three books that make up the work *History of Babylon (Babyloniaka)*, which was dedicated to King Antiochus I and is now lost. Fragments of some importance have survived thanks to other authors such as Abidenus and Alexander Polyhistor (1st century AD) who told the history of the world from its origins to the author's time.

Berossus divides the history of humanity essentially into two great epochs, before and after the Flood. During the first part, ten antediluvian kings ruled over very long periods, measured in *saroi* (the *sar* of the Sumerians?), periods of 3,600 years. The list of Greek king names is as follows: Aloro, Alapro, Malone, Ammenone, Magalaro, Daono, Euerodesco, Amempsino, Parte, Xisutro (the Sumerian Ziusudra, the biblical Noah?). During their time, fish with human heads and feet had emerged from the sea (the first was Oannes) and had taken the role of advisors to the rulers, teaching people all the elements of civilization.

After the Flood, the duration of the rule of the various kings decreased and was measured in neroi, that is, periods of 600 years. Eventually, we come to the historical figures, especially from Nebuchadnezzar II and Nabonidus; important fragments have been preserved.

— Cargo Cult

This phenomenon, studied by anthropologists, is characterized by Pacific Islanders paying homage to airplanes that landed on their islands, which they considered to be of "magical" or "divine" origin. It developed mainly in New Guinea, Melanesia, and Micronesia. We have discussed this at length in the "Introduction."

— Carmel, Mount

This mountain appears in the sacred texts of Judaism, Christianity, and other traditions. It must be said that it is not a discovery of Judaism but was inhabited since prehistoric times, as early as 150,000 BCE, and funerary objects indicate that it was considered a sacred place since that remote antiquity.

There is also evidence of Egyptian origin. In 1400 BCE, Pharaoh Tutmosis III conducted military campaigns in Palestine, and his reports also mentioned Mount Carmel, calling it the "Holy Mountain."

In the Bible, we find the following references:

– Joshua 12:22: Mount Carmel is conquered by Joshua, and King Jokneam is defeated.

– 1 Kings 18: Mount Carmel appears in the story of Elijah, which we have treated in a separate chapter.

After this episode, Mount Carmel does not appear again in biblical history, except in hints (Isaiah 35:2, Song of Songs 7:6, and Nahum 1:4).

In 66 AD, Vespasian sacrificed on Mount Carmel to the local god, whom Tacitus and Suetonius describe as a faceless god.

Various traditions then report that numerous hermits continued to retreat to the caves of this mountain, in perfect union with Elijah, Elisha, and their disciples. In the Elijah cave (in the church of the present monastery), there were monastic settlements since the Byzantine period, as testified by inscriptions found during excavations.

In the second half of 1100, some veterans of the Crusades gathered on Mount Carmel to begin a contemplative life dedicated to prayer and seclusion. The Patriarch of Jerusalem established the rules of the new order, which emerged from the union of various cenobitic communities.

In 1200, this monastic movement came to Europe under the Order of Saint Mary of Mount Carmel. It was based on contemplative solitude, prayer, poverty, and work.

The order changed from a hermit to a mendicant order in 1247 when Pope Innocent IV published the modified Rule of the Carmelites.

— Duranki (STA)

The "Sky-Earth link."

A pillar used by Enlil to "speak to heaven" stood in the center of Nippur, the capital of the god Enlil. It is also called Ekur, denoting the place where Enlil planted the seed of humanity.

— Eden, Edin (STA)

Cf. Genesis 2:10: the word Eden was translated into Greek as *paradeisos*, "paradise," and is derived from *pairidaeza* of the Zoroastrian religion (whose origin can be traced to the land of Eden). The Avestan word means "enclosed place." The Hebrew word for "garden," *gan*, derives from the root *ganan*, meaning "to enclose."

The גןבעדן [Gan be-eden] means "fenced garden in Eden," which would be located east of the Palestinian territory where the Old Testament was written. We do not consider addressing the question of its location here because it requires specific and analytical discussion.

— El

Semitic term: god of the Canaanites, the most important Ugaritic deity (pre-Jewish culture in Canaan and Sinai); name also used in the Bible as El Elyon or El Shaddai, "The One Above," "Lord of the Mountains," "Lord of the Steppe."

— Enki, Ea (STA)

"Lord of the Earth," "He who reveals secrets," and "Lord of Water." (Was this the same god that the Egyptians knew as Ptah?)

God of the Abzu, son of Anu; brother of Enlil; patron deity of Eridu; commander of the Anunnaki; the god who creates man at the urging of his mother Nammu, who encourages him to form a being similar to the gods, able to serve them and work for them. Enki creates man: he creates male and female just as the Hebrew god creates man and then woman.

He had as his emblem the two intertwined serpents; this symbol is reminiscent of the structure of DNA, the serpent [nachash] of the Bible tempting Eve.

Also referred to as "Lord of Water," he is linked to ancient Mesopotamian tales about half-fish, half-human beings, or individuals covered in scales (suits with scaly surfaces?), also sometimes described as "sentient animals" mentioned by several ancient chroniclers.

— Enlil (STA)

"Lord of heaven," "lord of command," "lord of the wind," son of Anu; brother of Enki; patron deity of Nippur (see Nibruki). After Anu, he was indeed the most powerful of the gods. After a certain time, he seemed to have replaced Anu, who was always absent. He was considered the "king of heaven and Earth," the "king of all lands," and the various local rulers claimed to have received, directly from him, dominion over the lands entrusted to their care. Enlil was the one who "pronounced the name of the king" and "gave him his scepter."

— Enmeduranki (STA)

"The Lord whose ME (Sumerian untranslated term) connects heaven and Earth."

Priest of the ME of Duranki who officiated at the sacred temple of Nippur. This character is reminiscent of the biblical Enoch, who was taken up to the skies.

— Enoch, Book of

An apocryphal text of Jewish origin, accepted only by the Coptic tradition, its definitive version dates from the 1st century BCE and has come down to us in a version written in an ancient literary language of Ethiopia (ge'ez).

Other versions of the Book of Enoch are the Aramaic version in the Qumran scrolls and the excerpt given by the monk George Syncello in a book from the 9th century.

The Book of Enoch may be the result of the union of earlier texts, as it consists of several sections: the "Book of Watchers" (cc. 1-36), the "Book of Parables" (cc. 37-71), the "Book of Astronomy" or the "Book of Heavenly Luminaries" (cc. 72-82), the "Book of Dreams" (cc. 83-90), the "Epistle of Enoch" (cc. 91-104), and the concluding section (cc. 105-108), also known as the "Apocalypse of Noah."

— Enuma Elish (STA)

A Babylonian poem known by the title "Epic of Creation," although the exact meaning of the term is "On High," relates the myth of the creation and deeds of the Babylonian god Marduk.

The time of its composition has yet to be discovered with certainty (19th century BCE), but it contains many elements typical of earlier Sumerian narratives. The clay tablets on which it is written are marked as a "copy of a Sumerian text." Various adaptations are preserved: the Neo-Babylonian, the Neo-Assyrian, an older Assyrian, and a pre-Babylonian.

The number of tablets containing the creation account, namely seven, corresponds precisely to the division of the days of creation in Genesis 1, and this detail suggests a direct dependence of the biblical text on the much older Sumerian-Babylonian text.

— Eridu (STA)

The oldest settlement of the "gods" of Sumer. The term evokes a dwelling far from the original dwelling place. The name possibly refers to the biblical Irad/Iaràd, the son of Enoch, the "builder of cities."

Genesis 4:17 speaks of a settlement in the plain and the founding of a city by Enoch, who is said to have named the settlement after his son Irad/Iaràd: this name means "the descended one" and seems to refer to a migration from the upper regions to the lower plain, or again to those who descended from above.

It was the place of worship of the god Enki, who had provided for the reclamation of the marshes. It was also called Haaki, "house of the water fish," because it was built on a system of canals and swamps.

It is also called Eduku, the "house of the sacred hill," where there is a "temple that rises to the sky." It was also known as Nunki: the land of Nun. Among the Egyptians, the term Nun denoted the primordial waters of chaos, and it was from these waters that Eridu arose as the first structure in the marshes of lower Mesopotamia (i.e., chaotic and uncontrolled, from the Abzu, the primordial waters). It corresponds to today's Tell Abu Shahrain (315 km southeast of Baghdad).

— Gilgamesh (STA)

Sumerian hero, ruler of Uruk (the biblical Erek), son of the goddess Ninsun and descendant of Shamash. He was two-thirds god and one-third man. He is also called the son of Lugalbanda and the grandson of Enmerkar. The Epic of Gilgamesh is a poem written in cuneiform on clay tablets. The known version dates from the 12th century BCE, but the content was inspired by the story of Atrahasis and other older Sumerian tales. His epic is about his quest for a long life reserved for the gods and the so-called Sumerian-Akkadian Noah: Ziusudra-Utanapishtim.

— Grapevine, wine

This plant has a special significance in the Bible, and in Genesis 9, it appears as the first agricultural crop after the Flood. This importance is due to its many properties, both physical and psychological. It has a therapeutic effect on the digestive and cardiovascular systems; it calms and produces a euphoria that can also be useful in certain areas and situations. In particular, from a physical point of view, it performs several functions: antioxidant, anti-inflammatory, antimicrobial, anticarcinogenic, and a regulator of platelet aggregation with a reduction in cardiovascular disease.

Of particular importance is resveratrol, one of the components of grapes.

The Elohim proved on several occasions that they had considerable medical knowledge, so it is not surprising that they paid particular attention to a product that could serve as a healing and preventive agent in various situations where there were no more effective alternative remedies. The history of the plant's spread also overlaps in an extraordinarily curious way with the events we have analyzed. Recent research dates the appearance of the vine back 140 million years, and according to the fossil record, there were about forty varieties of the genus vitis on Earth before the arrival of man, many of which disappeared during the ice ages. Some of them were saved by surviving in so-called "natural climatic refuges," one of which is located in Asia between the Black Sea and the Caspian Sea and is known as the "Pontic refuge."

The story of Noah is set on Mount Ararat in Armenia, that is, in the area where the "domestication" of the plant by man and the resulting production of wine seems to have originated.

Paleobotany has found that the transition from the wild grapevine (Vitis silvestris) to the cultivated grapevine (Vitis vinifera sativa) took place in the Syrian-Anatolian-Mesopotamian area. In 2010, French researchers in Armenia found traces of grape cultivation dating back some 8,000 years! If this discovery is confirmed, it would be another proof of the historicity of the biblical data.

The Sumerians knew not only about beer but also about grapevines, distinguished the characteristics of wines, and discovered, for example, that grapevines growing in hilly terrain yielded better wine than those growing in the plains. They brought wine from the Caucasian regions to the surrounding areas. They got the product to the market as early as 3000 BCE, although a real regulation of the "market" was introduced only later by the Assyrians and Babylonians.

— Igigi, Igigu (STA)

"Those who observe." This is how the Anunnaki astronauts who stayed in orbit were defined. Igi means "eye" and, with it, the act of looking; gu means "area, region;" gi has the meaning of "confidence, trust."

— Ilu (STA)

"He who is up above," "Lord."

— Flavius Josephus

He was born around AD 37 in Jerusalem into a noble family and received his education in the Jewish tradition but with influences from Greek and Latin culture. He was a Torah-observant Jew close to the Pharisaic movement and hostile to nationalist movements. In AD 64, he traveled to Rome and received a strong and positive impression.

During the First Jewish War (AD 66) he held the military office of governor of Galilee. When the rebels realized they could no longer resist the Romans, they committed suicide. Josephus managed to stay alive and surrender to the Romans. He had a very positive encounter with the military commander Titus Flavius Vespasian, whom he predicted would become emperor; due to this happy premonition, the future ruler of the Romans spared his life, and Josephus became related to the emperor's family, even taking the name of the gens Flavia.

His priestly family was among those who gave the temple treasury to the Roman generals and, in return, received a prosperous life. With this gift, General Vespasian bought the vote of his military to become emperor. He then lived in Rome and wrote strongly pro-Roman works but also spread elements of Jewish culture.

His writing text the *Jewish War* is the most important historical source about the war against Rome and also describes the last days of the Jewish fortress of Masada. The book *Jewish Antiquities* also contains references to the figure of Jesus (considered by scholars to be later insertions) and important information about the religious movements of Judaism at that time. He died in Rome around AD 100.

— Jubilees, Book of

This text, called Little Genesis, is considered canonical only by the Coptic Church. Probably written in Hebrew toward the end of the 2nd century BCE, it has been preserved in its entirety only in an Ethiopian translation and was listed with the Book of Enoch as a sacred text in the Bible from which it originated. It tells the story of the world, from creation to the Exodus from Egypt, dividing events into periods of 49 years — the Jubilees, hence the name — which is divided into further periods of seven years.

— Lulu, Lullu (STA)

"Mixed." The new being created by the Anunnaki/Elohim.

— Manetho

He was an Egyptian priest of the Serapis cult and was commissioned in 270 BCE by King Ptolemy Philadelphos to write the history of ancient Egypt. The three volumes, known as Aegyptiaca, were kept in the Library of Alexandria and were lost after numerous unfortunate events that led to the destruction of one of the most important ancient centers of world culture. Their contents are known thanks to the quotations of other authors, including Flavius Josephus, Sextus Africanus, and Eusebius of Caesarea.

In writing the work, he noted that since the beginning of time, the dynastic lists consisted of gods and demigods who ruled long before the pharaohs. The gods, with the duration of their respective reigns, were as follows: Ptah (9,000 years), Ra (1,000 years), Shu (700 years), Geb (500 years), Osiris (450 years), Seth (350 years), Horus (300 years). This was followed by a dynasty of 30 demigods who ruled for 3,650 years. After that, a period of chaos ended with the installation of the first exclusively "human" dynasty: the first pharaoh was Men (Menes).

The list of pharaohs that followed Menes was considered fanciful, and it was Champollion, the father of modern Egyptology, who noted that the information provided by Manetho was remarkable. Much more so than had previously been assumed: over time, concrete evidence was found for the existence of some of the rulers mentioned exclusively by Manetho.

— Masoretes

The Masoretes were the guardians of the "tradition" (masorah) who edited the biblical texts to complete the canon in the first millennium after Christ. To this end, they carried out various works. They corrected spelling and pronunciation, added vowels, divided the texts into words, books, sections, paragraphs, and verses, and corrected the texts to avoid misinterpretation.

Among the texts proposed by the various Masoretes over the centuries, the one that stands out is the codex compiled by the Ben Asher family of the school of Tiberias (8th century CE), which was recognized at the time as the standard text of the Bible and whose version has come down to us in the Codex Leningradensis (Leningrad Codex): a manuscript on parchment, dated AD 1008. The author, Samuel ben Yaaqov, claims to have copied it in Cairo from an original manuscript by the Masoretic leader Aaron ben Moshe ben Asher.

This manuscript is kept in the Russian National Library in St Petersburg (formerly Leningrad, hence the name), cataloged as "Firkovich B 19 A," and is the official reference version of the Hebrew-Aramaic biblical text for Jews and Christians. The Masoretes called themselves "pointers" (naqdanìm) because they developed and applied a system of dots and dashes to the consonantal text to mark the vowel sounds to read the sacred text with the correct pronunciation. The result was a precise but complex system of vocalization, which for this reason, is not discussed here.

— Moab

Moab was the son of Lot, born of the incestuous relationship between him and his eldest daughter after the destruction of Sodom and Gomorrah: he is presented as the eponym of the Moabites (Genesis 19:37). The term referred to the region between the Dead Sea on the west and the Syro-Arabian desert on the east; it ended on the south at the river Zéred (today's Wadi el Kesa).

— Nibruki (STA)

"Crossroads on Earth."

The Sumerian name for Nippur, the city from which Enlil ruled, was also called Duranki.

There were fifty Anunna and seven gods who "determined the destinies."

From the root IBR, which means "to cross over," perhaps the term "Hebrew" is derived.

Before man was created, the city was built for the gods.

The most important gods of Nippur were Enlil, Ninlil, and his mother, Nunbarshegunu.

The city of Nibruki/Nippur is located 150 km southeast of Baghdad.

— Sarai (STA)

"Princess."

Sarah is also a Semitic term: this is the name of Abraham's wife (Genesis 12-13).

— Septuagint, Version of the Seventy

The Seventies Version (Septuagint in Latin, which is also given in Latin numerals with LXX or the Greek letter omicron and a superscript) is the Greek language version of the Bible.

According to tradition, it results from a translation by 70 (72) sages working in the 3rd century BCE in Alexandria, a city with a significant Jewish community.

The commission allegedly came directly from the Hellenistic ruler Ptolemy II Philadelphus (285-246 BCE). This text still forms the liturgical version of the Old Testament for the Eastern Orthodox churches of Greek tradition and is not accepted by Protestant Orthodoxy.

— Shiimti (STA)

"Breath," "Wind," "Side," "Life," "Clay."

The house where the "wind of life" was transmitted: Shi corresponds to the Hebrew [nephesh], "soul."

— Shuruppak (STA)

"Place of supreme well-being."

The medical center run by Ninharsag/Sus, Enki's sister.

The dwelling of the Sumerian Noah, corresponding to the priest Ziusudra (Utnapishtim in Semitic, Atra-Hasis in Akkadian).

One of the five antediluvian cities that was built when Enlil decided to "take the people out of the caves" and give them a more human and civilized life with cities, agriculture and livestock. In these cities, kingship was exercised by the gods.

In the 1930s, numerous public buildings were discovered there, including schools with benches made of mud bricks and tablets with information about daily life, fieldwork, public administration, and also about events before the Flood. Cuneiform accounts say that people at that time did not eat bread, did not dress, were naked, ate grass by tearing it with their mouths, and drank water directly from the ditches.

It corresponds to present-day Tell al-Fara (180 km southeast of Baghdad).

— Stuttgartensia Bible

The *Biblia Hebraica Stuttgartensia*, or BHS, is an edition of the *Hebrew Bible* published by the German Bible Society in Stuttgart.

The text is an exact copy of the Masoretic text in the *Codex Leningradensis* (L) and is the official reference for the Hebrew-Aramaic biblical text for Jews and Christians. The text also corresponds to the *Letteris Bible* published by the British and Foreign Bible Society in London.

— Ugarit

City on the northern coast of Syria, corresponding to the present site of Ras Shamrah, a few kilometers north of the current city of Latakia.

The capital of the ancient kingdom of the same name was located at the mouth of an important caravan route from Mesopotamia to the Mediterranean, on the border between Hittite territory to the north and Egyptian-controlled areas to the south.

— Ur

A city mentioned in the Bible as "Ur of the Chaldeans" (Genesis 11:28-31), the home of Abraham, who left it with his father, Terah, to go to Canaan.

This site was continuously inhabited from the 4th millennium to 300 BCE. At the beginning of the 3rd millennium, it became one of the most important Sumerian cities.

It acquired particular importance through Ur-Nammu, who founded the Third Dynasty, whose rule extended over Babylon, Assyria, Elam, and the middle Euphrates.

It was destroyed in the 18th century BCE.

It corresponds to present-day Tell al-Mukayyar (300 km southeast of Baghdad). It must be said that, according to modern scholars, Abraham came from an area in northwestern Mesopotamia.

— Uruk

A center of worship of Anu and Inanna, whose temple Eanna descends directly from heaven.

According to the Sumerian royal list, it was the seat of the second post-Diluvian dynasty (after Kish).

The name of this city seems to derive from Akkadian Uruk and Sumerian Unu (g) and means "city of Unuki," i.e., "city of Enoch," the biblical patriarch mentioned in Genesis 4 and probable builder of Eridu, to which he would give the name of his son Iràd/Iaràd.

The Bible mentions it as "Erek" (Genesis 10:10).

It corresponds to today's Warka (250 km southeast of Baghdad).

At this site, archaeologists have excavated finds from the Eanna, the ziggurat of the white temple, the Sinkasid palace, and numerous cuneiform tablets.

— Utu/Shamash (STA)

"The god who shines and ascends, in fire, to the heavens (Shumu)."

The son of Nannar and Ningal; brother of Inanna.

The patron deity of Ur and Larsa: he was responsible for the property of the gods and justice; he was essentially the lord of the law.

Antediluvian king of Sippar.

— Ziusudra (STA)

"The days of his life lengthened," "His life like that of god."

The Sumerian Noah.

He was the son of Ubartutu, the last king of Shuruppak before the Flood.

He corresponds to the Babylonian Utnapishtim (as narrated in the epic of Gilgamesh, king of Uruk), the Atrahasis of the Semites of the Akkadian Empire, and the Deucalion of classical Greece.

He is warned of impending disaster by the Anunnaki Enki, who also gives him instructions on building a boat with which to save himself.

Ziusudra also sends a raven from the ark, a parallelepiped (tebah, "breast") like Noah's. After the Flood, Ziusudra was granted "life like that of the gods," hence the meaning of his name.

Ziusudra corresponds to Xisutros, mentioned by Berossus, the tenth and last Sumerian king before the Flood.

WORKS CITED AND CONSULTED

Alford, Alan. *When the Gods Came Down: The Catastrophic Roots of Religion Revealed*. Hodder & Stoughton, 2000.

———. *Gods of the New Millenium*. Hodder & Stoughton, 1997.

Anati, Emmanuel. *Har Karkom: Montagna sacra nel deserto dell'Esodo*. Jaka Book, 1984.

———. *La montagna di Dio. Har Karkom*. Jaka Book, 1986.

Andresen, Jensine, and Octavio A. Chon Torres, editors. *Extraterrestrial Intelligence. Academic and Societal Implications*. Cambridge Scholars Publishing, 2022.

Armstrong, Karen. *A History of God. From Abraham to the Present: the 4000 Year Quest for God*. Heinemann, 1993.

Artom M. Emanuele. *Corso pratico di morfologia ebraica*, Unione delle comunità israelitiche italiane, 1975, Rome, Italy.

Baccarini Enrico, *I Vimana e le guerre degli dei*, Secreta Edizioni, 2014, Siena, Italy

Baldacci, Massimo. *La scoperta di Ugarit. La città-Stato ai primordi della Bibbia*. PIEMME, 1996, Casale Monferrato (Alessandria, Italy).

——— *Il libro dei morti della antica Ugarit*. PIEMME, 1998, Casale Monferrato (Alessandria, Italy).

———. *Prima della Bibbia*. PIEMME, 2000 Casale Monferrato (Alessandria, Italy).

———. *Il diluvio*. Arnoldo Mondadori Editore, 2000 Milan, Italy.

Barbiero, Flavio. *La Bibbia senza segreti*. Magazzini del caos, 2008, Grosseto, Italy.

———. *Ufo. L'ipotesi terrestre. L'altra umanità*. Magazzini del caos, 2008 Grosseto.

———. *The Secret Society of Moses: The Mosaic Bloodline and a Conspiracy Spanning Three Millennia*. Inner Traditions, 2010, Rochester (Vermont, USA).

Basant, Dwivedi, and Maxwell C. Brockmann. "Meat flavour." *Critical Reviews in*

Food Technology, 5: 487-535, 1975.

Bat, L. Adam. *Esodo. Ovvero contrabbando di Know-how dalle Piramidi a Gerusalemme*. Robin Edizioni, 2010, Rome, Italy.

Bauval, Robert, and Graham Hancock. *The Message of the Sphinx: A Quest for the Hidden Legacy of Mankind*. Crown Pub, 2010.

Bauval, Robert, and Adrian Gilbert. *The Orion Mystery: Unlocking the Secrets of the Pyramids*. Crown, 1995.

Benner, A. Jeff. *The Ancient Hebrew Language and Alphabet: Understanding the Ancient Hebrew Language of the Bible Based on Ancient Hebrew Culture and Thought*. Virtualbookworm.com Pub, 2004, College Station, Tx.

———. *Ancient Hebrew Lexicon of the Bible*. Virtualbookworm.com Pub, 2005, College Station, Tx.

———. Ancient *Hebrew Dictionary. 1000 Verbs and Nouns of the Hebrew Bible*. Virtualbookworm.com Pub, 2009, College Station, Tx.

Benzine, Vittoria. "Archaeologists Ask Netflix to Reclassify Graham Hancock's 'Unfounded' Netflix Docuseries 'Ancient Apocalypse' as Fiction." *Artnet News*, 2 Dec. 2022, news.artnet.com/art-world/archaeologists-graham-hancocks-ancient-apocalypse-fiction-2222060?utm_campaign=artnet-news.

Beretta, Pier Carlo, editor. *Bibbia Ebraica Interlineare. Genesi*. San Paolo edizioni, 2006, Cinisello Balsamo (Milan, Italy).

———. *Bibbia Ebraica Interlineare. Esodo*. San Paolo edizioni, 2007, Cinisello Balsamo (Milan, Italy).

———. *Bibbia Ebraica Interlineare. Levitico*. San Paolo edizioni, 2003, Cinisello Balsamo (Milan, Italy).

———. *Bibbia Ebraica Interlineare. Numeri*. San Paolo edizioni, 2004, Cinisello Balsamo (Milan, Italy).

———. *Bibbia Ebraica Interlineare. Deuteronomio*. San Paolo edizioni, 2002, Cinisello Balsamo (Milan, Italy).

Bibbia Emmaus. San Paolo Edizioni, 2005.

Biglino, Mauro, and Lorena Forni. *La Bibbia non l'ha mai detto*. Mondadori, 2017.

Biglino, Mauro, and Giorgio Cattaneo. *La Bibbia nuda*. Tuthi, 2021.

Biglino, Mauro, and Giorgio Cattaneo. *The Naked Bible*. Tuthi, 2022.

Biglino Mauro, translator. *Cinque Meghillôt. Rut, Cantico Dei Cantici, Qohelet, Lamentazioni*, Ester. San Paolo Edizioni, 2008.

———. Il libro dei dodici. San Paolo Edizioni, 2009.

Biglino, Mauro. *La Bibbia non parla di Dio. Uno studio rivoluzionario sull'Antico Testamento*. Mondadori, 2016.

———. *Il Falso Testamento. Creazione, miracoli, patto d'allenza: l'altra verità dietro la Bibbia*. Mondadori, 2017.

———. *Le Dieu de la Bible vint des etoiles*. Editions Nouvelle Terre, 2011, France.

———. *La Bible comme vous ne l'avez jamais lue*. Les Editions Atlantes, 2014, France.

———. *Biblija nije sveta knjiga*. TELEDISK, 2015, Croatia.

———. *Kamen die Gotter aus dem Weltall?* KOPP, 2015, Germany.

———. *A Biblia nao è um livro sagrado*. Misty Forest, 2017, Portugal.

Black, Matthew, editor. *The Book of Enoch or I Enoch a New English Edition With Commentary and Textual Notes. With an Appendix on the "Astronomical" Chapters* (72-82) by O. Neugebauer. Brill, 1985.

Blech, Benjamin. *The secrets of Hebrew Words*. Roman & Littlefield, 2001, Lanham (USA).

Blumenthal, Jacob, et al., editors. *Etz Hayim Study Companion*. Jewish Publication Society, 2005.

Bock, Michael. "NASA to Set up Independent Study on Unidentified Aerial Phenomena." *NASA*, 9 June 2022, www.nasa.gov/feature/nasa-to-set-up-independent-study-on-unidentified-aerial-phenomena/

Bottero, Jean, and Samuel N. Kramer. *Uomini e dèi della Mesopotamia*. Einaudi, 1992, Turin, Italy.

Brown, Francis, et al. *The Brown-Driver-Briggs Hebrew and English Lexicon: With an Appendix Containing the Biblical Aramaic: Coded with the Numbering System from Strong's Exhaustive Concordance of the Bible*. Hendrickson Publishers Marketing, 2005.

Bürgin, Luc. Geheimakte Archäologie: Unterdrückte Entdeckungen, verschollene Schätze, bizarre Funde. Bettendorf, 1998, München, Germany.

Castellino, Giorgio, editor. *Testi Sumerici ed accadici*. UTET, 2017.

Celso, Aulo Cornelio. *Il Discorso Vero*. Adelphi, 1987.

Ceram, C. W. Gods, Graves and Scholars: *The Story of Archaeology*. Revised, Vintage, 2012.

Cerny, Christoph, and Werner Grosch. "Quantification of Character-impact Odour Compounds of Roasted Beef." *Zeitschrift für Lebensmittel-Untersuchung Und Forschung*, vol. 196, no. 5, Springer Science and Business Media LLC, May 1993, pp. 417–22. https://doi.org/10.1007/bf01190805.

Clark, Matityahu. *Etymological Dictionary of Biblical Hebrew*. New York, Feldheim Pub, 2000.

Cohen, Shaye. *The Beginnings of Jewishness: Boundaries, Varieties, Uncertainties*. University of California Press, 2001.

Colin, Wilson. *Alien Dawn: An Investigation Into the Contact Experience*. Virgin Books, 1998.

Collins, Andrew. *Gli ultimi dei. Alla ricerca dell'eredità negata degli angeli*. Sperling & Kupfer, 1997.

Corrias, Gian Matteo. *Prima della fede. Antropologia e teologia del culto romano arcaico*. Tuthi, 2022.

Cremo, Michael, and Richard Thompson. *Forbidden Archaeology: The Hidden History of the Human Race*. Bhaktivedanta Book Publishing, 1998.

Dalla preistoria all'antico Egitto, Gruppo Editoriale L'Espresso, 2004.

Daniélou, Jean. *La teologia del giudeo-cristianesimo*. Translated by C. Prandi, EDB, 2016.

Deiana, Giovanni, and Antonio Spreafico. *Guida allo studio dell'ebraico biblico. Con chiave degli esercizi. Con analisi grammaticale della crestomazia*. Claudiana, 2018.

Demontis, Alessandro. *Nibiru e gli Anunnaki*. 2009, Rome, Italy.

———. *Testi sumeri tradotti e commentati*. 2010, Rome, Italy.

———. *Il fenomeno Nibiru*. Vol. I, 2011, Rome, Italy.

———. Il fenomeno Nibiru. Vol. II, 2012, Rome, Italy.

De Giorgio, Santillana, and Hertha Von Dechen. *Hamlet's Mill: An Essay Investigating the Origins of Human Knowledge and Its Transmission Through Myth*. David Godin, 2015.

De Young, Mary. *The Sexual Victimization of Children*, McFarland & Co, 1983.

Disegni, Dario, editor. *Bibbia Ebraica*, Giuntina, 2013, Florence, Italy.

Di Segni, Gianfranco, editor. *Talmud babilonese: Trattato Berakhòt*. Giuntina, 2017

Downing, Barry. *The Bible and Flying Saucers*. Lippincott, 1968 Philadelphia, USA.

Feuerstein, Georg, et al. *In Search of the Cradle of Civilization: New Light on Ancient India*. Motilal Banarsidass, 2008.

Enciclopedia Della Bibbia. Elledici, 1969.

Evangelical Dictionary of Theology. Edited by Walter Elwell, Baker Academic, 2001.

Fagan, Brian. From Black Land to Fifth Sun: *The Science of Sacred Sites*. Basic Books, 1998, New York, USA.

———. *Le origini degli dei*. Sperling & Kupfer, 2000 Milan, Italy.

Flavius, Josephus. *The Jewish War*. Edited by Martin Goodman, Translated by Martin Hammond, 1st ed., Oxford UP, 2017.

Freud, Sigmund. *Moses and Monotheism: Three Essays*. Translated by James Strachey, Vintage/Ebury, 1974.

Fukuda, Kei, et al. "Regional DNA Methylation Differences Between Humans and Chimpanzees Are Associated With Genetic Changes, Transcriptional Divergence and Disease Genes." *Journal of Human Genetics*, vol. 58, no. 7, Springer Science and Business Media LLC, June 2013, pp. 446–54. https://doi.org/10.1038/jhg.2013.55.

Furlani, Giuseppe. *La religione babilonese-assira*. Zanichelli, 1929, Bologna, Italy.

———. *Miti babilonesi ed assiri*. Sansoni, 1958 Florence, Italy.

———. *Riti babilonesi e assiri*, Istituto Edizioni Accademiche, 1940 Udine, Italy.

Garbini, Giovanni. *Storia e ideologia nell'Israele Antico*. Paideia, 1986.

———. *Note di lessicografia ebraica*. Paideia Editrice, 1998 Brescia, Italy.

———. *Mito e storia nella Bibbia*. Paideia Editrice, 2003 Brescia, Italy.

Garbini, Giovanni, and Olivier Durand. *Introduzione alle lingue semitiche*. Paideia, 1994.

Gartler, Stanley M. "*The Chromosome Number in Humans: A Brief History*." Nature Reviews Genetics, vol. 7, no. 8, Springer Science and Business Media LLC, Aug. 2006, pp. 655–60. https://doi.org/10.1038/nrg1917.

Genesi-Bereshìt. Mamash, 2006.

Gesenius, Wilhelm. *Gesenius's Hebrew and Chaldee Lexicon of the Old Testament Scriptures*. Translated by Samuel Prideaux Tregelles, Andesite Press, 2015.

Goldhagen, Daniel. *Hitler's Willing Executioners: Ordinary Germans and the Holocaust*. Vintage, 1997.

Graves, Robert, and Raphael Patai. *Hebrew Myths: The Book of Genesis*. Cassell, 1964, London, UK.

Guth, H., and W. Grosch. "*Comparison of the Juices of Stewed Beef and Stewed Pork by Instrumental Analyses of the Odorants and by Sensory Studies.*" Bioflavour, no. 95, 1995, pp. 201–05.

Halloran, John. *Sumerian Lexicon: A Dictionary Guide to the Ancient Sumerian Language*. Logogram Publishing, 2006.

Hancock, Graham *Fingerprints of the Gods: The Evidence of Earth's Lost Civilization*. Three Rivers Press, 1996.

———. *The Mars Mystery: The Secret Connection Between Earth and the Red Planet*. Broadway Books, 1999.

Hancock, Graham, and Santha Faiia. *Heaven's Mirror: Quest for the Lost Civilization*. Three Rivers Press, 1998.

Hanhart, Robert, and Alfred Rahlfs. *Septuaginta Editio altera*. Deutsche Bibelgesellscaft, 2006.

Hendel, Ronald S. "Of Demigods and the Deluge: Toward an Interpretation of Genesis 6:1-4." *Journal of Biblical Literature*, vol. 106, no. 1, Mar. 1987, p. 13, https://doi.org/10.2307/3260551.

Herodotus. *The Histories*. Translated by Tom Holland, Penguin Classics, 2015.

Hesiod. *Theogony. Works and Days. Testimonia*. Translated by Glenn W Most, Harvard UP, 2018.

Il libro dei Giubilei, UTET, 1993.

Infranca, Giuseppe Claudio. *L'Arca Dell'Alleanza. Il Tabernacolo Di Dio. Diario Di Una Scoperta*. Gangemi Editore, 2008.

Inglis, Judy. "Cargo Cults: The Problem of Explanation." *Oceania*, vol. 27, no. 4, Wiley, June 1957, pp. 249–63. https://doi.org/10.1002/j.1834-4461.1957.tb00703.x.

Jacobsen, Thorkild. *Sumerian King List*. 2nd Edition, University of Chicago Press, 2022.

Jaeger, Nicola. *Il diritto nella Bibbia : giustizia individuale e sociale nell'Antico e nel Nuovo Testamento.* Pro Civitate Christiana, 1960, Assisi (Perugia, Italy)

Jebens, Holger. *Cargo, Cult, and Culture Critique.* University of Hawaii Press, 2004.

Jenkins, Keith. *Re-thinking History. With a New Preface and Conversation with the Author by Alun Munslow.* Routledge, 2004.

Jucci, Elio, translator. *Gli Apocrifi. L'altra Bibbia Che Non Fu Scritta Da Dio.* PIEMME, 1992.

Klein, Ernest. *A Comprehensive Etymological Dictionary of the Hebrew Language for Readers of English.* Carta, 1987.

Klein, Isaac. *A Guide to Jewish Religious Practice. Jewish Theological Seminary of America,* 1979.

Koestler, Arthur, and Herbert Butterfield. *The Sleepwalkers: A History of Man's Changing Vision of the Universe.* Penguin Books, 1990.

Kramer, Samuel Noah. *The Sumerians: Their History, Culture, and Character.* University of Chicago Press, 1971.

———. *From the Tablets of Sumer.* The Falcon's Wing Press, 1956, Indian Hills, USA.

———. *Mythologies of the Ancient World.* Doubleday & Company Inc., 1961, New York, USA.

———. *Sumerian Mythology.* Harper & Brothers, 1961, New York, USA.

———. *L'histoire commence a Sumer.* Flammarion, 1975, Paris, France.

———. *The Sacred Marriage Rite.* Indiana University Press, 1969, Bloomington, USA.

———. *I Sumeri. Alle radici della storia.* Newton & Compton, 1979, Rome, Italy.

———. *I Sumeri agli esordi della civiltà.* Aldo Martello Editore, 1958 Milan, Italy.

Kuhn, K. G. Rabbinische Texte. 2. Reihe, *Tannaitische Midrasch Sifre zu* Numeri. Kohlhammer Verlag, 1959, Stuttgart, Germany.

Labat, René. *Manuel d'epigraphie akkadienne.* Geuthner, 1976, Paris, France.

La Bibbia concordata. Antico testamento. Pentateuco. Arnoldo Mondadori Editori, 1982.

Lambert, Wilfred, et al. Atra-Hasis. *The Babylonian Story of the Flood.* Clarendon Press, 1969 Oxford, UK.

Langdon, Stephen. *Le Poème Sumérien du Paradis, du Déluge, et de la Chute de l'Homme*. Leroux, 1919, Paris, France.

Lawrence, Peter. *Road Belong Cargo: A Study of the Cargo Movement in the Southern Madang District*, New Guinea. Waveland Press, 1989.

Lexicon Recentis Latinitatis: Volumen 1. Et 2. Urbe Vaticana, Libraria Editoria Vaticana, 2003.

Lieber, David, et al., editors. *Etz Hayim: Torah and Commentary*. The Jewish Publication Society, 2004.

Lindstrom, Lamont. *Cargo Cult: Strange Stories of Desire from Melanesia and Beyond*. University of Hawaii Press, 1993.

Liverani, Mario. *Oltre la Bibbia. Storia antica di Israele*. Laterza, 2003.

Loeb, Avi. "Daring to Look through New Telescopes." *Projects.iq.harvard.edu*, projects.iq.harvard.edu/galileo/home; on the search for extraterrestrial life see also: Avi Loeb. *Extraterrestrial: The First Sign of Intelligent Life beyond Earth*. Houghton Mifflin Harcourt, 2021.

Marrs Jim. *Our Occulted History: Do the Global Elite Conceal Ancient Aliens?* HarperCollins, 2013.

McCall, Henrietta. *Mesopotamian Myths*. University of Texas Press, 1990.

Mittler, Doron. *Grammatica ebraica*, Zanichelli, 2001 Bologna, Italy.

Neri, Umberto, editor. *Genesi. Biblia. I libri della Bibbia interpretati dalla grande tradizione*. Gribaudi, 1986, Bologna, Italy.

Neugebauer, Otto. *The Exact Sciences in Antiquity*. Brown University Press, 1957, Providence, USA.

New American Bible Revised Edition. US Conference of Catholic Bishops, 2011.

Newberg, Andrew, et al. *Why God Won't Go Away: Brain Science and the Biology of Belief*. Ballantine Books, 2002.

Newberg, Andrew, and Eugene D'Aquili. *The Mystical Mind. Probing the Biology of Religious Experience*. Fortress Press, 1999, Minneapolis USA.

O'Brien C. A. E., and Barbara Joy O'Brien. *The Genius of the Few*. Borgo Press, 1985.

Office of the Director of National Intelligence. *Preliminary Assessment: Unidentified Aerial Phenomena*. 2021, www.dni.gov/files/ODNI/documents/assessments/Prelimary-Assessment-UAP-20210625.pdf

Paipetis, Alkiviadis. *The Unknown Technology in Homer*. Springer, 2012.

Peri, Chiara. *Il regno del nemico*. Paideia, 2003, Brescia, Italy.

Pettinato, Giovanni, editor. *La saga di Gilgamesh*. Rusconi, 1992, Milan, Italy.

Pettinato, Giovanni. *Mitologia sumerica*. UTET, 2001

——. *Mitologia Assiro Babilonese*. UTET, 2005, Turin.

——. *Sumeri. Rusconi*, 1994, Milan, Italy.

——. *La scrittura celeste*. Mondadori, 1999, Milan, Italy.

——. *I re di Sumer*. Vol. I, Paideia, 2003, Brescia, Italy.

Pevsner, J., et al. "Isolation and Characterization of an Olfactory Receptor Protein for Odorant Pyrazines." *Proceedings of the National Academy of Sciences*, vol. 82, no. 9, May 1985, pp. 3050–54. https://doi.org/10.1073/pnas.82.9.3050.

Picknett, Lynn, and Clive Prince. *The Stargate Conspiracy*. Little, Brown & Co., 1999, London, UK.

Pinotti, Roberto, and Maurizio Blondet. *Oltre. Dal Seti agli UFO. Viaggio fra i fenomeni non classificati alla ricerca del pensiero alieno*. Olimpia Editoriale, 2002, Florence.

Pinotti, Roberto. *Atlantide. Il mistero dei continenti perduti*. Mondadori, 2001, Milan, Italy.

——. *UFO. Top secret. Tutta la verità sugli extraterrestri*. Bompiani, 2001, Milan.

——. *Oggetti volanti non identificati. Nuovo rapporto su avvistamenti e ricerche in Italia*. Mondatori, 2003, Milan, Italy.

——. *Oggetti sommersi non identificati. 1947-2003: rapporto sugli UFO del mare*. Editoriale Olimpia, 2003, Florence, Italy.

——. *Spazio. I segreti e gli inganni. Breve controstoria dell'astronautica*. Editoriale Olimpia, 2003, Florence, Italy.

——. *Strutture artificiali extraterrestri. I fenomeni lunari transitori, i monumenti di Marte, gli artefatti sugli asteroidi e sulle lune di Saturno*. Editoriale Olimpia, 2005, Florence, Italy.

——. *La guerra di due mondi. Dagli scenari della fantascienza all'incubo della realtà*. Editoriale Olimpia, 2005, Florence, Italy.

——. *Ufo. Il fattore contatto. Alieni, intelligence ed esopolitica*. Mondadori, 2007,

Milan, Italy.

———. *Ufo e extraterrestri*. De Vecchi, 2011, Florence, Italy.

Popper, Karl Raimund. *The Poverty of Historicism*. Hassell Street Press, 2021.

Pritchard, James. *Ancient Near Eastern Texts Relating to the Old Testament With Supplement*. 3rd Revised ed., vol. I–IV, Princeton UP, 1969.

Quinzio, Sergio. *La Sconfitta Di Dio*. Adelphi, 2019.

Ramachandran, Vilayanur, and Sandra Blakeslee. *Phantoms in the Brain: Probing the Mysteries of the Human Mind*. HarperCollins, 1999, New York, USA.

Rashi di Troyes. *Commento alla Genesi*. Marietti, 1999.

Ravasi, Gianfranco. *500 curiosità della fede*. Mondadori, 2010.

Rendich, Franco. *Dizionario etimologico comparato delle lingue classiche indoeuropee. Dizionario indoeuropeo (sanscrito-greco-latino)*. Palombi Editori, 2010, Rome, Italy.

Reymond, Philippe. *Dizionario di ebraico e aramaico biblici*. Società Biblica Britannica e Foresteria, 2001, Rome, Italy.

Rohl, David. Legend. *The Genesis of Civilisation*. Century, 1998, London, UK.

———. *La Genesi aveva ragione*. PIEMME, 2000, Casale Monferrato, (Alessandria, Italy).

Roux, Georges. *Ancient Iraq*. Allen & Unwin, 1964, London.

Sacchi, Paolo, editor. *Apocrifi dell'Antico Testamento*. UTET, 2013.

Sagan, Carl, and Iosif Shklovskii. *Intelligent Life in the Universe*. Holden-Day, 1966.

Salibi, Kamal. *The Arabia Bible revisited*. Cadmus Press, 2008, Beirut (Lebanon).

Schökel, Luis Alonso. *Dizionario di Ebraico Biblico*, San Paolo, 2013, Cinisello Balsamo (Milan, Italy).

Schroeder, Gerald. *Genesis and the Big Bang: The Discovery Of Harmony Between Modern Science And The Bible*. Bantam Books, 1990 New York, USA.

Scott, William, and Harold Scanlin. *A Simplified Guide to BHS: Critical Apparatus, Masora, Accents, Unusual Letters & Other Markings*. BIBAL, 1987 Richland Hills, Texas (USA).

Scarpa, Marco, and Mara Filippi, editors. *La Bibbia di Gerusalemme*. EDB, 2009.

Sefer Torah Nevijm u-Ketuvim. The British and Foreign Bible Society, London, UK.

Sitchin, Zecharia. *The Complete Earth Chronicles: The 12th Planet; The Stairway to Heaven; The Wars of Gods and Men; The Lost Realms; When Time Began; The Cosmic Code; The End of Days: Armageddon and Prophecies of the Return.* Bear & Company, 2004.

——. *Is Modern Science Catching Up With Ancient Knowledge?* Avon Books, 1990.

——. *The Lost Book of Enki: Memoirs and Prophecies of an Extraterrestrial god.* Bear & Company, 2001.

——. *Divine Encounters: A Guide to Visions, Angels and Other Emissaries.* Avon Books, 1995.

——. *There Were Giants Upon the Earth: Gods, Demigods, and Human Ancestry.* The Evidence of Alien DNA. Bear & Company, 2010.

Smith, George. *The Chaldean Account of Genesis.* Sampson Low & C., 1876, London.

Socken, Paul, editor. *Why Study Talmud in the Twenty-first Century?* The Relevance of the Ancient Jewish Text to Our World. Lexington Books, 2009 Lanham, USA.

"Space Smells like Fried Steak." *Www.telegraph.co.uk*, 16 Oct. 2008, www.telegraph.co.uk/news/worldnews/northamerica/usa/3210415/Space-smells-like-fried-steak.html.

Spedicato, Emilio. "Galactic Encounters, Apollo Objects and Atlantis: A Catastrophical Scenario for Discontinuities in Human History." *Episteme*, no. 5, Jan. 2002, pp. 215–47. www.cartesio-episteme.net/episteme/epi5/epist5.html.

——. "A new chronology for Egyptian and related ancient histories." *Har Karkom e Monte Sinai, Archeologia e Mito.* Atti Convegno di Studi. Associazione Lombarda Archeologica, 1997 Milan, Italy.

Stiebing, William. *Ancient Near Eastern History and Culture.* Pearson, 2004 New York, USA.

Strong, James. *Strong's Hebrew Dictionary of the Bible.* BN Publishing, 2012.

Tacitus, Cornelius. *The Histories. Edited by Rhiannon Ash,* Translated by Kenneth Wellesley, Penguin Classics, 2009.

Tanakh: A New Translation of the Holy Scriptures According to the Traditional Hebrew Text. Jewish Publication Society, 1985 Philadelphia.

Tipler Frank. *La fisica dell'immortalità.* Mondadori, 1995 Milan, Italy.

Tov, Emanuel. *Textual Criticism of the Hebrew Bible: Third Edition, Revised and*

Expanded. Fortress Press, 2011.

Van der Toorn, Karel, et al. *Dictionary of Deities and Demons in the Bible.* W. B. Eerdmans, 1999.

Verbrugghe, Gerald, and John Wickersham. *Berossos and Manetho, Introduced and Translated: Native Traditions in Ancient Mesopotamia and Egypt.* University of Michigan Press, 2001.

Volterri, Roberto. *Narrano antiche cronache. Ricordi dal futuro.* Acacia, 2002, Rome, Italy.

——. *Archeologia dell'impossibile. Tecnologie degli dei.* Eremon Edizioni, 2010, Italy.

Von Däniken, Erich. *Chariots of the Gods.* Berkley Books, 2018.

——. *History is Wrong.* Career Press, 2009.

——. *Odyssey of the Gods.* Career Press, 2011.

——. *Aliens of the Ancient World.* Rosen Young Adult, 2016.

——. *The Gods Never Left Us: The Long Awaited Sequel to the Worldwide Best-seller Chariots of the Gods.* Career Press, 2017.

——. *Eyewitness to the Gods: What I Kept Secret for Decades.* Career Press, 2019.

——. *The Gold of the Gods.* Adventures Unlimited Press, 2020.

——. *War of the Gods: Alien Skulls, Underground Cities, and Fire from the Sky.* Career Press, 2020.

——. *Impossible Truths: Amazing Evidence of Extraterrestrial Contact.* Watkins Media, 2021.

——. *Confessions of an Egyptologist: Lost Libraries, Vanished Labyrinths & the Astonishing Truth Under the Saqqara Pyramids.* New Page Books, 2021.

——. *L'impronta di Zeus.* PIEMME, 2001 Casale Monferrato (Alessandria, Italy).

——. *Gli dèi erano astronauti.* PIEMME, 2003 Casale Monferrato (Alessandria, Italy).

——. *Gli occhi della Sfinge.* PIEMME, 2000 Casale Monferrato (Alessandria, Italy).

Wallace, Alfred Russel. *Contributions to the Theory of Natural Selection.* White Press, 2016

Webster, Noah, editor. *Webster Bible* (1833). Baker Pub Group, 1988.

Wells, Spencer. *The Journey of Man: A Genetic Odyssey*. Princeton University Press, 2003.

West, John Anthony. *Il serpente celeste*. Corbaccio, 1999.

Wilson, Colin. *Alien Dawn: An Investigation Into the Contact Experience*. Virgin Books, 1998.

——. *From Atlantis to the Sphinx*. Weiser Books, 2004.

Woolley, Leonard. *The Sumerians*. Clarendon Press, 1928.

——. *Ur dei Caldei*. Einaudi, 1958, Torino.

Zorell, Franz. *Lexicon Hebraicum Veteris Testamenti*. Pontifical Biblical Institute, Rome, 1984.

Printed in Great Britain
by Amazon

23713538R00187